THE THEORY AND PRACTICE OF PEACEKEEPING

INDAR JIT RIKHYE

Major-General, Indian Army (retd)

The Theory &
Practice of
Peacekeeping

Published for the International Peace Academy by

ST. MARTIN'S PRESS, NEW YORK

Library of Congress Cataloging in Publication Data

Rikhye, Indar Jit, 1920-
  The theory and practice of peacekeeping.

  Includes bibliographical references and index.
  1. United Nations—Armed Forces. 2. Security, International. I. Title.
JX1981.P7R528   1984   341.5'8   83-40193
ISBN 0-312-79718-4

*To my children Ravi Indar and Bhalinder
and theirs, Evan Mahinder and Kiran*

PREFACE

During a meeting in London in the spring of 1980, the British publisher Christopher Hurst suggested that there was a need to keep abreast of new developments and political trends in the maintenance of an international system of peace and security, and therefore a successor-volume was required to *The Thin Blue Line: International Peacekeeping and its Future*, written by Brigadier Michael Harbottle, Major-General Bjørn Egge and myself.

The International Peace Academy has published a series of papers by distinguished peacekeepers to be included in *Peacekeeping: Appraisals and Proposals*, edited by Dr Henry Wiseman, Professor in the Department of Political Studies, University of Guelph, Canada, and who for the two previous years served as Director of Peacekeeping Programs of the Academy. This publication is an important contribution to peacekeeping literature but does not include a historical analysis of peacekeeping operations and the discussion in the UN relating to its future.

It took only a few minutes of discussion with Mr Hurst for me to agree that a new publication was needed and that I would undertake the writing; whereas it has taken me more than two years to prepare the MS.

I have based my writing not only on reports by international and regional organizations and governments, and other sources of information, but also to a large extent on my personal knowledge of events and personalities. I have visited Cyprus and the Middle East to observe the UN operations and the US Sinai Support Mission. I have met the diplomatic and military leaders involved in these operations and have brought many of them to participate in the Academy's seminars and workshops, where these problems were discussed.

I have closely followed the events at the United Nations, the Organization of American States, the Organization of African Unity, the Association of South-East Asian Nations, the Gulf Cooperation Council and the South Asian Forum. I have travelled extensively to crisis areas to understand those conflicts. I have met political and military leaders involved in the conflicts, as well as the main third-party role actors. Except where I have used quotations, the views expressed are mine.

I am grateful to the Board of Directors of the Academy, who have facilitated my task, and to the Academy's staff who have assisted me in many ways, especially Mrs Celia Seggel Pangalis, Director for Training, for the preparation of the study on the Southern Sahara; Mr Nosakhare Obaseki, Assistant Director for Research, for the study on Namibia; and Colonel Peter C. Harvey, Executive Director, who has made available the maps (drawn by the Cartographic Department, Ministry of Defence) that he had specially prepared for his thesis on UNEF II at the University of Keele, England. I also wish to thank Mr Milkos Pinther, Cartographer, and Mr Michael Dulka, Map Librarian, of the United Nations for their assistance.

I could not have completed this MS. without advice and assistance in editing from Mr Hugh Hanning, the Academy's UK Representative, and, last but not least, the enormous help of Miss Dolores Fenn, my special assistant and the Academy's Librarian. She has not only typed and retyped a number of drafts but has helped to collate, edit and index this MS.

New York,
April 1984

I.J.R.

CONTENTS

MAPS

(Detail of UN Map 1477.1, Oct. 1963.)

(Details of: [*above*] Map 1654(b)X, made by the Cartographical Institute
of the Autonomous University of Santo Domingo, 1963: [*right*] UN Map
1898 Rev. 3, May 1980.)

ABBREVIATIONS

ADL	Armistice Demarcation Line
ADF	Arab Deterrent Force
AKTUR	Action Front for the Retention of Turnhalle Principles (Namibia)
ANC	*Armée Nationale Congolaise*
ANIL	Integrated National Army (Chad)
ASEAN	Association of South-East Asian Nations
AWACS	Airborne Warning and Control System
BET	Borkou-Ennedi-Tibesti region, Chad
CENTO	Central Treaty Organization
DTA	Democratic Turnhalle Alliance (Namibia)
DZ	Demilitarized Zone
EIMAC	Egyptian-Israeli Mixed Armistice Commission
EOKA	Greek-led National Organization of Cypriot Fighters
FAN	*Forces Armées du Nord*
FAP	*Forces Armées Populaires*
FAT	*Forces Armées Tchadiennes*
FDL	Forward Defended Locality
Frolinat	*Front National de Libération du Tchad*
GAA	General Armistice Agreement
GUNT	Traditional Government of National Unity (Chad)
IADB	Inter-American Defense Board
IADC	Inter-American Defense College
IAPF	Inter-American Peace Force (Dominican Republic)
ICRC	International Commission of the Red Cross
IDF	Israel Defence Force
ICJ	International Court of Justice
ILMAC	Israel-Lebanon Mixed Armistice Commission
IPKO	International Information Center on Peacekeeping Operations
ISMAC	Israel-Syria Mixed Armistice Commission
NATO	North Atlantic Treaty Organization
J & K	Jammu and Kashmir
MAC	Mixed Armistice Commission
MFO	Multinational Force and Observers (Sinai)
MNF	Multinational Force (Beirut)
OCAM	*Organisation Commune Africaine, Malagache et Mauricienne*
OPs	Observation Posts
OGS	Observer Group Sinai
OAS	Organization of American States
OAU	Organization of African Unity
ONUC	*Opération des Nations Unies au Congo*
POC	Peace Observation Commission
PLO	Palestine Liberation Organization
Polisario Front	*Frente Popular para la Liberacion de Saguia el Hamra y Rio de Oro*
POW	Prisoner of War
PPT	*Parti Progressiste Tchadien*
RSF	Rhodesian Security Forces
SADF	South African Defence Forces
SADR	Saharan Arab Democratic Republic
SEATO	South East Asia Treaty Organization
SFM	Sinai Field Mission

SSM	Sinai Support Mission
SWAPO	South West African People's Organization
UAM	*Union Africaine et Malagache*
UDI	Unilateral Declaration of Independence (Rhodesia, 1965)
UNCIP	United Nations Commission for India and Pakistan
UNDOF	United Nations Disengagement Observer Force (Syria)
UNEF	United Nations Emergency Force (Sinai)
UNFICYP	United Nations Peacekeeping Force in Cyprus
UNIFIL	United Nations Interim Force in Lebanon
UNIPOM	United Nations India Pakistan Observation Mission
UNITA	*União Nacional para a Independência Total de Angola*
UNMO	United Nations Military Observer
UNMOGIP	United Nations Military Observer Group in India and Pakistan
UNOGIL	United Nations Observation Group in Lebanon
UNRWA	United Nations Relief Works Agency (for Palestine refugees in the Near East)
UNSF	United Nations Security Force (West Irian)
UNSCOB	United Nations Special Committee on the Balkans
UNSCOP	United Nations Special Committee on Palestine
UNTAG	United Nations Transition Assistance Group (Namibia)
UNTEA	United Nations Temporary Executive Authority (West Irian)
UNTSO	United Nations Truce Supervision Organization in Palestine
UNYOM	United Nations Yemen Observation Mission
UPT	*Union pour le Progrès du Tchad*
ZANU	Zimbabwe African National Union
ZAPU	Zimbabwe African People's Union

1

THE EVOLUTION OF PEACEKEEPING

Origin and definition

The origin of peacekeeping, as that term is tentatively defined below, can be traced back to the League of Nations. The League provided for timely action to deal with situations that were a threat to peace. Right from the start, it established methods and procedures that helped to prevent a threatening situation from developing into international conflict. But the theory was better than the practice, and the League failed to take action over the war in Manchuria between China and Japan (1931–3). When the great powers, France and Great Britain, were in agreement, it could act positively. But, when Italy invaded Abyssinia, the two great powers tried to deal with Italy outside the League Council, and little was achieved. By the middle of the 1930s, the League had been made ineffective by the growing militarism of Japan, Italy and Germany.

One of the methods by which it tried to prevent escalation of a crisis was peace observation, whereby the organized international community initiates a third-party intervention as early as possible with a view to permitting calmer judgments to resolve the potential or actual conflict.[1]

Although the term 'peacekeeping' only came properly into use when the United Nations (hereafter 'UN') established its first emergency force, UNEF I, after the Suez war in 1956, it was formalized in February 1965 when the UN General Assembly established a special committee to deal with peacekeeping matters, and named it the Special Committee on Peacekeeping Operations. Up till then, the UN, like the League, had used peace observation as an international instrument to prevent or end hostilities. Peacekeeping, as a form of collective action, uses military contingents for this purpose, although a peacekeeping force generally includes observation functions. Both peace observation and peacekeeping may be related to, or even include, peacemaking responsibilities, i.e. resolution by diplomatic means. Peace observation may use one person, a small fact-finding mission, or a substantial presence including a small staff, to become the eyes and ears of a regional or international organization.

In spite of several attempts, the term 'peacekeeping' has still not been formally defined. This lack of clear definition provides a measure of flexibility that serves political and operational purposes. But there are corresponding disadvantages in that the term can be loosely used and vaguely understood. The International Peace Academy has defined it as 'the prevention, containment, moderation and termina-

1

tion of hostilities between or within states through the medium of third-party intervention, organized and directed internationally, using multinational military, police, and civilian personnel to restore and maintain peace.'

Some UN members use the term to cover any action by the world organization in the maintenance of international peace and security as provided by the Charter. Others give it a more restricted interpretation. In practice, only the experience of the UN and regional organizations can establish the limits and nature of the concept.

Peacekeeping operations can be of a military, para-military and non-military character. Their nature has always been non-mandatory and non-coercive and they require the invitation or consent of parties to the conflict. The nature of these operations varies according to their mandate and organization. There is not, and never has been, any need for a coercive mission in situations where a third-party presence is interposed, or is deployed to prevent a breach of the peace — employing means selected by the parties, within the meaning of Article 33, or measures recommended by the General Assembly under Article 14.

Military presences have been used to observe a ceasefire, to separate rival forces, to maintain a neutral demilitarized zone, to investigate and fact-find, and to prevent external interference, and they have ranged in size from a handful of observers to military forces of between 3,000 and 20,000 men. These are all non-coercive measures, seldom creating serious threats to the personnel involved. However, the need to deploy combat units for peacekeeping has arisen when a stronger military presence was needed. Furthermore, assistance to a country for the maintenance of law and order can require the use of force, although this has been strictly limited to the requirement for self-defence. Such exceptional peacekeeping operations are generally held to fall between Chapters VI (Pacific Settlement of Disputes) and VII (Enforcement Action) of the Charter. However, there are member-states which take the view that this use of troops falls within the purview of Chapter VII.

The mediation and conciliation missions of the UN and of the regional organizations, as well as the transfer of power in Zimbabwe, are all referred to as peacekeeping operations.   .

United Nations responsibility

When the signatories of the UN Charter met in San Francisco in 1945, they were determined to provide the new organization with the capability to maintain world peace, which the League of Nations had so clearly lacked.

Foremost among the purposes of the UN is 'to maintain international peace and security, and to that end: to take effective collective measures for the prevention and removal of threats to the peace, and for the suppression of acts of aggression or other breaches of the peace, and to bring about by peaceful means, and in conformity with the principles of justice and international law, adjustment or settlement of international disputes or situations that might lead to a breach of the peace.'[2]

Warned by the experience of two world wars in recent history, the members of the United Nations, determined to save succeeding generations from the scourge of war,[3] brought into the Charter of the organization machinery to keep peace by force, if necessary. A Security Council, including the world's strongest powers, was created in order to ensure prompt and effective action, and entrusted with the primary responsibility for the maintenance of international peace and security.[4] The General Assembly, comprising all the members, may discuss any questions or any matters except as provided in Article 12[5] of the Charter and may make recommendations to the members of the United Nations or to the Security Council, or both, on any such questions or matters.[6]

The subsequent UN efforts to build an effective machinery for peace have followed a long and tortuous path. The Cold War during the early life of the UN prevented the Security Council from fully developing its potential. The Charter envisaged that a unanimity of purpose would be available to keep and even enforce peace when necessary. Instead, the use of the veto accorded to the five permanent members blocked many efforts to use the Council as an effective instrument for peacekeeping.

Only in the case of Korea, during the absence of the Soviet delegation caused by a walk-out over the Council's refusal to agree to the Soviet proposal to allow the representative of the People's Republic of China to participate in the debate, did the Council decided to enforce peace under Chapter VII of the Charter. The only other example of enforcement, during the Congo operation, was in a different category and purely *ad hoc*: the Council agreed to use force in the last resort to implement the mandate given to ONUC to end the secession of Katanga.[7] When UNEF II and later UNDOF were established after the October 1973 Arab-Israeli war, the Security Council authorized the troops to defend their posts.[8]

The Council was authorized by the Charter to call on member-states to provide, on a systematic basis, military assistance and facilities, including rights of passage, to keep the peace.[9] No such agreement has yet been reached. Instead, each case is dealt with on its own merits. A Military Staff Committee was established to advise the Council on all questions relating to military requirements.[10] But after immediately disagreeing on the size and nature of the forces required, this Committee has met twice a month without any substantive item on its agenda.

The Council has, however, authorized several fact-finding, truce, armistice or ceasefire observation and supervision missions, such as UNMOGIP, UNTSO, UNOGIL, UNYOM and others. These missions, by their very nature, may only report to the Council for such actions as it may decide upon. But by their presence they contribute to peace and quiet in their areas of responsibility.

For peacekeeping proper, the real debut came in 1956. Faced with a possibility of dangerous confrontation between the United States and the Soviet Union following the Suez war, the Council determined on swift action. Threatened with a veto by France and the United Kingdom, whose troops were involved in the fighting, it called for a Special Session of the General Assembly to deal with the crisis.[11]

When, in July 1960, fighting broke out in the newly-independent Congo, the Security Council decided to provide massive civilian assistance and authorized a UN force to help maintain law and order. Since then the Security Council has established several peacekeeping operations. In 1962 in West Irian (former Dutch New Guinea) a United Nations Security Force was established to maintain law and order over the six-month period during which the UN had agreed to administer the territory before turning it over to Indonesia. In 1964, a force was set up in Cyprus (UNFICYP) to keep the peace between the Greek and Turkish Cypriots. In 1965, when civil war broke out in the Dominican Republic, a representative of the Secretary-General and military observers were sent to Santo Domingo. Later the same year, following fighting between India and Pakistan, UNIPOM was established to supervise the ceasefire and other arrangements to restore peace.

The Security Council faced a major test when fighting again broke out between the Arabs and Israel in October 1973. The first ceasefire, backed by the United States and the Soviet Union, failed to hold. The Israeli forces, having crossed the Canal, threatened Suez and cut off the supply lines of the Egyptian Third Army deployed east of the Canal between Ismailia and Suez. The Soviet Union determined to resupply this Army, which conjured up the danger of a clash between Israeli and Soviet military aircraft. This caused the United States to order a worldwide nuclear alert. Like the Berlin blockade, Suez and the Cuban missile crisis, the October War threatened a military confrontation between the two superpowers. It was on the initiative of its non-permanent members that the UN Security Council agreed to order a second ceasefire and to introduce UNEF II[12] between Egyptian and Israeli forces to implement its decisions. In 1974, the UN Disengagement Observation Force (UNDOF) was introduced between Israeli and Syrian forces on the Golan Heights.

As already noted, while the Security Council was charged with the primary responsibility for keeping the peace, the General Assembly can have this authority delegated to it. This is under the Uniting for

Peace Resolution of 1950 (see below). In addition, the Assembly may discuss any questions relating to the maintenance of peace and security brought before it by any member-state or by the Security Council, or by a non-member-state except as provided by Article 12 of the Charter.[13] The Assembly also may make recommendations to the member-states or to the Security Council, or to both, on any question or matter.[14]

The Assembly receives annual and special reports from all organs of the United Nations, including the Security Council.[15] It is the Assembly that approves the budget of the organization and apportions the organization's expenses to member-states. Thus, not only is residual authority for peacekeeping vested in the Assembly, but also its approval is essential for expenditures and to apportion expenses to member-states.

The experience of the Korean operation, which as we have seen would have been vetoed but for the chance absence of the Soviet Union, caused many member-states to consider how to make the UN an effective instrument for peace despite the veto. In 1950, on an initiative of the United States, the Assembly approved a 'Uniting for Peace'[16] resolution permitting the Assembly to take whatever action it felt was necessary for the maintenance of international peace and security. This was contrary to Article 12 of the Charter, and later emerged as a serious issue when the authority of the Security Council was the subject of debate between the superpowers.

In the case of Korea, this resolution helped to maintain the operation. But it was the Suez war of 1956 that provided an opportunity for the full application of this formula. It was under the 'Uniting for Peace' resolution that the Assembly on 5 November 1956 authorized the establishment of the first peacekeeping force in the history of the organization: UNEF I. But subsequently, controversy broke out over the question of relative authority of the Council and the Assembly, and it is unlikely that the Assembly will act in such a manner again.

When UNEF I was removed at the request of President Gamal Abdel Nasser on 16 May 1967, it caused widespread disappointment in the UN's capability to maintain peace. Its withdrawal became a key factor leading to the June 1967 war, which left the Arabs humiliated and the Israelis in occupation of the Golan Heights, the West Bank and Sinai. In consequence, the membership of the UN suffered a loss of confidence in the peacekeeping system which had been so carefully nurtured by Dag Hammarskjöld and his successors. The Israelis, always sceptical of the UN role in their conflict with the Arabs, preferred to do without any international presence in the future. Even Nasser, who called for the removal of UNEF, later blamed the UN for leaving. But seven years later, after the October 1973 war, the world witnessed a revival of international peacekeeping. It became an important instrument in Dr Henry Kissinger's step-by-step diplomacy, which led to the withdrawal of Israeli forces from east of the Suez Canal in the Sinai, and in Syria from the very gates of Damascus. Later in 1978, a new peacekeeping force had to be introduced in Southern Lebanon to keep the Palestine Liberation Organization (PLO) and leftist elements apart from the Israelis and Lebanese Christians; and when the UN failed to renew UNEF II as part of the Camp David Egyptian-Israeli accord, even the Israelis were disappointed.

Elsewhere, too, peacekeeping has at least retained its former importance. A UN peacekeeping force — UNFICYP — remains in Cyprus keeping the Turks and Greeks apart. UN observers (UNTSO) continue to play a useful role along the armistice lines between Israel on the one side and Lebanon and Syria on the other. Similarly, UN observers in Kashmir (UNMOGIP) maintain a UN presence along the ceasefire line between Indian and Pakistani troops.

The role of regional organizations

Early in 1978, a Commonwealth Monitoring Force performed an important function in the transition to independence of Zimbabwe. The future of Namibia is tied to a UN peacekeeping role to ensure a similar transition of the territory from South African control to independence.

Both the Organization of American States (hereafter OAS) and the Organization of African Unity (hereafter OAU) have employed military observers for peacekeeping with varying degrees of success. The OAS sent observers to El Salvador and Honduras after the so-called 'football war' in 1976. It was the OAS, too, that set up the peacekeeping force in the Dominican Republic in 1965–6, following an initial intervention by the United States; the OAS force was, in fact, built around the US troops.

The OAU established an observer operation between Algeria and Morocco in 1963. In 1981, the Assembly of the Heads of State decided to launch a peacekeeping operation in Chad, envisaging the alternative possibility of a UN intervention.

The Arab League, too, has peacekeeping experience. An Egyptian force under the League was sent to Kuwait in 1961, and another League force has been in Lebanon since 1978. Like the OAS force in the Dominican Republic, the Arab League troops in Kuwait were from a single nation, while the Lebanon force, which originally consisted of a large Syrian contingent with token contributions from other Arab countries, later consisted only of troops from Syria.

The UN has employed a one-person fact-finding mission; small and large observer groups to report on armistice, ceasefires and limited arms zones; and peacekeeping forces of up to 20,000 men. Not only does it have more experience than regional organizations in peacekeeping, but it has also shown a greater capacity to organize, operate, support and finance these operations. The UN Security Council,[17] the Office of the Secretary-General and the Secretariat have acquired considerable skill with successive operations. Although the UN Special Committee on Peacekeeping, established in 1964,[18] has yet to resolve remaining questions of procedure, there was enough consensus by 1973 to permit a renewal of UN peacekeeping in the Middle East and its smooth conduct by the Secretary-General under the direction of the Security Council. The regional organizations have yet to match the UN's ability to keep peace.

The role of peacekeeping in the strategy of nations

The evolution of international and regional machinery for international peace and security has by no means met global needs. The great alliance of the Second World War came apart during the flush of victory. The Russians brought most of Eastern Europe into their orbit, the Baltic states disappeared within the Soviet Union itself, and by the 1950s the Central European states had become part of the Moscow-led socialist system. An iron curtain divided Eastern Europe from the West. Seeking protection against the incursion of Communism and the growing military potential of the Soviet Union, the Western democracies entered into a military and political treaty and established NATO. The Russians formalized their relationships with the East European socialist states through the Warsaw Pact.

The two military blocs, through a balance of nuclear terror, have kept peace in Europe for a period unprecedented in its recent history. The Soviet Union kept its influence and peace from Berlin to Vladivostok according to its own dictate and has not called for any assistance from the international system for peace and security. However, the Atlantic alliance, a compact of free democracies, has had its problems. After the defeat of the Axis, the Western European nations, with the hesitant consent of the United States, were committed to restoring their authority to those of their colonial territories which had been temporarily occupied by the enemy. But the war and occupation had fuelled hopes and aspirations for self-determination. Hardly had the Western European powers returned to their former colonies than they had to cope with demands for change, and with revolution, civil strife and insurrection. The perceived threat of Soviet and Chinese Communism further provoked the United States to help Western European states to assert control over their colonies, but the colonial powers were exhausted by the war, and generally lacked the means and the political will to maintain their hold over these territories. Gradually, independence came to many lands. The process of change caused conflicts and sometimes wars, which the colonial powers had no desire to fight. Instead, they increasingly relied on international peacekeeping to cope with their conflicts, such as those in Indonesia and Palestine.

In order to isolate these conflicts as much as possible from East-West relations, the United States gave strong support to the UN system. The Soviet Union, never enthusiastic, acquiesced because it was committed to change and because peacekeeping had proved useful in the decolonization process.

The process took an unusual turn in Indochina where the French were unwilling to relinquish the territory until they finally met with military defeat at the hands of Ho Chi Minh in 1954. The United States later stepped in to keep the area free of Communism, but after a costly and prolonged war, it too had to withdraw.

In their other colonies the French, determined to maintain their own manifest destiny, followed their rule of self-reliance in keeping the peace. Having learned from the Indochinese experience, however, President de Gaulle, in a surprise move, granted independence to the French African colonies in 1958, except for Algeria. Under treaty arrangements, France mainly kept responsibility for peace and security in her former African territories, although there have been some hesitations, as in Chad.

The Belgians followed the French example, but their expectations of similar results turned sour after they had granted independence to the Congo (now Zaire) and Rwanda-Burundi. The Congo, one of the largest countries in Africa, threatened to fall apart when Belgium withdrew, and a major UN peacekeeping and civil assistance operation was needed to restore a measure of law and order. The Belgians returned but never again as the sovereign power.

The Portuguese and the Spanish were the last to give up their colonies: Portugal through liberation wars in the colonies and revolution at home, and Spain by a voluntary process after the death of General Franco.

Thus in spite of its limitations, the UN system of peace and security proved most effective in the decolonization process and became a major instrument of United States policy. The Belgians, British and Dutch accepted this arrangement, but the Portuguese and Spaniards placed little reliance in the system, to their own detriment. The French remained sceptical until the emergence of the crisis in Southern Lebanon and the introduction of UNIFIL in 1978, an operation in which they have participated.

The passing of the colonial era, however, has not ended conflict in those areas. Past rivalries and religious, ideological, ethnic, economic and social tensions have erupted into new wars. These have often become proxy wars in which one or the other superpower has been involved, thereby endangering peace on a global scale.

After Stalin, the relaxations in Soviet policy gave rise to new hopes for a peaceful resolution of East-West differences. In 1962,

Khrushchev was ready to recognize that the presence of Soviet missiles in Cuba was intolerable to the United States and withdrew them after assurances that the United States would not take military action against Cuba. However, the Soviet Union never ceased building up its military strength, both nuclear and conventional, and it has maintained large forces along its borders with the West. For security during this period, the Americans and the West placed their major reliance on their nuclear superiority. In the 1970s, the Soviet Union caught up with the nuclear capability of the West, and its long-range nuclear missiles have made the United States no longer defensible. This, added to mutual mistrust and competition, has led many to believe on both sides that armed force alone would eventually determine the outcome of their differences. Thus it is no longer the Soviet capacity to promote social revolution that is seen as the main danger, so much as the spectre of the Soviet Union as an aggressive military power.[19]

The Soviet Union's support of Vietnam's action in Kampuchea and its military intervention in Afghanistan have further damaged relations with the West. And during the economic unrest in Poland in the early 1980s, the constant possibility of a Soviet intervention caused further disquiet in the West. The administration of President Jimmy Carter, towards its end, had put aside détente and increased military spending. The Reagan administration came to office with a promise to change the military balance in favour of the West. Yet neither side wants a third world war. There seems to be no rationale for the further militarization of the Cold War.

In the late 1970s it became evident that the superpowers were unable to deal with conflicts outside their immediate spheres of influence owing to limits on their available resources and their inability to co-operate. Thus, conflicts on the edges of their influence, or in the grey areas outside them, have stagnated into long-drawn-out wars causing much suffering and loss of life. The conflicts in Chad and Western Sahara fall into this category. The Americans have been unable to influence the situations in Kampuchea, the Ogaden or Afghanistan because those places are on the extremities of their own influence. So too is the Persian Gulf, where the vulnerability of the West's oil supply lines, the revolution in Iran, the war between Iran and Iraq and other developments combine to form a serious threat to the Western and Japanese economies.

Accepting that both East and West will be careful to avoid a war in Europe, it is the Third World, with so many current and potential conflicts, which provides the setting for dangerous manoeuvres by the two blocs. The Soviet Union has indicated by its actions that it will continue to exploit available opportunities in this area. The oil-rich states, after their first flush of independence and the rise in oil prices, now fear threats of disintegration from tribal rivalries and other internal challenges. Other states in Asia as well as in Africa, South America and the Caribbean, embody historic conflicts resulting in new demands for social change.

The generally high rate of inflation and the deterioration in the world economy, particularly in the West, are likely to cause conflicts over resources that may lead to new wars. The Soviet Union has its problems too. The socialist states have not escaped the impact of global recession and increases in oil prices. Their appetite for raw materials from the Third World and for markets for their manufactured goods is expanding. Last but not the least, there is a growing desire in the Soviet bloc for decentralization, personal freedom, greater availability of food and better material conditions.

Western strategic analysts believe that, as members of the next generation take over power in Moscow from the generation of Brezhnev, Andropov and their contemporaries, they are likely to want to make the Soviet Union the most powerful nation in the world. During the 1970s the Soviets, through armed intervention, placed pro-Moscow parties in power in South Vietnam, Laos, Kampuchea, Afghanistan, Ethiopia, Angola and South Yemen. They have also shown that once a pro-Moscow party gains power in a country, as in Kampuchea and Afghanistan, they will go to any limits to support it.

In Asia the Soviet Union retains control of disputed islands adjacent to Japan's northernmost province of Hokkaido, retains influence in Outer Mongolia and North Korea, and remains active in support of Communist parties throughout the continent. It has a powerful position in the Middle East, where it is the major supporter of Syria and a friend of Iraq, and enjoys diplomatic relations with almost all the conservative states, and strong links with the Tudeh party in Iran. The Soviet Union has also increased its military potential significantly. It has established a naval fleet at Vladivostok, and has access to Cam Ranh Bay (Vietnam) and bases in the Red Sea.

In Africa, besides its close ties with Angola and Ethiopia, the Soviet Union is the major arms supplier to Libya, which has in the past few years crossed swords with Egypt and Tunisia, opposed Sudan, attempted to support the former President Amin in Uganda and, early in 1981, despatched a force to Ndjamena to assist President Goukouni of Chad. In Central and South America, the Soviet Union maintains its close ties with Cuba and, through Fidel Castro, with left-wing and Communist groups throughout these lands.

Some analysts fear that the Soviet Union may well continue to exploit its military advantage over the West before parity is achieved again. They believe that several options are available to Moscow. First, it could intervene in situations like that in Poland to restore party control, knowing that the West could not react militarily. Secondly, it could encourage the Tudeh party in Iran, move more troops into the south of the Soviet Union, and encourage dissent in the sheikhdoms, threatening the West's interests and causing it to divert military resources to the area, and then, taking advantage of the United States being overstretched, advance over the Elbe and the Rhine to the Channel. It might be especially tempted to do that if it believed that revolts in Poland and other East European dependencies made it essential to remove West European 'contagion'.[20]

Thirdly, Moscow could react in several ways to the growing possibility of a United States-Japan-China axis. There is the option of taking out the Chinese nuclear capability with or without invading Sinkiang. Again, trouble could be made between the two Koreas, or the Soviets could encourage military action in Indochina, either against China or against Thailand.

Fourthly, the Soviets could destabilize Pakistan by aiding dissident Pakhtoons and Baluchis. Such action could be in support of activities in South-West Asia or Sinkiang. Such are Moscow's offensive opportunities.

On the other hand, the Soviets are faced with real and perceived threats that could cause them to act more cautiously. They see their greatest danger from the Western encouragement of dissidence in the East European states, which could spread to the Soviet Union itself. Secondly, they suspect the West of designs to support right-wing regimes in order to gain greater, if not complete, control of markets and resources as the solution to its economic crisis. Thirdly, they fear growing ties between China and Japan as part of a Western attempt to encircle them.

Thus the needs of the two power blocs could easily lead them on to a collision course, fuelled by further militarization leading to greater possibilities of the use of force. The interplay of Third World currents with the East-West conflict presents an awesome picture.

Reason should dictate that nobody would wish to be involved in a nuclear war under any circumstance. But history has proved that reason does not always prevail, and that power can blind decision-makers. Neither East nor West has always conducted itself in a rational manner.

President Jimmy Carter's attempt to take the hostages out of Iran by force could have touched off a war if the US helicopters had reached their destination. On his side, Leonid Brezhnev seriously over-reacted to political developments in Afghanistan, and the Soviets now face a prolonged war that seriously endangers peace in South Asia. These two examples, while greatly varying in scale, indicate the inherent dangers of the rash use of power. A way must be found to cope with this. Fortunately, there are grounds for believing that the interests of the superpowers have much in common, and that in each case the desire for peace transcends all other interests. The Russian people are constantly reminded of their 20 million dead in the Second World War — an experience they do not wish to repeat. Their casualties in Afghanistan, though much less than American losses in Vietnam over a similar period, have already prompted them to seek a political solution. Similarly, the Vietnam experience has persuaded the American people to make greater use of diplomacy and to avoid gunboat diplomacy in situations like those in Nicaragua or El Salvador.

The two blocs share economic problems with the rest of the world. There is no lack of realization that in this interdependent world there must be sharing of global resources. There is universal demand for improvement in the quality of life and the satisfaction of human needs.

These arguments suggest that the underlying interest of both parties is not military confrontation but negotiation. Thus, where security considerations arise, if military confrontation is to be avoided, an alternative system of maintaining peace and security must be sought. Peacekeeping as evolved by the UN offers such an alternative.

NOTES

1. David W. Wainhouse and Associates, *International Peace Observation* (Baltimore: Johns Hopkins University Press, 1966), p. 1.
2. Charter of the United Nations, Article 1, para. 1.
3. *Ibid.*, p. 1, para. 1.
4. *Ibid.*, Chapter V.
5. While the Security Council is exercising, in respect of any dispute or situation, the functions assigned to it in the present Charter, the General Assembly may not make any recommendations on that question unless the Security Council so requests.
6. Charter of the United Nations, Chapter IV.
7. Security Council Resolution 169, 1961.
8. S/11052 Rev. 1, 27 October 1973.
9. Charter of the United Nations, Article 43.
10. *Ibid.*, Article 47.
11. This was the only occasion when a peacekeeping operation was launched by the General Assembly.
12. UNEF I was established Nov. 5, 1956, and withdrawn on May 18, 1967. UNEF II was established in October 1973 and ended, after the Camp David agreement, in 1979.
13. Charter of the United Nations, Article 11.
14. *Ibid.*, Article 10.
15. *Ibid.*, Article 15.
16. UN General Assembly Resolution 377 (V), Nov. 3, 1950: 'Resolves that if the Security Council, because of lack of unanimity of the permanent members, fails to exercise its primary responsibility for the maintenance of international peace and security in any case where there appears to be a threat to the peace, breach of the peace, or act of aggression, the General Assembly will consider the matter immediately with a view to making appropriate recommendations to the members for collective measures, including in the breach of the peace or act of aggression, the use of armed force when necessary to maintain or restore international peace and security.'

17. Only UNEF was organized by the General Assembly under 'Uniting for Peace Resolution'. 377 (V).
18. UN General Assembly Resolution No. A/Res/2006 (XIX), 18 February 1965.
19. George F. Kennan, 'Cease the Madness', *Atlantic Monthly*, January 1961.
20. Norman Macrae, 'President Reagan's Inheritance', *The Economist*, Dec. 27, 1980–Jan. 2, 1981, p. 15.

2

PEACE OBSERVATION

General

The League of Nations developed and was able to use peace observation in a number of situations. These arrangements included peace observers, commissions of inquiry, plebiscite commissions, administrative commissions and judicial panels. The League used international forces only twice, in Upper Silesia in 1921 and in the Saar in 1935. In general the League dealt with disputes arising from claims over frontiers. It proved successful in preventing war and restoring peace whenever Great Britain and France, then the great powers, were in agreement.

The use of Commissions of Enquiry, now known as fact-finding missions, had salient features[1] which proved helpful as a guide to similar United Nations missions. The League Council set down the powers and duties, and designated the personnel. The Commissions were asked by the Council to suggest solutions and, as a rule, enjoyed freedom of movement; persons appointed to them were not only eminent but experienced. Usually there were five members supported by Secretariat experts; the members were paid for by the League, were from disinterested countries, and acted in their individual capacities. The Council generally adopted the reports provided by the Commissions together with their recommendations.

The UN Charter provides that parties to any dispute likely to endanger the maintenance of international peace[2] shall first seek a solution by peaceful means of their own choice. However, except for a few situations when this practice has been followed, peace observation has mostly been established by an organ of the UN. Having established a Security Council to maintain international peace and security, the Council has been authorized[3] to 'investigate any dispute, or any situation which might lead to international friction or give rise to a dispute'. Although this procedure has been invoked, only the superpowers agree that a 'decision to investigate' article is legally binding by the UN. The Security Council may also 'recommend procedures or methods of adjustment',[4] and if the continuance of a dispute is likely to endanger peace and security, it may 'recommend such terms of settlement as it may consider appropriate'. This provides for the use of peace observation if the Council should recommend it as a procedure or as a term of settlement.

Under the procedure of the Security Council described in Article 29, the Council may establish such subsidiary organs as it deems necessary for the performance of its functions. Here too the approval of the five

14

powers exercising the veto is essential. The enforcement authority provided under Chapter VII of the Charter to the Security Council authorizes the Council to employ various means not involving the use of force, i.e. peace observation to prevent aggression. However, this does not require the approval of the five 'veto powers', and as such was done only in Palestine and Korea — the Soviets' veto could not be applied because of their absence from the Council (in protest at the Council's refusal to accept the representative of the People's Republic of China as a participant in the debate).

The General Assembly can recommend peace observation under the authority provided by the Charter[5] to discuss any questions relating to the maintenance of international peace and security brought before it in accordance with the Charter procedures. However, peace observation instituted by an Assembly recommendation is not binding on the parties.

Lastly, the UN Secretary-General, under Article 99 of the Charter, may bring to the Security Council's attention any matter that he believes may threaten the maintenance of international peace and security. The Secretary-General has maintained that in order to carry out his functions under this article, it may be necessary for him to dispatch personnel from the Secretariat to disturbed areas to determine whether a particular matter sufficiently threatens the maintenance of international peace and security to justify his bringing it to the attention of the Security Council.

The evolution of peace observation by the UN first relied on the Security Council, with its primary responsibility for the maintenance of international peace and security, to authorize it. However, as the Cold War severed relations between the two superpowers, the General Assembly became the convenient forum for such sessions. By the 1950s even this practice lost favour with the great powers, who encouraged arrangements outside the UN.

Within the UN system, the Secretary-General's role, starting in the time of Dag Hammarskjöld, has emerged as central. Depending on the situation, the Security Council and (when it is unable to act) the General Assembly have authorized peace observation, making the Secretary-General responsible in every case for supervision and for reporting to the UN organ concerned.

Early in its life, the UN realized that after an agreement for the settlement of a conflict, some form of supervision or observation was needed to ensure that the parties concerned were complying with the commitments made by them. Depending on the nature of the task, the UN may help in the implementation of an agreement by providing a one-person supervisor to a number of observers. Supervision by the UN is more useful when combatants have to be separated and withdrawn to agreed-to lines. The presence of the UN can help in arranging for the parties to meet or, as a face-saving device, to agree to an otherwise unpalatable arrangement. The UN can prevent an incident from escalating further by the calming effect of its presence. UN supervisory functions can assist in confidence-building before or after an agreement has been reached.

It is possible that UN peace observation may not actually lead to a settlement of the dispute, but it certainly creates a positive environment when an agreement is possible. The UN mission reports to the Security Council (or sometimes to the General Assembly). The report is sent through the Secretary-General, who can bring it to the attention of the UN organ either openly or by a restricted method. The open approach can result in international response. Thus, reporting to the UN organs can be used as a means of assuring compliance by the parties to an agreement.

Lastly, UN missions are the eyes and ears of the Security Council and can provide accurate information on developments. Such information is vital for the Council to act judiciously and with speed.

The UN Security Council established its first peace observation mission on 19 December 1946,[6] to ascertain facts relating to alleged violations of Greek territory by Albania, Bulgaria and Yugoslavia. This precursor of future peace observation, now generally covered by the term 'peacekeeping', became a novel style of diplomacy for the resolution of conflicts through peaceful means. It has been effectively used by the UN, by regional organizations, and in multinational arrangements.

With the reduction in the Cold War after the death of Stalin, the superpowers, in order to by-pass Security Council involvement, agreed to multinational arrangements outside the UN. The Neutral Nations Supervisory Commission, as part of the Korean armistice agreement, and the International Control Commission in South-East Asia were set up under such arrangements. But neither of these missions proved effective.

The subsequent years witnessed an increasing involvement by the UN Secretary-General in the operations authorized by the Security Council or the General Assembly. Typical examples are the peace observation missions in Indonesia; the 1958 Lebanese crisis; the UN operations in the Congo and Rwanda-Burundi in 1960–4; the conflict in West Irian in 1962; and the UN observer mission in Yemen in 1962–4. Although it would be appropriate to discuss in this chapter the UN's observer mission in the Dominican Republic in 1965–66, this mission is remarkable in that 'it was established to observe a peace-keeping operation by a regional organization — the Organization of American States (OAS) — and as such was the first of its kind. It is therefore discussed in Chapter 5 on Regional Organizations (pages 131–78).

While it is not always easy to separate peace observation and peacekeeping operations, various types of observer operations are described below, with important examples, in order that their usefulness in the peaceful settlement of disputes can be judged.

Investigation

For the observer mission during the civil war in Greece in 1947, the UN Special Committee on the Balkans (UNSCOB) was set up to deal with the alleged border violations. Greece had been under Axis occupation during the Second World War, and the British, after landing in 1944, had assisted local forces to regain control. At the end of the war, when the authority of the Axis powers was removed, two rival groups claimed sovereignty. A non-Communist group formed a government of national unity with the support of the Greek army, a guerrilla group (EDEDS) and the British forces; while the resistance movement, under the control of Communists, organized a National Liberation Front (EAM) consisting of leftist parties and ELAS, another guerrilla group. In their attempt to gain full control, the Communists encouraged their guerrilla groups, who operated in the northern part of the country where they could receive aid from the Communist regimes of neighbouring states.

The Soviet Union first complained to the Security Council in January 1946 that the continued presence of British troops was a threat to international peace. Later the Ukraine complained of incidents along the Greek-Albanian border. In December 1946, the Greek government brought a complaint before the Security Council that Albania, Bulgaria and Yugoslavia were assisting the guerrillas in northern Greece. The United States proposed to set up a Commission of Investigation, and this went through without Soviet veto. However the Soviets were clearly determined to destroy the project by other means.

The three neighbouring states declined to co-operate with the Commission; and when the Commission upheld the Greek government's complaint, the Soviets vetoed three Council resolutions to accept its report and implement its recommendations. On an initiative of the United States, this item was removed from the Security Council agenda and a resolution by the second General Assembly in October 1947[7] created a new Committee in place of the earlier Commission.

The terms of reference of the Committee were broader than those of the abrogated Commission. It could perform its functions wherever it deemed fit; it would report to the Assembly; it would remain in existence at the will of the Assembly, and it would use its good offices to settle disputed matters and observe the maintenance of peace. Further, a novel provision was added requiring the UN Secretary-General to provide staff for the Committee, and to negotiate with each of the four governments concerned what later came to be known as 'status agreements' for peacekeeping operations.

The Third General Assembly in 1948, in addition to calling for an end to external interference in Greece, condemned the three neighbouring Communist states; authorized[8] UNSCOB to utilize the services and good offices of one or more persons, whether or not members of their Committee; and called on the four governments to settle frontier questions in accordance with previous conventions, or conclude new ones; and to settle the problem of refugees.

When the Fourth General Assembly met, the Yugoslav border was no longer available to guerrillas, as a result of the rift between Yugoslavia and the Soviet Union. All the three Communist states reported that Greek guerrillas entering their territories were being disarmed. The situation improved during 1950.

The Commission of Investigation established by the Security Council had met in Athens, visited Salonika and travelled to the three neighbouring states to examine witnesses and hear testimony, and before it was abolished it had begun to investigate border incidents. It exercised these functions of consultation and peace observation with moderation and tact.

UNSCOB, obliged to observe from within Greek territory alone, interrogated witnesses and monitored radio broadcasts of the 'Free Greece' radio station located in Yugoslavia, as well as broadcasts from the three neighbouring states. The UN had little experience in organizing peace missions at that time, and the operation of observer posts presented totally new problems. The UN flag and identification badges were used for the first time; administrative and logistical arrangements had to be made; and, since the UN Secretariat could not provide all the staff, extra personnel were employed including military attachés from nations represented in the Committee with embassies in Athens. The expenses of the delegates were paid by their own governments. These delegates took orders from their respective countries and not from the Secretary-General — the latter practice was only to develop later. However, the observer team members did act as individuals, and reported to UNSCOB. When, on a recommendation by the Greek Government, the sixth General Assembly session in 1951 terminated UNSCOB, its responsibilities were assigned to a subcommission of the Peace Observation Commission[9] (POC). These observers reported both to the POC and the Secretary-General, and their reports were circulated as General Assembly documents directly to the member-states.

Initially, this mission was given an investigative responsibility. Later, the UNSCOB role was expanded to provide good offices to negotiate and to maintain peace. While its main purpose was to investigate complaints and report first to the Security Council and later to the General Assembly, UNSCOB was given additional tasks. It established processes that were to become generally adopted;

already peace observation operations by the UN were laid on firm foundations for the future.

Maintenance of ceasefire

The United Nations Yemen Observation Mission (UNYOM) was established by the Security Council in 1963 following an agreement between Egypt, Saudi Arabia and Yemen to end the fighting there.[10] Saudi Arabia also agreed to suspend aid to the forces of the Imam of Yemen, who had sought its help after being removed from power by a pro-Nasserite military coup. The Egyptians agreed to withdraw their troops which had been sent at the request of the military rulers.

UNYOM arrived in the area on June 13, 1963, but it left on 4 September 1964 without having accomplished disengagement. This was because the Egyptians and Saudis did not comply with the agreement. Since the cost of the operation was being borne by these two governments, and they did not wish to continue it, UNYOM was terminated.

The UN Military Observer Group in India and Pakistan (UNMOGIP), established in 1949, has been the observer mission to remain longest in service. On the division of the sub-continent into two, most of the Indian princely states chose to join either India or Pakistan. The status of only three states was left undetermined: Hyderabad, Junagarh, and Jammu and Kashmir (hereafter 'J & K'). J & K has been a major source of conflict between India and Pakistan, leading to two wars in 1947–8 and 1965 respectively.

In the middle of the nineteenth century the British defeated the Sikh princes who ruled northern India, and gave J & K to a loyal Hindu prince to end the Sikh dominance over this region. Geographically J & K consists of five regions: the north-east; the strategically important region of Ladakh, bordering Sinkiang in China and Tibet, with Buddhists forming a majority of the population; the north-west which, like Ladakh, borders Sinkiang and is predominantly Muslim; the central region, Poonch and the Kashmir Valley, mostly with a Muslim majority; and Jammu, predominantly Hindu. Maharaja Hari Singh vacillated over which side to join: if he joined Pakistan he could not, as a Hindu, remain a ruler; if he chose India, the introduction of democratic institutions would spell the end of his family rule.

The Governor-Generals of India and Pakistan, Lord Mountbatten and Muhammad Ali Jinnah respectively, agreed on a Standstill Agreement for six months. But J & K could not remain isolated from the religious disturbances and fighting across the sub-continent which preceded partition. Soon Poonch, the Kashmir Valley and Jammu became affected. Many Hindus from the plains of the Punjab had escaped to Jammu to save themselves from the marauding Muslims. In September 1947, Pathan tribesmen from Pakistan's frontier belt

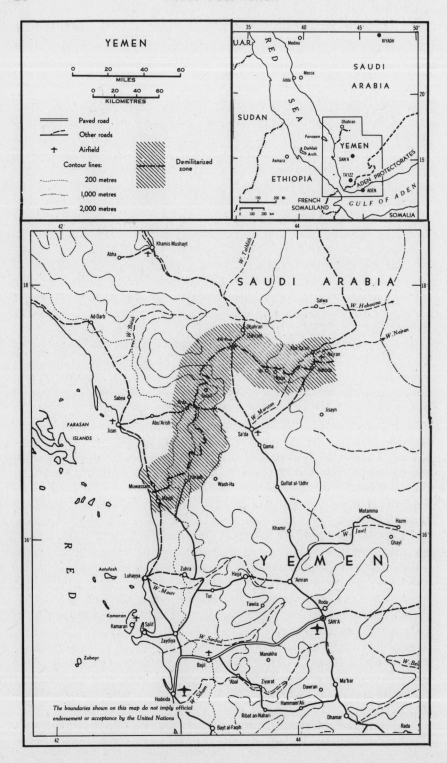

The boundaries shown on this map do not imply official
endorsement or acceptance by the United Nations

with Afghanistan and Iran were able to swarm into Kashmir to help their co-religionists, committing murder, rape and arson as they advanced up the Kashmir Valley to the outskirts of Srinagar. In face of this mass tribal invasion, Maharaja Hari Singh acceded the state to India, called for military assistance and fled from the capital. The National Conference, the majority political party in the State, then invited Sheikh Mohammed Abdullah, a Muslim and a national hero of Kashmir, to establish a provisional government. With the gradual build-up of the Indian forces, the tribesmen were pushed back, triggering the direct involvement of Pakistani forces within J & K territory in their support.

On January 1, 1948, in the Security Council, India accused Pakistan of assisting the raiders who had attacked J & K, which now belonged to India. On 20 January, the Council established a UN Commission for India and Pakistan (UNCIP)[11] composed of Argentina, Czechoslovakia and United States representatives. The Council resolution directed UNCIP to 'proceed to the spot as quickly as possible' with the dual function of 'investigating the facts pursuant to Article 34[12] of the Charter', and exercising a 'mediatory influence likely to smooth away difficulties'.

In April 1948, two more members from Belgium and Canada were added to the Commission. After reaching the sub-continent and fully apprising itself of the situation, UNCIP adopted a resolution calling for a ceasefire and truce agreement, and indicated that a plebiscite would follow the truce. The Security Council, anticipating a ceasefire in J & K, asked the Secretary-General to appoint and send a high-ranking officer to act as a military adviser to the Commission and to arrange the despatch of military observers at short notice to supervise the ceasefire.[13] By the end of the year India and Pakistan agreed to their proposals, and a ceasefire came into effect on 1 January 1949. The next day Lt.-Gen. Maurice Delvoie of Belgium with some observers began the supervision of the ceasefire.

On 15 January 1949 the military commanders of India and Pakistan agreed to the following (known as the Karachi Agreement):[14] (1) slight adjustments in troop dispositions to avoid minor incidents; (2) use of specified supply roads by both armies; (3) withdrawal of all 'raiders' from J & K as soon as possible; (4) the Azad Kashmir (Pakistan-supported) force to be relieved in the forward areas, and (5) both Indian and Pakistani armies to give UNCIP all the facilities it required to establish observer teams in the area of J & K. Each neutral observer team would include an Indian and Pakistani officer. The plan was put into effect on the Pakistan side on February 3 and on the Indian side on February 10, by which time twenty military observers had been deployed.

The terms of reference of the military observers have not changed much since January 1, 1949, despite the many efforts to transform the

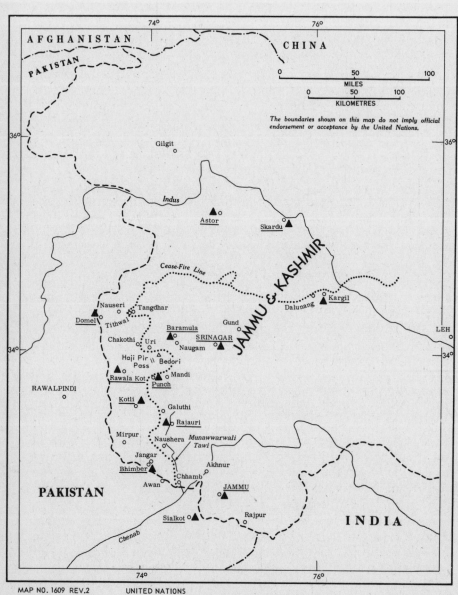

MAP NO. 1609 REV.2   UNITED NATIONS
FEBRUARY 1971

ceasefire into a truce and to arrange for a plebiscite. A ceasefire line was established[15] on July 29, 1949. The Agreement specifies: (1) the observers to be stationed by UNCIP when it seems necessary; (2) the ceasefire line to be verified mutually on the ground by local commanders on each side with the assistance of UNMOs; (3) disagreements to be referred to the UNCIP Military Adviser whose decision will be final; (4) the Military Adviser to be responsible for issuing the final map indicating the ceasefire line; (5) certain activities — e.g. strengthening defences, increasing troop levels, increasing military potential — were prohibited.

In September 1949 the ceasefire was effectively in place. On September 19, UNCIP left the sub-continent, informing the two governments that the Military Adviser and UNMOs would of course remain and pursue their normal activities.[16]

On March 14, 1950, the Security Council established a UN Representative: (1) to assist in the preparation, and to supervise the implementation, of the programme of demilitarization; (2) to make suggestions for solution of the disputed matters; (3) to exercise all powers of the UN Commission as hitherto agreed; and (4) to arrange for a plebiscite administrator to assume his functions. This resolution terminated UNCIP.[17] Dr Frank Graham was appointed UN Representative and later Admiral Nimitz was chosen as the Plebiscite Administrator. By July 1949 General Delvoie had thirty-two observers from the United States, Canada, Belgium, Mexico and Norway. Later the number of observers was increased to sixty-five, from Chile, Denmark and Sweden as well as the five countries just named.

On March 30, 1951, the Security Council decided that the military observer group should continue to supervise the ceasefire in J & K, and requested the two governments to ensure that their Agreement regarding the ceasefire should continue to be faithfully observed.[18] The UN Representative subsequently reported that the debate in the Council on this resolution indicated that the Council meant the Representative to deal only with the question of the demilitarization of J & K. The responsibilities for the ceasefire and other clauses of the Karachi Agreement were placed upon UNMOGIP.[19]

As part of the January 1949 agreement, India and Pakistan had agreed (1) to hold the line of forward defended localities as at the time of the ceasefire; (2) no further advance to be made in positions; (3) no patrolling forward of these positions; (4) to carry out troop reliefs as ordered before; (5) a 500-yard demilitarized zone on both sides of the ceasefire to be patrolled by civilian police; and (6) to help local refugees to settle in their homes.

In 1954 the United States extended military aid to Pakistan. Then India requested that the United States observers and air crew be replaced, as they were no longer considered neutral.

The cost of UNMOGIP averaged between $500,000 and $600,000

per year. The military personnel were paid travel, subsistence and $100 kit allowance, their own countries being responsible for their basic salaries and allowances.

The organisation of UNMOGIP is shown in the table below. The group had the following three functions: (1) investigation of complaints, (2) determination of the order of battle of the two armies and other troop information, and (3) control of civilians.

UNMOs operated in groups of two or three, and a network of radio communications was established. Messages were sent by code to protect information regarding troop movements.

Incidents are investigated by observers on both sides of the line. In the event of fighting, military observers proceed to the area 'to calm the troops on their respective side',[20] and frequently UN jeeps flying the UN flag move into the line of fire to stop the clashes. The second function is to report on troop movements to guard against dangerous build-ups. This last has required secrecy. The sparseness of published reports from UNMOGIP indicates the 'top secret' nature of this work. The third function relates to the problem of civilians in the 500-yard zone. Often local commanders intervene with troops, but both sides have indicated confidence in the UN observers by inviting them to resolve violations.

The general tranquillity along the ceasefire lines ended early in 1961. Politically, there was an impasse. India insisted that Pakistani troops withdraw from territory occupied by them before a plebiscite could be held, and although this was not written in the arrangement, Pakistan insisted that India too withdraw all its forces so that a free plebiscite could be held in areas occupied by them. United States military aid to Pakistan, and the latter's participation in CENTO and SEATO, had altered the US position and made India even more insistent on Pakistan withdrawal from J & K. Following India's war with China in 1962, Pakistan seemed to apply pressure on the United States, and to influence India by rectifying the boundary between China and Pakistan-occupied J & K. In fact, this accord even included the part of J & K held by the Indian forces.

The incident of the stolen hair of the Prophet from a mosque in Srinagar, and differences between Sheikh Mohammed Abdullah, the popular Kashmir leader, and the Indian government all created conditions enabling large infiltrations by civilians from Pakistan-held territory, resulting in violence in Indian-held areas. This escalated into war between India and Pakistan during the summer of 1965. Unlike 1947–8, fighting this time was not confined to J & K alone. This was because India had made it known that any attack against J & K would be considered as an attack against sovereign Indian territory. So when fighting erupted along the ceasefire line, India launched its operation against Pakistan's mainland towards Sialkot and Lahore.

After about ten days of fighting, the UN Security Council was able to arrange a ceasefire.[21] The UN India Pakistan Observer Mission (UNIPOM) under Maj.-Gen. Bruce MacDonald of Canada was introduced to separate the two armies and to arrange a withdrawal to their new territory. However, UNMOGIP remained responsible for the restoration of the ceasefire line in J & K, with some strengthening of UNMOs,[22] and co-operation between the two missions was established.

Before the end of the year, on a request by the two parties, the Security Council extended UNIPOM for a second period of three months, and the Secretary-General extended the added personnel with UNMOGIP for the same period. The Tashkent Agreement between India and Pakistan, achieved through the mediation efforts of the Soviet Prime Minister Kosygin, decided on withdrawals by both sides to the positions held by them up to August 5, 1965, to be completed by February 25, 1966.[23] These withdrawals applied to the ceasefire line in J & K under the Karachi Agreement, and to the international border between India and Pakistan. On February 26, 1966, the Secretary-General reported that this task had been completed. Since that date the basis of the activities of UNMOGIP has been exclusively the Karachi Agreement and arrangements related to it.

The 1971 war between India and Pakistan, leading to the independence of Bangladesh, did not materially influence the situation in J & K. Since that war India has emphasized the importance of bilateral relations with Pakistan, as exemplified by the Simla talks in 1972 between the Indian Prime Minister Indira Gandhi and Pakistan's leader Zulfiqar Ali Bhutto. India has shown little interest in the continuing UN presence in J & K, while Pakistan attaches great importance to it: UNMOGIP observers remain deployed in Pakistan–occupied areas whereas, on the Indian side, UN observers are now

Peace Observation

only permitted at divisional headquarters level.

Although there is little chance of a solution, or indeed even of a resumption of negotiations, Pakistan insists on maintaining UNMOGIP, whereas India has agreed to its presence only 'because the UN wants it'. The presence of UNMOGIP keeps the question of J & K alive within the UN and provides a UN presence in a serious conflict which remains unresolved. While some consensus has evolved between India and Pakistan, serious differences remain.

Most of the area under Pakistan occupation was always largely populated by Muslims. Buddhists form a large majority in Ladakh, which prefers to be part of India. Similarly most of the Indian-held part of Jammu province had a Hindu majority, and now few Muslims remain. Thus, with the exception of some small areas along the cease-fire line, only the former minor princely state of Poonch, which had a majority of Muslims (now living in Pakistani-held territory), and the Muslim-dominated Valley of Kashmir remain contentious. Since the 1962 war between India and China, the Kashmir Valley has become vital to India's strategic needs because it provides the best routes to the frontier with China (Sinkiang province) and Western Tibet, and the only important surface approach to Ladakh.

To win Chinese support against India, Pakistan entered into an agreement to cede most of the border territory claimed by China in the Pakistani-held part of J & K. This has not only weakened India's case in its border dispute with China but exasperated India, since Pakistan has made this agreement in respect of military-occupied territory in violation of international law.

Pakistan continues to call for a plebiscite to decide the future of J & K. India responds by contending that a number of free elections have been held in Indian-controlled territory; and a duly elected state government controls the state. By contrast there have been no elections by Pakistan in the territory under its control.

The organization and deployment of the UN mission has remained unchanged since the start. The observers were divided into two groups, one attached to each side under a Control Headquarters in close liaison with the Commander of the operation theatre. The two Control Headquarters were under the direct command of the Military Adviser till his departure, and then the Chief Military Observer. There have been no fatal casualties in the line of duty. The Chief Military Observer deals directly with the Chief of Staff of the Indian Army and the Commander-in-Chief of the Pakistan Army. The observer teams are attached to army formations of each side.

The financial arrangements of UNMOGIP were made by the Secretary-General under the authority granted to him by the General Assembly Resolution 252 (III C) paragraph (*a*) on unforeseen and extraordinary expenses (A/C/5/275, last paragraph). However, expenses were covered in 1949 by the regular budget of the organization, as they have been ever since (from 1950 Sec A/C 5/338 and General Assembly Official Records XXIII, Session Supplement no. 5, part VI, section 16, chapter II). Supplementary budgets for additional costs in 1965 were approved by the General Assembly (Resolutions 2124, 2125 [XX] and 2195 [XXI]).

The functions and operating procedures of UNMOGIP 'have been incorporated in its Field Regulations, and have become the practice with all UN military observer operations. In carrying out these responsibilities UNMOs report their findings and observations to both sides and to the Secretary-General, who in turn may inform the Security Council if appropriate. The observers are expected to abide by the Karachi Agreement, but are not entitled to seek enforcement of the terms.

Contrary to normal practice, UNMOGIP does not submit regular reports to the UN organs, and its existence is often forgotten. From the early days it was agreed that reporting to the Security Council should be on a confidential basis to avoid prejudice against UNMOs who are rotated between both sides. This practice proved disadvantageous to India in 1965 when Pakistani agents slipped into the Valley, leading to military escalation and a new war for which India was blamed because the facts had not been placed on record by the UN Secretariat.

UNMOGIP, in more than thirty years of existence, has enjoyed the confidence of both sides. Although, as we have noted, Pakistan has shown more enthusiasm for it than India, certainly since the 1971 war, both governments have provided the observers with the agreed facilities and support. General Delvoie left the area in November 1949 and Brig. Henry Angle of Canada, Acting Chief Military Observer, assumed command, but this fine Second World War Armoured Corps officer was killed in an air accident. Lt.-Gen. R. H. Nimmo of Australia was appointed in 1950, and after his death was replaced by Lt.-Gen. Luis Tassara Gonzales of Chile. Nimmo and Tassara served ably through many crises, including the 1965 and 1971 wars. Brig.-Gen. Stig Waldenström of Sweden, a veteran peacekeeper, was appointed Chief of Staff in June 1978, and Brig.-Gen. Thor A. Johnsen of Norway in May 1982. Observers from fourteen countries and aircraft from the United States, Italy, Canada and Australia have participated in this mission.

The Kashmir problem remains a major hurdle in the normalization of relations between India and Pakistan. The Simla Agreement of 1971 emphasised bilateral relations between the two countries. The Janata Government of Morarji Desai and, since 1980, Indira Gandhi's Government in Delhi and Gen. Mohammed Zia ul Haq's regime in Islamabad have done much to harmonize relations; yet Pakistan has brought the Kashmir question to the attention of international forums. Taking into account the global strategic environment and relating it to the Soviet military intervention in Afghanistan, renewed large-scale United States military aid to Pakistan, Indo-Soviet relations, the friendship between Pakistan and China since the early 1960s and the possibility of the United States attempting to establish some joint military arrangement with China and Pakistan against the Soviet Union (which could not fail to affect India), a crisis over Kashmir could easily spark off another war between India and Pakistan. Such a war is not only a real danger in itself but is more likely than its predecessors to bring serious involvement by the two superpowers and China, with all its inherent dangers. Although UNMOGIP's role is only a presence and a confidence-building measure, it does provide eyes and ears for the Security Council, thereby usefully serving the cause of peace.

Armistice supervision

The United Nations Truce Supervision Organisation (UNTSO) provides a suitable example of armistice supervision responsibilities.

The seeds of the conflict between Arabs and Jews were planted during the First World War. The British were fighting the Turkish empire, which included all the Arab territories in West Asia except Saudi Arabia. Jewish settlements in Palestine, started in the late nineteenth century, were gradually increasing; the Jews sought a national home. The Sykes-Picot treaty of 1916 enacted that the Arab territories then under Turkish rule would be divided between Britain and France after their victory, and among other territories the British would inherit Palestine. The importance of Jewish support to the Allied war effort led to the Balfour Declaration in 1917, which promised the Jews a homeland in Palestine. At the same time the British made promises to the Arabs concerning their independence because of the support they had given to the war effort against the Turks.

Subsequently Jewish persecution in Europe, the colossal massacre of Jews by the Nazis in the Second World War, the strong Jewish support for the Allied war effort, including manpower for the armed forces, and the influence of Jews in the United States, all led to pressure for the early establishment of a Jewish national home.

The fighting in Palestine between Jews and Arab nationalists, which had already erupted in the 1930s but been kept under control by the British mandatory power, reopened with great ferocity after the Second World War as the immigration of Jewish victims of Nazi crimes in Europe increased. In April 1947 the United Kingdom brought the problem to the General Assembly and announced its desire to give up the mandate. A special session of the General Assembly held in April-May 1947 established a Special Committee in Palestine (UNSCOP) to investigate the question,[24] and after receiving

UNSCOP's report[25] the General Assembly recommended the termination of the mandate, and the partition of Palestine into an Arab and a Jewish state. Jerusalem was to be placed under international control, and the territories were to be linked in a plan of economic union.[26]

The Jewish leaders accepted this, but the Arabs rejected it and resorted to fighting to prevent its implementation. The Security Council was charged with the problem of stopping the war in February 1948. In April it called for a truce[27] and established a Truce Commission composed of the Belgian, French, United States and Syrian Consuls in Palestine. The last refused to serve, since the Syrian forces had joined the Arab armies in attacking Israel. In May the General Assembly appointed a Mediator with responsibilities overlapping those of the Truce Commission: Count Folke Bernadotte of Sweden.[28]

The British terminated their mandate in accordance with the General Assembly's resolution at midnight on May 14–15, 1948, and at the same time the Jewish people of Palestine declared the independence of the state of Israel. The Palestinian Arabs and the neighbouring Arab states immediately attacked the new Jewish state.

After six weeks of fighting, the Security Council was able to obtain a four-week ceasefire;[29] it also increased the authority of the Mediator to supervise the ceasefire with the help of military observers. Fighting resumed at the end of the ceasefire, and in June the Council again called for a halt to the bloodshed.[30] However, sporadic fighting continued while the Mediator tried to find a way around the impasse. Before his proposals could be submitted to the UN suggesting some changes to the Partition Plan (the news of some of which had leaked out), he was assassinated by Jewish terrorists, but already he had done valuable work. The Truce Commission had been joined in early May by four staff members from the UN Secretariat, including a military adviser. The duties of the Commission relating to a ceasefire were confined to Jerusalem where, after the arrival of the Mediator, they were assisted by his staff.

Count Bernadotte obtained fifty-one observers from the states making up the Truce Commission to observe the first truce, between June 11 and July 9. The Commission and the Mediator were responsible for determining whether Arabs and Jews were observing the Truce and the Council's ceasefire terms. The observers were deployed in five areas: Jerusalem, Western, Central, Southern and Northern. They were based respectively at Jerusalem, Tel Aviv, Ramallah, Gaza and Arfula. Additional observers were located in Amman, Baghdad, Beirut, Jbail (Byblos, Lebanon), Cyprus, Damascus and Egyptian ports. The observers were to prevent either side from gaining military advantage and were authorized to demand 'that acts contrary to terms of truce be not committed, or be rectified', but had no power to enforce such demands. They were to settle disputes by direct approaches to local commanders and authorities and, when possible, by bringing them together.[31]

The second truce, which started on July 18, could not be fully implemented. During this period the number of observers from the same three countries was raised from 51 to 682, and communications equipment was supplied by France, the United Kingdom and the United States. The Mediator, through a Chief of Staff, was entirely responsible for the operations. He deployed 127 observers with the Israeli defence forces; 79 in Jerusalem; 40 with Palestinian Arabs; and 69 with Arab forces.

In the situation of extreme hostility between Arabs and Jews, the task of the observers was far from easy. In the Arab Sector of Palestine there was no administrative authority. The lines between the Arab and Jewish forces kept changing, and Arab refugees were an added problem. However, the Mediator did enjoy the Council's full support, and the rapid availability of personnel and equipment eased his task.

The Mediator and Truce Commission could obtain information and examine witnesses, had the right to inspect all types of transport, and enjoyed excellent communications within mission areas and with New York. They were to perform many different tasks which have since become typical of peace observation (or peacekeeping) responsibilities: observing ceasefire and armistice lines, establishing and supervising demilitarized zones (DZs), establishing procedures to deal with violations and maintain the truce, keeping contacts with the parties, removing mines and obstructions along essential roads and areas needed for operations, transferring prisoners and protecting minorities. Observation was conducted by mobile patrols and at fixed posts.

The duties of the Mediator and Truce Commission reinforced each other. Count Bernadotte enjoyed great prestige, unlike the Consuls constituting the Commission. The co-operation between them was made easier as the Commission confined its role to Jerusalem, whereas the Mediator had wider responsibilities. After Bernadotte's murder, Dr Ralph Bunche, who had been his assistant, was appointed Acting Mediator. Between May 1948 and July 1948, about fifteen serious violations were reported, yet the Truce was maintained. This in itself speaks for the success of the operation.

In November 1948, the Security Council called on the parties directly involved to seek agreement for an immediate armistice including the delineation of armistice demarcation lines.[32] The General Assembly established a Conciliation Commission including representatives of France, Turkey and the United States to assume the functions formerly assigned to the Mediator or to the Truce Commission.[33] Ralph Bunche as the Acting Mediator plunged ahead to secure armistice agreements between the belligerents, but he soon learned that an agreement between Arabs as one party and Israel was impossible because of disunity among the Arabs. He then succeeded, by July 1949, in concluding separate agreements with each of the Arab belligerent states and with Israel.

On August 11, 1949 the Security Council discharged the Acting Mediator from further responsibility; noted the provisions of the Mixed Armistice Agreements establishing Mixed Armistice Commissions (MACs); requested the Secretary-General to continue to provide personnel for UNTSO, assist the parties to observe the terms of the agreements, and supervise their application; and required the Chief of Staff to report to the Council on the observance of the cease-fire, and to keep the Palestine Conciliation Commission informed in matters of mutual concern.[34]

With this Council Resolution the third phase of UNTSO operations was set in motion. Ralph Bunche returned to New York, and with the departure of Swedish officers after Bernadotte's death, General William Riley of the US Marine Corps, who had first been appointed acting Chief of Staff, was made permanent in this position. With headquarters in Jerusalem, he was assisted by a Political Adviser and other civilian staff from the UN Secretariat together with military staff assigned by contributing countries, as were the military observers. The basic organization of UNTSO remained the same as before. However, the observers came from several countries instead of from only one, as was the case in the beginning when Bernadotte had only Swedish officers.

The armistice agreements removed the embargo on military shipments and entry of military personnel, thereby obviating the need to observe ports and transportation. Once the armistice lines were marked, the number of observers was reduced to about fifty. Thereafter the main tasks of observers were to prevent incursions and supervise the demilitarized zones: around Jerusalem on Mount Scopus, the Mount of Olives, the Latrun pumping station, and Government House where the UNTSO headquarters was located; the Gaza strip (the south-western part of Palestine which had been occupied by Egyptian forces during the 1948 hostilities); El Auja (Nitzana) on the international frontier near El Arish in Egypt; south of Lake Huleh and then along the River Jordan to Lake Tiberias; and along the eastern shore of Lake Tiberias, starting about the middle of the eastern shore of the lake and extending to El Hamma. Another important function was to provide Chairmen for the Mixed Armistice Commissions (MACs).

Whenever the ceasefire was violated, the Chief of Staff was able to act quickly, avoiding delays and restrictions imposed by MACs. He might decide to send observers immediately to the place where an exchange of fire had started, and a ceasefire might be arranged before

the observation and investigation machinery of the armistice agreements could be set in motion.[35]

Most of the work of the observers was the investigation of incidents involving breaches of the armistice agreements.[36] Each MAC could have three to five delegates from Israel and the Arab state concerned, with an UNTSO military observer as Chairman. In practice each side nominated three, except for the Egyptian-Israeli MAC (EIMAC) which had two each.

The third phase ended with the Suez war in October 1956. This period was marked by an increase in tensions. The General Armistice Agreement (GAA) of 1949 was intended to promote the return of permanent peace to Palestine, and the armistices were accepted as an indispensable step towards that end. The UN, with the willing agreement of the parties directly involved, envisaged that a cessation of hostilities would provide conditions for starting negotiations to achieve permanent peace. This did not happen because of a number of obstacles to peace.

The most important matter to be resolved was the future of Arab Palestine refugees.[37] They lived in camps in the Gaza strip, on the West Bank and in the neighbouring Arab states, and thus were a constant reminder that there could be little peace till they were given the right to return and settle in what they believed was their usurped homeland. But the Israelis maintained that they had fled their homeland on the advice of the Arab Higher Committee, and had therefore forfeited the right to live in the country. At first Israel was willing to permit 100,000 refugees to return, but later this offer was withdrawn.

A second question related to compensation claims for Arab property left in Israel. The Israelis agreed in principle but needed outside financial help which could be made available by interested great powers.

A third question related to the future of Jerusalem. The UN plan called for international control. The Israelis rejected this plan, Arabs generally accepted it, but Jordan, which was in occupation of Jerusalem, wished to retain the city.

The last but not the least important problem related to the question of boundaries. The Arabs wished to return to the Partition Plan boundaries. Israel's position was that since the Arabs had rejected the Partition Plan, the boundaries should generally conform to the GAA lines, with equitable exchanges to eliminate some inconvenient lines that had been drawn arbitrarily. The armistice line along the Israeli-Lebanese border followed the old international frontier, and was generally accepted by the inhabitants. Furthermore, the Lebanese government wanted quiet along the border so that its people could pursue their economic life in peace. Thus the Israel-Lebanon Mixed Armistice Commission (ILMAC) had few complaints to deal with. The armistice line between Egypt and Israel also generally followed the international frontier except for the demilitarized zone at El Auja and where, from a point just south of Rafah, it ran along the Gaza strip.

There were three areas which required a special watch; the Gaza strip, where about 200,000 Palestine Arab refugees lived in UNRWA camps and sought ways to violate the armistice lines; El Auja; and the southern tip of the frontier on the Gulf of Aqaba, where the Israelis were developing a port at Elath and were being prevented from using it by Egyptian military action from across the border. Though EIMAC was never over-burdened with complaints or incidents, this area witnessed some serious violations resulting in heavy casualties to both sides. As the situation worsened between the Arabs and Israel, the Gaza strip became an important *fedayeen* (guerrilla) base, and hence one of the main causes of the 1956 war.

The political tensions between a weak government in Syria and a determined Israel led only to few incidents, but they were very serious ones. Here too the armistice line ran along the old frontier except for the two demilitarized zones which were the cause of most of the inci-dents. The DZs had been established because there were areas awarded to Israel under the 1947 Partition Plan which were under Syrian occupation when the ceasefire was established. The GAA provided for separation of the two military forces to avoid incidents, and restoration to normal life within the zones. Chairman ISMAC (Israel-Syria MAC) was made responsible for the implementation of relevant articles in the GAA. Israel held the view that it had full sovereignty over the zones, subject only to the commitment of keeping their military forces out of them. Israel also insisted that the Chairman of ISMAC (an appointment held by the Chief of Staff UNTSO) was responsible, and not ISMAC itself. Consequently Israel refused to participate in this MAC. On the other hand, Syria held the view that all activity in the DZs should have their prior consent. The UN policy directives to the Chief of Staff decreed that the Chairman MAC could determine whether any activity violated the GAA, subject to review by the Security Council.

An added factor resulting in incidents was that the armistice line along Lake Tiberias was a few feet away from the frontier, resulting in both sides shooting at each other's ships. Furthermore, where the Israeli, Jordanian and Syrian frontiers met in the DZ there were two Israeli *kibbutzim* providing easy targets for the Arabs.

There were two major incidents in the DZs, and one along the frontier. Early in 1951 Israel began dredging operations to dry the marsh by Lake Huleh. As a result of a Syrian complaint, the Chief of Staff UNTSO recommended that the operation be halted until a MAC could deal with it but the Israelis refused to comply. Not only did they decline to participate in ISMAC but they also alleged that the Chief of Staff was biassed and therefore denied his authority in the DZs.

Meanwhile, the exchange of firing continued. On May 8, 1951, the Security Council, acting on the Chief of Staff's recommendation, called for a ceasefire, reaffirmed the authority of the Chief of Staff as stated in the GAA, and called on the two parties to attend MAC meetings. Both sides agreed to this, but Israel refused to participate in the MAC.

In 1953 Israel decided to divert the Jordan waters in the northern DZ for a power project. The Chief of Staff declared that such a diversion would alter the nature of the zone in a way that would be unfavourable to Syria. When Israel again denied the authority of the Chief of Staff as Chairman of ISMAC, the Security Council insisted that such changes required Syrian consent.

On December 11, 1955, Israeli troops crossed the frontier in force and attacked a Syrian post, causing heavy casualties. The Security Council blamed Israel and was able to deal with the incident. Its significance was that, in spite of previous knowledge by the Chief of Staff, UNTSO, that military preparations were being made by Israel, any UN action was stymied by Israel's refusal to participate in the MAC which provided the machinery to deal with such situations.

Israel's intransigence resulted in incidents and violations being dealt with by the Security Council, which greatly limited the role of UNTSO in this area. At this time the Cold War was at its height, and all actions by the superpowers in the area were largely influenced by their own conflict. Hereafter the Arab-Israeli conflict was very much part of the Cold War, with the Soviets gradually gaining influence over the Arabs and siding with their cause by using, or threatening to use, the veto in the Council.

The Israel-Jordan armistice line was about 300 miles long and included the sensitive DZ around Jerusalem. The GAA had left Jordan with a large gain for King Abdullah and his army, Jordan being the only Arab nation to have kept a large part of Palestine, including Jerusalem. It was therefore in Jordan's interests to maintain quiet along this armistice line. In fact this sector had the largest number of incidents, and by August 1955 the number of unsettled complaints stood at 2,150.[38]

General Burns, Chief of Staff in 1954–6, wrote: 'The cases individually were of little moment, . . . but the effect of having so many unsettled was to discourage subtly the members of the MAC and the observers, and tend to make them feel that it was not of much consequence whether a complaint was or was not investigated, and dealt with by the MAC. It gave the feeling that the machinery of MAC was clogged, and grinding to a standstill — which in fact it was. The enormous backlog obliged the MAC to deal with the more serious cases on an emergency basis so that when both sides wanted the organization to be effective, it could.'[39]

The main problems along the armistice line were the following. (1)

More than 100 villages had been cut off from their lands, so that every attempt by the farmers to reach their lands constituted a violation. The population and the police were sympathetic to the farmers, and the Jordan government, despite its determined efforts to prevent infiltrations, had to understand the emotions aroused. (2) There were infiltrations to visit relatives, and for smuggling. (3) Egypt, Saudi Arabia and the ex-Mufti were helping groups in Damascus to enlist and train men to carry out sabotage in Israel. Lastly, (4) the area around Jerusalem was extremely sensitive.

Despite these difficulties, the number of serious incidents along this sector was far less than with Egypt or Syria. This was largely due to the efforts of King Abdullah, who worked for a permanent peace. General Sir John Glubb, the able and renowned Commander of the Arab League, and the Jordan government continued this policy even after King Abdullah was assassinated in July 1951. However, this situation changed considerably in the early 1960s when Jordan willy-nilly provided a haven for Palestinian guerrillas.

Wainhouse and Associates,[40] in analysing the role of UNTSO, stated that it was obvious that the peace observation functions of the MACs, UNTSO and the Chief of Staff were far less than those of the Mediator and the Truce Commission. With the existence of armistice lines, the main activity of peace observation was detecting violations of these lines. In due time certain interpretations were given to the Mixed Armistice Agreements, and the August 11 Security Council Resolution (1) confined the jurisdiction of the MACs to the consideration of violations of the armistice agreements that had already taken place and had been brought before it by one of the parties; (2) limited the functions of UNTSO to providing personnel and services to MACs, and (3) limited the functions of the Chief of Staff to acting as or designating the Chairmen of the MACs, acting as Chairman of the Special Committee, and reporting to the Security Council. In the event the consideration by the MACs of violations after they had taken place was insufficient to maintain the ceasefire, and the Security Council remained the final authority to decide future action.

The GAA had given UNTSO more responsibilities than just carrying out such investigations as might be directed by MACs. The supervision of the ceasefire required many more duties, which the Arabs and Israelis had gradually prevented UNTSO from carrying out. UNMOs were being denied their freedom of movement without which they could not adequately perform their responsibilities. Similarly UNTSO was denied its freedom to post UNMOs in sensitive areas. Apparently, these restrictions were being placed with the intention not of eroding the GAA but of preventing the passing by UNMOs of military information about one side to the other side. With some exceptions, military observers have proved their caution and neutrality. The new cases of violation of this trust did not justify limiting the effectiveness of UNTSO in a way which permitted an escalation of the conflict.

Indeed Arab emotionalism, at least surreptitiously, supported infiltration and raids into Israel, and for its part Israel, surrounded by hostile states and with no end in sight to the Arab raids, let alone recognition by them, developed a siege mentality. On becoming Chief of Staff, IDF, General Moshe Dayan persuaded his Minister of Defence Ben Gurion (later Prime Minister) to adopt a policy of retaliation. The necessity for this policy was based on the premise that any Arab infiltration had to be authorized by Arab governments in control of territories adjoining Israel. If the Arab governments failed to authorize it, then they still condoned it either willingly or secretly, and thus deserved to be punished. In fact, retaliation failed to prevent raiding. It was this policy which also set the Arabs and Israelis irreversibly on course for the next war.

The relations between the Arabs and Israel steadily worsened during 1954. In the summer a series of incidents on the Israel-Jordan armistice demarcation line (ADL) led General Burns to warn the Security Council that 'unless such violations were checked they could spread like bushfire'. On February 28, 1955, Israel, in a retaliatory operation against infiltrations from the Gaza strip, attacked the Egyptian military camp near Gaza, leaving thirty dead and many wounded. President Nasser called this raid a turning-point in the Arab-Israeli conflict. In May 1955 Egypt approached the Soviet Union for arms, and there began a steady stream of Soviet bloc weapons and advisers to arm and train the Egyptian forces. The Soviets had already shifted their position from support of Israel to vetoing an attempt by the Security Council to reaffirm its 1951 Resolution calling on Egypt to provide complete freedom of navigation through the Suez Canal.[41]

As the situation worsened during the first quarter of 1956, the Security Council requested the Secretary-General to undertake a survey of the various aspects of enforcement of, and compliance with, GAA and past related Council resolutions,[42] and to arrange with the parties for adoption of any measures which would reduce existing tensions along the ADLs. After a month of visiting Middle Eastern capitals, Hammarskjöld returned to New York and reported[43] that he had obtained agreements for compliance with the ceasefire, that the parties could advance to deal with the main issues, and that the initiative was then in the hands of the governments who were parties to the GAA. In a press statement he said he believed that the present situation offered unique possibilities. The final settlement was still far off, but even a partial solution to the harassing problems would contribute to peace.[44]

By July 1956 a series of developments was to supersede Hammarskjöld's mission to the Middle East. Nasser had provided active

Arab support to the Algerians in their war against France, resulting in a swing in French policy in favour of Israel, and had put pressure on Britain to evacuate the Suez Canal. The Soviets had by now changed to full support for the Arabs. As events hurtled towards a major crisis over the nationalization of the Canal, Nasser antagonized all the signatories (France, the United Kingdom and the United States) to the 1950 Tripartite Declaration (unconnected with the GAA) which had been designed to maintain the *status quo* and deter aggression by any of the Arab governments against Israel. In fact France and the United Kingdom were to join Israel in the Suez war against Egypt. In analysing these events, Burns later wrote: 'Looking back, one can see that by the spring of 1956 the currents which were bearing antagonists in the Middle East towards the whirlpool of war were too strong to be stemmed just by diplomatic interventions, or changed by simple mediation by third parties, including the United Nations and its agent the Secretary-General. If the Three Powers had remained firmly determined to enforce their declaration, peace could have been maintained — but in a few months Nasser's nationalization of the Suez Canal would put an end to that, making enemies of two of the three powers that had undertaken to keep the peace.'[45]

The fourth phase of UNTSO started at the end of the Suez war with the establishment of UNEF I between Egypt and Israel. The presence of UNEF altered the situation in the Gaza strip and on the Sinai frontier. Other than minor infiltrations, both Egypt and Israel co-operated in enabling UNEF to accomplish its responsibilities. This helped to calm the situation and significantly contributed to the general stability of the area. During the Lebanese crisis in 1958 and the simultaneous coup in Baghdad, which in turn threatened the future of the Hashemite Kingdom in Jordan, it was UNEF's presence which prevented a further escalation of the crisis.

After the deployment of UNEF the Israeli government declined to recognize EIMAC. In establishing UNEF the General Assembly had taken cognizance of the GAA. Therefore, the Secretary-General's interpretation of his mandate was that since the GAA provisions remained unaffected, EIMAC could and should continue its operations. This view was supported by the Egyptians, who accordingly continued reporting to EIMAC, besides their dealings with UNEF. Israel dealt only with UNEF until it was withdrawn in May 1967.

In order to overcome this problem, the Secretary-General placed EIMAC for operations under General Burns, Commander UNEF, so that the operations of the two UN peacekeeping operations in this sector could be co-ordinated. Thereafter complaints by Egypt made to EIMAC, or Israeli reports made to UNEF, were examined by both peacekeeping missions. After co-ordination and analysis, Burns had two channels available for reporting to New York, i.e. the UNEF channel, if the matter were strictly within its mandate, or the UNTSO channel by authorizing Chairman EIMAC to report to the Chief of Staff UNTSO.

UNMOs of EIMAC were also used as independent observers when UNEF was involved in a sensitive incident. This independent reporting proved a useful means of satisfying the Commander on facts when he wanted to submit authenticated reports to New York. After Burns's departure, since the relationship between UNEF and EIMAC had become well established, the two missions operated independently but in perfect harmony.

After the outbreak of the June 1967 war, the Security Council demanded an end to hostilities on June 9.[46] Since the fighting had not ended by June 12, the Council called for a return to previous ceasefire lines and co-operation with General Odd Bull of Norway, Chief of Staff UNTSO, and UN observers in implementing a ceasefire.[47] General Bull was asked to make the necessary arrangements with the parties. A ceasefire on the Suez Canal was finally made effective by July 17, 1967, supervised by ninety-one UNMOs. Similarly, observers were redeployed on the Golan Heights. Later, in 1972, following incidents in Southern Lebanon, three observer posts were established there at the request of the Council.

Thus three ceasefire arrangements were established after the June 1967 war. The first was effective on June 10 *in situ*; the second, along the Canal, in July; and the third in Lebanon in 1972. The role of the UN observers was crucial during the war of attrition between Egypt and Israel. When attempts to negotiate Israeli withdrawal from the occupied territories failed, Nasser, unable to permit continued occupation of Sinai, authorized shooting across the Canal. This was followed by Israeli attacks on the Canal cities and air raids on Cairo. US Secretary of State William P. Rogers was able to negotiate an end to this fighting, and the UN authorized Ambassador Gunnar Jarring, its Middle East negotiator, to use his good offices and UNMOs to implement the arrangement.

UNTSO had to be reorganized to cope with its new responsibilities after the June 1967 war. Chief of Staff UNTSO was able to return to his headquarters in Government House, Jerusalem. On the Syrian front Quneitra was occupied by the Israelis. UNTSO established sixteen OPs along the new ceasefire line. MAC headquarters remained in Damascus, and Tiberias Control Centre was also retained. EIMAC headquarters was maintained by a skeleton staff, and a liaison officer remained in Cairo. Eight OPs were kept on the east and seven on the west side of the Canal, each under a control centre. The east was first controlled from Qantara but later from Rabah and the west from Ismailia. Bull recommended helicopters and towers to improve observation along the Canal but did not get the agreement of the parties. ILMAC headquarters remained in Beirut with an outstation at Naqoura. A total of five OPs were established in 1972 and the number of observers was increased.

After the October 1973 war, UNTSO observers were deployed to effect the ceasefire on the Egyptian and Syrian fronts. On the establishment of UNEF II, UNMOs in Sinai were placed under the operational control of the force, and when UNDOF was established, control of UNMOs on the ceasefire line between Israel and Syria passed from Chief of Staff UNTSO to Commander UNDOF. Again after UNIFIL was established, UNMOs in South Lebanon were placed under the operational control of the force Commander.

When UNEF was in operation from October 1973 until July 1979, UNTSO observers in the Egypt-Israel sector assisted and co-operated with UNEF in fulfilment of the latter's tasks. They manned certain checkpoints and conducted patrols in the buffer zone in Sinai. They also carried out inspections of the area of limitation of forces and armaments in the peninsula. During the initial period of UNEF, UNTSO observers also undertook the search for bodies of soldiers killed during the October 1973 hostilities. It may also be recalled that during the formative days of UNEF, the then Chief of Staff of UNTSO, General Siilasvuo, was appointed as Interim Force Commander, and several UNTSO observers, including the Senior Staff Officer, were temporarily assigned to UNEF headquarters pending the appointment of its regular staff. After the withdrawal of UNEF and in accordance with a statement made by the Secretary-General on July 24, 1979, a number of UNTSO observers in the Egypt-Israel sector continued to be stationed there to maintain a UN presence in the area. These were withdrawn when Israel completed withdrawal of its forces from Sinai in April 1982.

In the Israel-Syria sector, UNTSO observers have been assigned to assist UNDOF. Specialized tasks performed by those observers include manning of UNDOF observation posts, and patrolling and inspection of the area of limitation of forces and armaments on the Golan Heights. Selected observers are assigned to staff positions at UNDOF headquarters in Damascus. In addition to the duties mentioned above, observers assigned to ISMAC assist UNDOF in non-operational matters as occasion requires.

UNTSO observers in the Israel-Lebanon sector are organized into two elements. First, the headquarters of ILMAC in Beirut has been maintained and now also functions as a liaison office for UNIFIL. And secondly, observers in south Lebanon perform various tasks under the operational control and supervision of the Commander of UNIFIL. In this connection, observers man the UNTSO observation posts along the armistice demarcation line, conduct patrols as necessary and provide liaison teams with various parties. In addition, UNTSO continues to provide some administrative support for UNIFIL. It should be mentioned also that in pursuance of Security

Council Resolution 467 (1980), the Secretary-General had initiated an
effort aimed at the reconvening of ILMAC and the reactivation of the
GAA between Israel and Lebanon. These efforts were overtaken by
subsequent events leading to a major Israeli military intervention in
Lebanon.

As indicated earlier, the armistice observation operations in the
Egypt-Israel, the Israel-Syria and the Israel-Lebanon sectors were
terminated after the establishment of UNEF, UNDOF and UNIFIL
respectively.

UNTSO observers in the Egypt-Israel sector, whose duties were
to assist and cooperate with UNEF in the fulfilment of the latter's
tasks, formed the 'Observer Group Sinai' (OGS). The observers of
OGS were directed by a Chief Military Observer stationed at Ismailia
with UNEF headquarters. An outstation was maintained at Rabah at
the location of the former Qantara Control Centre. EIMAC headquarters at Gaza was maintained with a skeleton staff, and continues
to serve as a relay station. The Chief Military Observer of OGS also
acted as Chairman of EIMAC. Following the withdrawal of UNEF,
the 'Observer Group Sinai' was replaced by the 'Observer Group
Egypt'. The latter group, headed by an Officer-in-Charge, mans a
liaison office in Cairo and five stations located in Ismailia and in
western Sinai. EIMAC has been abolished.

The observers are assigned to assist UNDOF to form the 'Observer
Group Golan'. Some twenty-two observers are now included in
UNDOF as an integral part of the Force; other observers assist it as
occasion requires. ISMAC headquarters in Damascus and the
Tiberias Control Centre have been maintained and provide admin-
istrative support for those observers on their respective side. The
Quneitra outstation has become an UNDOF installation.

The structure of HKJIMAC (Hashemite Kingdom of Jordan and
Israel Armistice Commission) has remained unchanged.

Observers in the Israel-Lebanon sector, whose duties are to assist
and co-operate with UNIFIL in the fulfilment of its tasks, form the
'Observer Group Lebanon'. The structure of ILMAC headquarters in
Beirut, headed by the Chairman of ILMAC, has been maintained and,
as indicated above, functions also as a liaison office for UNIFIL.

UNTSO is under the exclusive command and control of the UN at
all times. The Chief of Staff is appointed by the Secretary-General; he
is responsible to the Secretary-General and reports to him. Lt.-Gen.
Emmanuel A. Erskine of Ghana returned to this position in 1981,
after three years' service as Commander, UNIFIL.

Cessation of fighting

The process of procuring a cessation of fighting involves negotiations
to establish a ceasefire; fact-finding; establishing a ceasefire, which

may involve disengagement and withdrawal; and observing ceasefire provisions. Suitable examples are the UN Observer Group In Lebanon (UNOGIL), the first phase of UN operations in West Irian before the UN Security Force (UNSF) was established, and the UN Yemen Observation Mission (UNYOM). The first phase of the UN operation in West Irian will now be described and analysed.

The negotiations leading to the independence of Indonesia ignored the future political status of West New Guinea, which was deferred for negotiations. (This territory was called West Irian at the time of the UN operation; the Indonesians then called it Irian Barat.) Indonesians maintained that West Irian was an integral part of Indonesia since it had been part of the Dutch East Indies. They brought the dispute before the General Assembly sessions of 1954–7, but without any conclusion; meanwhile the Netherlands government continued to administer the territory.

The Dutch were committed to protect the rights of the Papuans, who were ethnically different from the Indonesians. In 1961 they declared that they were prepared to place the territory under UN authority provided the Papuans were given the right of self-determination. The General Assembly was again unable to resolve this question. Before the end of the year Indonesian infiltrators started to land in the territory, and by the beginning of 1962 a number of clashes occurred between them and Dutch troops. Assisted by the United States, U Thant was able to arrange for Ambassador Ellsworth Bunker to act as a neutral mediator to work out a solution between Indonesia and the Netherlands. The Bunker Plan was duly agreed. It required the Dutch to hand over the territory to the UN for administration for less than one year, and the territory would then be transferred to Indonesian administration which, at a future date, would arrange for the people of West Irian to decide their own future. In fact, only a six-month period of UN temporary administration (UNTEA) was agreed — from October 1, 1962, to May 1963. A UN Security Force would be responsible for supporting local authorities in the maintenance of law and order.

Before the introduction of the Bunker Plan, the UN Secretary-General agreed (1) to arrange the observation of the implementation of the ceasefire, and the agreement that neither side would reinforce or resupply its military force; (2) to take steps to prevent acts which would threaten the security of the forces of either party; (3) to receive reports of incidents, and to take suitable measures to restore the situation in consultation with the parties; and (4) to make advance arrangements for the early establishment of UNTEA.

U Thant then entered into negotiations to arrange the immediate implementation of the ceasefire. He nominated his Military Adviser, the present author, to leave New York on August 15, 1962, and make his way to Hollandia without delay. Owing to heavy storms in Japan, the final stage of the Military Adviser's journey by a special charter KLM aircraft was delayed for forty-eight hours. On landing at Biak he was able to negotiate an immediate cessation of hostilities by the Dutch forces. However, the Dutch Officer-in-Charge at Biak reported the presence of two Indonesian (Soviet-made) submarines, adding that there had been an attempt to land commandos from them near Hollandia in rubber boats. The presence of these submarines seriously threatened the implementation of the ceasefire. The Military Adviser succeeded in contacting U Thant in New York by telephone through the United States military network, and the Secretary-General promised to call on President Soekarno immediately to withdraw the submarines. By the early morning they had left the area, enabling the ceasefire to go into effect.

UN representatives now faced some complex problems caused by the enormous land area of West Irian (412,781 sq. km.), the complete lack of surface communications, and the inadequacy of airfields other than in the five main coastal towns, where port facilities were also available. The Indonesians had landed between 800 and 900 paratroop volunteers who, according to the Dutch, were dropped haphazardly, and had been killed by the local tribes. Similarly the Indonesians had landed volunteers by small naval craft, and these too had largely been apprehended or had died in the bush.

The Military Adviser proceeded to Djakarta and obtained the approval of President Soekarno to the Indonesian radio stations informing the 'freedom fighters' that the ceasefire was in effect. In addition, the UN would arrange the dropping of pamphlets in the name of the Indonesian government to inform these fighters that they should report to the five ports for food, and medical and other assistance from the UN. Meanwhile, on the urgent request of the Military Adviser, the Secretary-General arranged to despatch twenty-one military observers (they were supplied by Brazil, Ceylon, India, Ireland, Nigeria and Sweden). A flight of Royal Canadian Air Force amphibious aircraft and US Air Force helicopters and transport aircraft were also made available. Soon the ceasefire was in effect, and the Indonesian fighters started to trickle into the five reporting centres. The Dutch forces had also begun their withdrawal. On September 21, 1962, the Military Adviser reported to the Secretary-General that the observer team's task had been completed. Thereafter the Secretary-General despatched his representative to start arrangements for the arrival of UNTEA and UNSF.

This mission was able to accomplish its task in only about two months for a number of reasons: (1) the two parties involved were anxious to solve the problem peacefully; (2) the Netherlands government was determined to accomplish the transfer of authority to the UN without any casualties to their armed forces; (3) the Indonesians only had to wait for a few months of UN administration before they

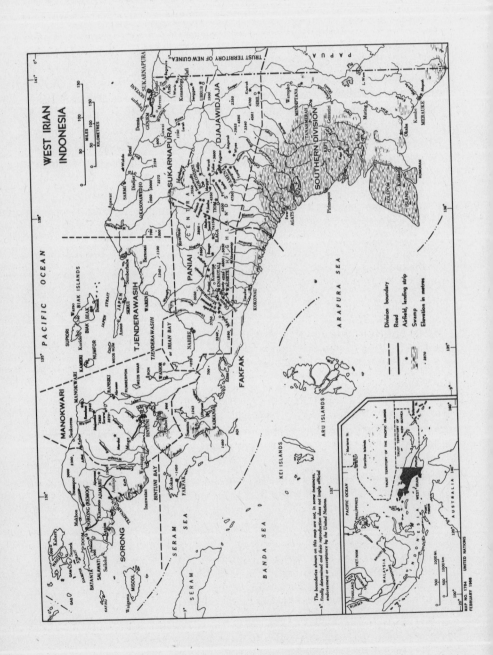

could establish their own authority; (4) the UN enjoyed the complete support of the United States, which carried enormous influence in the region; and (5) the nomination by the Secretary-General of his own Military Adviser demonstrated his personal commitment. Furthermore, the strong backing he gave to his nominee in carrying out his responsibilities greatly facilitated the mission.

Eventually the Bunker Plan was fully implemented. A referendum held later favoured retention of the territory by Indonesia. Some considered that the Papuans were robbed of their right to choose independence. At the time, however, President Kennedy was convinced that the war between the Dutch and Indonesians must be stopped before it got out of hand, and that a price had to be paid to end colonial rule in this region.

NOTES

1. David W. Wainhouse and Associates, *International Peace Observation* (Baltimore: Johns Hopkins University Press, 1966), p. 10.
2. UN Charter, Article 33.
3. UN Charter, Article 34.
4. UN Charter, Article 36.
5. UN Charter, Articles 11 and 12.
6. UN Security Council, Official Records, 1st Year, 2nd Series, no. 26, 86th and 87th Meetings, Dec. 19, 1946, pp. 700–1.
7. UN General Assembly Resolution 109 (II), Oct. 21, 1947.
8. UN General Assembly Resolution 103 (III), Nov. 27, 1948.
9. UN General Assembly, Ad Hoc Political Committee, A/AC. 53/L2.
10. UN Security Council Resolution S/5331, June 11, 1963.
11. UN Security Council Resolution no. 39, Jan. 20, 1949.
12. UN Charter, Article 34: 'The Security Council may investigate any dispute, or any situation which might lead to international friction or give rise to a dispute, in order to determine whether the continuance of the dispute or situation is likely to endanger the maintenance of international peace and security.'
13. UN Security Council Resolution S/1100, annex 25, July 20, 1949.
14. UN Security Council Document S/1430.
15. *Ibid.*
16. UN Security Council S/1430.
17. UN Security Council Resolution 80, March 14, 1950.
18. UN Security Council Resolution 91, March 30, 1951.
19. UN Security Council, S/2375, Oct. 15, 1951.
20. UNMOGIP Field Regulations.
21. UN Security Council Resolution 209, Sept. 6, 1965.
22. UN Security Council Resolution 210, Sept. 6, 1965.
23. UN Security Council, S/7221, Jan. 10, 1966.
24. UN General Assembly Document A/286, April 2, 1947.
25. UN General Assembly Document A/364 (1947).
26. UN General Assembly Resolutions 131, 132, A/519 (1947).
27. UN Security Council Resolution 727, April 23, 1948.
28. UN General Assembly Resolution 186, May 14, 1948.
29. UN Security Council Resolution 801, May 29, 1948.

30. UN Security Council Resolution 902, July 15, 1948.
31. UN Security Council Document no. 928, p. 1.
32. UN Security Council Resolution no. 1080, Nov. 16, 1948.
33. UN General Assembly Resolution no. 194 (III), Dec. 11, 1948.
34. UN Security Council Resolution no. 1376, Aug. 11, 1949.
35. Lt.-Gen. E.L.M. Burns, *Between Arab and Israeli* (New York: Obolensky, 1963), p. 27.
36. *Ibid.*
37. A United Nations Relief Works Agency (UNRWA) was established to support these refugees by the General Assembly Resolution 194 (III), December 11, 1948.
38. Burns, *Between Arab and Israeli*, p. 41.
39. *Ibid.*
40. Wainhouse and Associates, *International Peace Observation*, p. 258.
41. UN Security Council Resolution 95, Sept. 1, 1951.
42. UN Security Council Resolution 113, April 4, 1956.
43. UN Security Council S/3596, May 19, 1956.
44. Brian Urquhart, *Hammarskjöld* (New York: Knopf, 1972).
45. Burns, *Between Arab and Israeli*, pp. 143–4.
46. UN Security Council Resolution 235 (1967).
47. UN Security Council Resolution 236 (1967).

3

SEPARATION OF FORCES

General

The first peacekeeping operation by the UN designed to separate forces was UNEF I, established to end the Suez war of 1956.[1] By March 1957 UNEF was deployed along the Armistice Demarcation Lines in the Gaza strip and along the Egypt-Israel frontier.[2] In the Gaza strip it was given a 500-metre zone; and along the Sinai frontier the depth of the zones was 5 km. by day and 2 km. by night. The special responsibility of ensuring freedom of navigation through the Strait of Tiran was given to UNEF to eliminate a major cause of friction in the area. The experience of UNEF[3] provided the guidelines for all future peacekeeping operations. Since the author has already written extensively on this operation,[4] the present chapter will deal with UNEF II and UNDOF, which were established after the renewal of hostilities in 1973.

However, it is essential to outline the circumstances that led to the introduction of UNEF I and the hard bargaining and the conditions of acceptance that led to its approval, for these became the guiding principles for subsequent operations of a similar nature.

The Arab revolution in Egypt led by Colonel Gamal Abdel Nasser was intended to eliminate foreign domination, and this included removal of the British military bases in the Suez Canal zone. The revolution also required large-scale national development, which led to the planning of a new dam at Aswan for which the World Bank pledged a loan. In his search for arms to reorganize Egyptian forces after their poor showing in their war with the fledgling state of Israel, Nasser, spurned by the West, succeeded in arranging a deal with the Soviets, who agreed to military sales by Czechoslovakia. The United States, already displeased with Nasser for his refusal to join the southern tier of defence against communism which was being determinedly put together by Secretary of State John Foster Dulles, was now greatly angered by his purchase of arms, which of course enabled him to become a serious threat to the security of Israel, already a cornerstone of American foreign policy in the Middle East. It therefore persuaded the World-Bank to withdraw its offer to help build the Aswan dam. Nasser met this challenge by nationalizing the Suez Canal. Protracted negotiations by the Canal users and at the Security Council followed. Impatient with the lack of progress in the talks, the British and French, who owned the Suez Canal Company, decided on military action. Israel, anxious to end *fedayeen* raids from Gaza and El Arish, readily joined in the invasion in October 1956.

Egypt was incapable of resisting such a combination. Realizing that the Suez Canal was of greater strategic importance, the Egyptian forces withdrew from Sinai, giving the Israelis an easy victory, and concentrated around the main canal cities. In response to Nasser's appeals for help, the Soviets sent 'volunteers'.

The invasion of Egypt by two of its closest allies and by Israel had greatly embarrassed the United States, and with the memory of the role of the Chinese 'volunteers' in the Korean campaign fresh in everyone's minds, it determined not to allow a great power military confrontation over the Suez issue. President Eisenhower called on the invading forces to withdraw, threatened to send the US Southern Fleet to maintain peace in the region, and strongly backed the efforts by the UN to deal with the conflict. American policy prevailed, but a formula had to be worked out to provide the basis for the withdrawal of foreign forces.

The minimum conditions for withdrawal acceptable to the British and French were, first, that their forces be replaced by an international force, and secondly, that the safety and the use of the Canal be assured. Israel insisted on an end to all *fedayeen* raids and freedom of navigation through the Suez Canal and the Strait of Tiran. Egypt wanted the withdrawal of all foreign forces, respect for Egyptian sovereignty, and its own control of the Canal. The formula worked out by the Canadian Minister of External Affairs, Lester B. Pearson, and the UN Secretary-General, Dag Hammarskjöld, on the night of 4 and 5 November 1956 came closest to meeting those conditions. Because Britain and France, as permanent members, vetoed any Security Council action, the UN General Assembly in a special session authorized under the 'Uniting for Peace' resolution provided the mandate to establish UNEF I.

The conditions laid down by Britain and France were met by creating an international force under the UN. This force was given the responsibility for the clearance of the Canal, its safety and its protection. Furthermore, this force would assure free use of the Canal. Israel's conditions regarding the use of the Canal were met on the same basis as for the other two combatant parties, except that Egypt later forbad the use of the Canal to Israeli shipping. However, the UN was fully successful in keeping the Strait of Tiran open by placing its troops at Sharm el Sheikh, and it was able to prevent *fedayeen* raiding by deploying troops along the armistice demarcation line in the Gaza strip and along the international frontier in Sinai. Lastly, Egyptian demands were met with the withdrawal of foreign troops and restoration of Egyptian control over the Canal. However, Egypt had to accept the presence of an international force on its soil in order to satisfy all the parties. The negotiations to establish a UN peacekeeping force to separate the parties to an armed conflict and its continued presence to that end led to the evolution of a novel system of the use of military forces to keep peace by not waging war.

The Egyptians, of course, realized that they would have to accept the UN force to have their demands met. Yet there was no overlooking the fact that foreign troops were on its soil. In his negotiations with the Egyptians, Hammarskjöld came forward with suggestions that would satisfy the national pride and sovereignty concerns of the Egyptians. Thus, the first principle became Egyptian consent. By the same token the Israelis declined to have any part of the force located on their territory (little did they realize at that time that by doing so they were abrogating their ability to keep the force once Egypt had withdrawn its consent). The other main principle was that UNEF was not an occupation force, but a friendly force. The force was not there to fight but to maintain peace by agreement; it would not use force except in self-defence. These, then, became the guidelines for future peacekeeping.

After the October 1973 war, in a series of separation agreements skill-fully negotiated by the US Secretary of State, Dr Henry Kissinger, the importance of peacekeeping for the peaceful settlement of disputes was again established. After the 1979 Egyptian-Israeli peace treaty, the UNEF II mandate was not renewed beyond July 1980, leaving only the UNTSO military observers attached to this force to remain in the area. The US Sinai Support Mission assumed the major responsibility for peace observation in Sinai. Meanwhile, in the absence of any progress in dealing with the Israeli-Syrian situation, UNDOF continues to separate Israelis from the Syrians on the Golan Heights.

UNEF II

At the end of the June 1967 war, the Arabs had lost the Golan Heights, the West Bank of the Jordan including East Jerusalem, the Gaza strip and Sinai. Israeli forces were within striking distance of Damascus and on the east bank of the Suez Canal, blocking navigation. Immediately after victory, Israel declared its willingness to return all the occupied Arab lands in exchange for recognition and peace; but the Arab Summit meeting at Khartoum on September 1, 1967, rejected any peace negotiations or recognition of Israel.

In November 1967 the Security Council (1) affirmed the principles of Israeli withdrawal from the occupied Arab lands, termination of belligerence and acknowledgement of sovereignty of every state (including Israel) in the area; (2) affirmed further the necessity of guaranteeing freedom of navigation through international water-ways, achieving a just settlement of the refugee problem, guaranteeing territorial inviolability and political independence of states in the area through measures including the establishment of demilitarized zones; and (3) requested the Secretary-General to designate a Special Representative to promote agreement and assist in a peaceful and acceptable settlement.[5]

As his Special Representative U Thant nominated Gunnar Jarring, Sweden's Ambassador to the UN, who shuttled from one Middle Eastern capital to another for several years without achieving a breakthrough. An undeclared limited war — the so-called War of Attrition — broke out between the Egyptians and Israelis along the Suez Canal. As the war intensified, Israeli aircraft destroyed the refinery at Suez and raided Cairo. In 1970 the US Secretary of State William Rogers was able to negotiate a ninety-day ceasefire through the Security Council. Ambassador Jarring negotiated the arrangements in the area, and although no formal arrangements could be made, the ceasefire continued beyond ninety days and put a stop to the War of Attrition.

On Nasser's death in 1970, Anwar Sadat became President. He declared that it was his destiny to regain what Egypt had lost, by war if diplomacy failed, and warned that 1972 would be the 'year of decision'. Realizing the need for thorough preparation to avoid a repetition of the 1967 debacle, Sadat started earnest military consultation with Jordan and Syria. In a surprise attack on October 6, 1973, Egyptian forces launched the first large-scale water obstacle crossing, over the Suez Canal, since the Second World War. Simultaneously the Syrians attacked across the ceasefire lines.

The Arab objectives were limited: to regain as much of their lost territories as possible. They realized that the great powers would not allow the war to continue long. Egypt badly needed the Canal, and to rebuild the cities along it, and they all wanted negotiations to be resumed with determination.

The Security Council met between October 7 and 12 but failed to achieve a consensus because the parties to the conflict were not ready for a ceasefire. The heavy losses Israel suffered early in the war had persuaded the United States to arrange a large-scale re-supply. Later, when the Israelis managed to break through Egyptian forces on the east bank of the Canal, crossed the Canal, started their advance towards Suez and threatened Cairo, Egypt called for help from the Soviet Union — whose military technicians Sadat had expelled when it tried to restrain him from going to war — to supply their Third Army Corps which was cut off from its bases. Realizing that a Soviet attempt to air-supply the Egyptians would cause a clash between Soviet and Israeli aircraft, thereby seriously threatening world peace, the United States and the Soviets jointly agreed to sponsor a Security Council resolution calling for a ceasefire *in situ*, to be effective within twelve hours from the moment of adoption.[6] As the parties were already in agreement, the resolution was adopted.

The next day the Council requested the Secretary-General to despatch elements from UNTSO to observe the ceasefire, hoping thus to achieve an effective end to hostilities after an earlier call had proved abortive.[7] However, UNMOs were unable to persuade the parties to comply, since the Israelis were busy extending their bridgehead on the west bank of the Canal. Sadat asked the United States and the Soviet Union to provide a peacekeeping force to supervise the ceasefire. The United States declined. At this juncture, on an initiative by the non-aligned members, the Security Council decided to demand an immediate ceasefire, and requested the Secretary-General to increase UNMOs on both sides, set up a UNEF from member-states excluding the five permanent powers, and report to the Council within twenty-four hours on the steps taken to this end.[8]

Conscious of the differences between the superpowers, the Secretary-General Dr Waldheim placed his recommendations within the framework of the areas where there appeared to have been agreement during the discussions of the Special Committee on Peace-keeping. In his report Dr Waldheim proposed the following. (1) The Secretary-General should be responsible for the functioning of the force under the authority vested in him by the Security Council. In turn the Secretary-General undertook to keep the Council fully informed. (2) The Commander was to be appointed by the Secretary-General with the consent of the Council. (3) The guidelines for the force were to be along the same lines as those for other peacekeeping forces. (4) The composition of the new force was to be agreed upon by the Security Council. (5) While force might be used only for self-defence, a new approach was recommended in that self-defence could include 'resistance to attempts by forceful means to prevent UNEF from discharging its duties under the Security Council mandate'. (6) The organization of UNEF should proceed as follows: (*a*) Major-General E. Siilasvuo of Finland, Chief of Staff UNTSO, to be appointed interim Commander; (*b*) personnel from UNTSO, to provide initial staff for Headquarters UNEF; (*c*) the force should have a total of 7,000 men; (*d*) troops should immediately be made available from UNFICYP, to include Austrians, Finns and Swedes subject to the approval of their governments; and (*e*) the force should be initially authorized for a period of six months at an estimated cost of $30 million, to be borne by members in accordance with Article 17(2) of the Charter.[9]

Having obtained the approval of the Security Council[10] — China abstained from voting, stating that because the parties to the conflict had accepted the proposal they would not oppose it — Waldheim proceeded with the organization and establishment of the force. The credit for the preparation and despatch of the first batch of troops belongs largely to the UN Secretariat and to Headquarters UNFICYP. Cyprus was a short distance away, and there was a full-scale peace-keeping operation in the island with effective command control and logistics; and there were suitable airfields with all the necessary support services to organize a major airlift.

Once the approval of the troop-contributing countries had been obtained, the troops with matériel, vehicles and supplies started to move by air. The advance party of Austrians arrived late on October 26. General Siilasvuo, who had already arrived in Cairo with a nucleus staff drawn from UNTSO, assumed command, and UNEF II was established. The next day, about 200 men from each of the three contingents in Cyprus, forty-eight vehicles and about 200,000 kilos of stores had reached Cairo. Siilasvuo had moved troops from Finland to an area west of Suez, under Israeli control, and the first meeting took place at Kilometer 101 on the Cairo-Suez road, between Egyptian and Israeli officers in the presence of UNEF personnel. Preliminary steps were discussed for the implementation of the ceasefire, resupplying the beleaguered Egyptian Third Army Corps, and evacuation of the wounded. This led to the immediate opening of the road for the UN supply convoys to provide the immediate and essential needs of the Egyptians in Suez and across the Canal. Meanwhile, Siilasvuo had deployed UNTSO observers on both sides of the Canal — nine on the west side under Ismailia Control Centre, and six on the eastern side under Qantara Control Centre. Shortly afterwards, the Finns assumed responsibility for the area on the Suez road, the Austrians for the Ismailia area, and the Swedes for the area west of the Great Bitter Lake.

Back in New York, Dr Waldheim with his senior aides, headed by Brian Urquhart, were busy planning, preparing and organizing the force. Determined to have a correct geographical distribution of contingents, they approached Canada, Ghana, Indonesia, Ireland, Nepal, Panama, Peru, Poland and Senegal, and all agreed. Austria, Finland and Sweden had meanwhile agreed to raise their contribution to about 600 men each. By the end of the year UNEF strength had reached 5,467, and UNTSO had put 112 observers in the area.

The problem of logistic support, difficult enough for any peace-keeping operation (with the exception of UNFICYP, which was based primarily on British support), presented a novel development. The Secretary-General had asked the Canadians to undertake this responsibility, and they agreed, but the Soviets insisted that it should be shared between Canada and Poland. After protracted negotiations between the Secretariat, Canada and Poland a memorandum of understanding was recorded.[11] This document described the logistic organization and composition of units comprising the UNEF system. The responsibility for logistic support would be divided, although units of each contingent would be administered by their respective contingent commanders. The latter arrangement was along the same lines as that established between Indians and Canadians for logistic support of UNEF I, and for that of the Congo force where many nationalities were involved in carrying out these functions. Canada agreed to provide a signals communications unit, a service unit (including a supply company), a maintenance company, an aviation unit, a movement control unit and a postal unit. Poland assumed responsibility for providing an engineer unit (including mine clearance), a road transport unit with workshops, and a 100-bed hospital.

The UNEF maintenance base was established at Heliopolis, a Cairo suburb near the international airport with easy road access to the Canal area. The Canadians and the Poles worked well together, and the performance of the Poles, the first socialist nation to participate in peacekeeping, was second to none. The only problem arose when Israel refused to permit Polish personnel (road transport unit) to enter its territory. Obviously the importance of including a socialist member-state in UNEF was overriding, regardless of the problems that could arise with Israel. Eventually Canadian personnel had to drive Polish unit vehicles through Israeli-controlled territory, causing considerable administrative inconvenience to UNEF.

On November 9, Dr Kissinger, who had been tirelessly working to ensure the implementation of the ceasefire, informed Dr Waldheim that (1) both sides had agreed to comply with the ceasefire, (2) the question of a return to the positions as on October 22 would be discussed within the framework of an agreement on disengagement and separation of forces under UN auspices; (3) daily supplies of food for Suez and non-military supplies to the Third Army Corps would be permitted by the Israelis under agreed arrangements; (4) wounded civilians in Suez would be evacuated; (5) the UN would replace Israeli checkpoints on the Cairo-Suez road with Israeli supervision; and (6) once replacement as stated in (5) was completed, an exchange of prisoners-of-war including the wounded would be carried out.

As these arrangements and the establishment of UNEF went ahead, Dr Kissinger made progress with efforts to proceed to the next stage of negotiations. The talks at Kilometre 101, in the military group of the Geneva Peace Conference, and Kissinger's efforts resulted in the Egypt-Israeli Agreement on Disengagements of Forces, which was signed at Kilometre 101 on January 18, 1974. This agreement stated:

(1) Egypt and Israel will scrupulously observe the ceasefire on land, sea and air called for by the United Nations Security Council and will refrain from the time of the signing of this document from all military or para-military actions against each other.
(2) The military forces of Egypt and Israel will be separated in accordance with the following principles:
  (*a*) All Egyptian forces on the east side of the Canal will be deployed west of the line designated as line A on the attached map [see p. 55]. All Israeli forces, including those west of the Suez Canal and the Great Bitter Lakes, will be deployed east of the line designated as line B on the attached map.
  (*b*) The area between the Egyptian and Israeli lines will be a zone of disengagement in which the United Nations Emergency Force (UNEF) will be stationed. The

UNEF will continue to consist of units from countries that are not permanent members of the Security Council.

(c) The area between the Egyptian line and the Suez Canal will be limited in armament and forces.

(d) The area between the Israeli line (B on the attached map) and the line designated as line C [shown] on the attached map, which runs along the western base of the mountains to where the Gidi and Mitla Passes are located, will be limited in armament and forces.

(e) The limitations referred to in paragraphs 3 and 4 will be inspected by UNEF. Existing procedures of the UNEF will be continued.

(f) Air forces of the two sides will be permitted to operate up to their respective lines without interference from the other side.

(3) The detailed implementation of the disengagement of forces will be worked out by military representatives of Egypt and Israel, who will agree on the stages of this process. These representatives will meet no later than 48 hours after the signature of this Agreement at Kilometre 101 under the aegis of the United Nations for this purpose. They will complete this task within five days. Disengagement will begin within 48 hours after the completion of the work of the military representatives, and in no event later than seven days after the signature of this Agreement. The process of disengagement will be completed not later than 40 days after it begins.

(4) This Agreement is not regarded by Egypt and Israel as a final peace agreement. It constitutes a first step toward a final, just and durable peace according to the provisions of Security Council Resolution 338 and within the framework of the Geneva Conference.[12]

The signatories to the agreement were Maj.-Gen. Muhammad Abdul Ghani El-Gamasy, Chief of Staff Egyptian Armed Forces, and Lt.-Gen. David Elazar, Chief of Staff Israel Defence Forces (IDF). It was witnessed by General Siilasvuo for the UN.

The area between the Egyptian and Israeli lines became a UN buffer zone, left exclusively for UNEF operations. The area between the Egyptian line and the Canal, and that between the Israeli line B and the line designated as line C running through the western base of Gidi and Mitla Passes, became limited armament and forces zones. UNEF undertook these responsibilities with the help of UNTSO observers.

The disengagement operation began on January 25 and was completed by March 5. The Israeli withdrawal from each of the designated areas was carried out in phases. In each case, after the Israeli withdrawal UNEF held the area for a temporary period (buffer time) before turning it over to the Egyptians. During the disengagement process, UNEF interposed itself between the Egyptian and Israeli forces by establishing these temporary buffer zones.

UNTSO observers, under UNEF supervision, carried out the survey and completed the marking of the lines of disengagement, i.e. lines A and B. In this task they were assisted by Israeli and Egyptian surveyors respectively. In order to carry out these responsibilities, UNEF established a forward Headquarters at Kilometre 101 on January 26; this was moved forward again two days later, and by February 12 was established near El Ghala in the new temporary buffer zones. Once disengagement had been accomplished, UNEF manned the disengage-

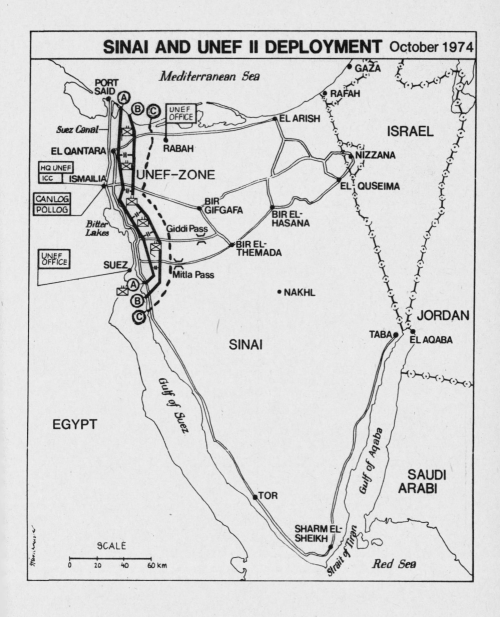

SINAI AND UNEF II DEPLOYMENT October 1974

ment zones and conducted inspections of areas of limited arms and forces.

In August 1974, UNEF Headquarters and the major part of the logistics base was moved to Ismailia. During the year the Irish troops were withdrawn in May, the Nepalese who came for six months arrived in February and left in August, and the Panamanians departed in November — all without replacement. The deployment of UNEF from mid-January 1974 to October 1975 in the zone of disengagement was as follows:

The *Swedish battalion* had its Headquarters at El Nagita (near Rabah), a forward command post and fifteen outposts from the Mediterranean Sea to a line north-east of Ismailia.

The *Indonesian battalion* had its Headquarters in Suez City, a forward command post and eleven posts from the southern limit of the Swedish Sector to a line east of the northern tip of Great Bitter Lake.

The *Ghanaian battalion* had its Headquarters at Fayid-Fanara, a forward command post and twelve outposts from the southern limit of the Indonesians to a line east of the southern tip of Great Bitter Lake.

The *Senegalese battalion* had its Headquarters in Suez City, a forward command post and eleven outposts from the end of the Ghana Sector to a line north-east of Suez.

The *Finnish battalion* had its Headquarters in Suez City, a forward command post and fourteen outposts standing south of the Senegalese to the Gulf of Suez, south-east of Suez City.

The *Canadian and Polish logistic units* were at El Ghala Camp near Ismailia, with a ration depot in Cairo, air transport at Ismailia and an UNTSO F-27 (Swiss) when required, movement control units in Alexandria, Tel Aviv and Beirut, and liaison officers in Cairo and Jerusalem.

As indicated by its deployment, UNEF's main task was manning checkpoints and observation posts and conducting patrols so as to control the zone of disengagement, and furthermore, with the assistance of UNTSO observers, to conduct weekly and later bi-weekly inspections of the areas of limited forces and armaments and to inspect other areas agreed to by the parties. UNEF also played a useful role in the exchange of prisoners-of-war, the transfer of civilians and the search for the remains of those killed in co-operation with the Red Cross.

UNDOF

After the initial Syrian success on the Golan Heights, the Israelis counter-attacked and, crossing the 1967 ceasefire lines, were heavily engaged around the Sassa salient threatening Damascus. After the ceasefire call by the Security Council in its resolutions 338 and 339 (1973), UNTSO observers available on the Syrian side were immediately deployed. The demarcation of the new ceasefire lines based on the Forward Defended Localities (FDLs) of Israeli and Syrian troops presented few difficulties.

The authorization of UNEF II did not specify whether the force would be deployed in both the Suez area and the Golan Heights, since the situation on the Egyptian front threatened superpower confrontation, and therefore this most dangerous sector received priority attention. The ceasefire held on the Golan Heights, and because there was little danger of a great power confrontation in that sector, its supervision was left to UNMOs.

In due course, efforts to bring about an exchange of Israeli and Syrian prisoners-of-war failed. A war of attrition which had broken out earlier increased in intensity. Having reached an understanding with President Sadat, Dr Kissinger increased his personal efforts, by what came to be known as 'shuttle diplomacy', to arrange a disengagement of Israeli and Syrian forces. On 31 May 1974 the Israel-Syria Disengagement of Forces Agreement was signed in Geneva. The text of the Agreement is as follows:

A. Israel and Syria will scrupulously observe the ceasefire on land, sea and air and will refrain from all military actions against each other, from the time of the signing of this document, in implementation of United Nations Security Council resolution 338 dated 22 October 1973.
B. The military forces of Israel and Syria will be separated in accordance with the following principles:
    1. All Israeli military forces will be West of the line designated as Line A on the map attached hereto [see p. 59], except in the Quneitra area, where they will be West of Line A-1.
    2. All territory East of Line A will be under Syrian administration, and Syrian civilians will return to this territory.
    3. The area between Line A and the line designated as Line B on the attached map will be an area of separation. In this area will be stationed the United Nations Disengagement Observer Force established in accordance with the accompanying protocol.
    4. All Syrian military forces will be East of the line designated as Line B on the attached map.
    5. There will be two equal areas of limitation in armament and forces, one West of Line A and one East of Line B as agreed upon.
    6. Air Forces of the sides will be permitted to operate up to their respective lines without interference from the other side.
C. In the area between Line A and Line A-1 [running just west of Quneitra and not shown] on the attached map there shall be no military forces.
D. This agreement and the attached map will be signed by the military representatives of Israel and Syria in Geneva not later than 31 May 1974, in the Egyptian-Israeli Military Working Group of the Geneva Peace Conference under the aegis of the United Nations, after that group has been joined by a Syrian military representative, and with the participation of representatives of the United States and the Soviet Union. The precise delineation of a detailed map and a plan for the implementation of the disengagement of forces will be worked out by military representatives of Israel

and Syria in the Egyptian-Israeli Military Working Group, who will agree on the stages of this process. The Military Working Group described above will start their work for this purpose in Geneva under the aegis of the United Nations within 24 hours after the signing of this agreement. They will complete this task within five days. Disengagement will begin within 24 hours after the completion of the task of the Military Working Group. The process of Disengagement will be completed not later than 20 days after it begins.

E. The provisions of paragraphs A, B and C shall be inspected by personnel of the United Nations comprising the United Nations Disengagement Observer Force under this agreement.

F. Within 24 hours after the signing of this Agreement in Geneva all wounded prisoners of war which each side holds of the other as certified by ICRC will be repatriated. The morning after the completion of the task of the Military Working Group, all remaining prisoners of war will be repatriated.

G. The bodies of all dead soldiers held by either side will be returned for a burial in their respective countries within 10 days after the signing of this Agreement.

H. This Agreement is not a Peace Agreement. It is a step towards a just and durable peace on the basis of Security Council resolution 338 dated 22 October 1973.

In a protocol to the Agreement, UNDOF's responsibilities agreed upon by the parties were given as follows:

1. It will use its best efforts for the scrupulous observation of the ceasefire.
2. It will supervise the Agreement and protocol regarding areas of separation and limitations. It will carry out regular inspections and report to the parties. These inspections will be not less than every 15 days or when requested by either party.
3. It will comply with Syrian laws and regulations and not hamper the functioning of local civil administration.
4. It will enjoy freedom of movement and communication and other facilities needed to perform its functions.
5. It will be mobile, provided with weapons of a defensive character and shall use such weapons only in self-defence.
6. The strength will be above 1,250 from non-permanent members, the contingents to be selected in consultation with the parties.
7. The Secretary-General will manage the force under the authority of the Security Council.

On May 31 the Security Council approved the establishment of UNDOF for an initial period of six months subject to further renewal by the Council,[13] and requested the Secretary-General to take the necessary steps to this effect.

Dr Waldheim, having obtained the approval of the Peruvians and Austrians to provide their units from UNEF, appointed Brig.-Gen. Gonzalo Briceno interim Commander. He also obtained the consent of Canada and Poland to detach logistic personnel for UNDOF. On June 3 Briceno assumed command of UNTSO observers already in the area and established Headquarters UNDOF in Damascus. By June 18 UNDOF had 1,218 men of all ranks deployed in the area.

The disengagement operation started on June 6. The Austrians were placed in the Sassa salient area, the Peruvians were deployed in the Quneitra area, and the Canadians were located with the Peruvians and the Poles with the Austrians. UNTSO observers based in Tiberias

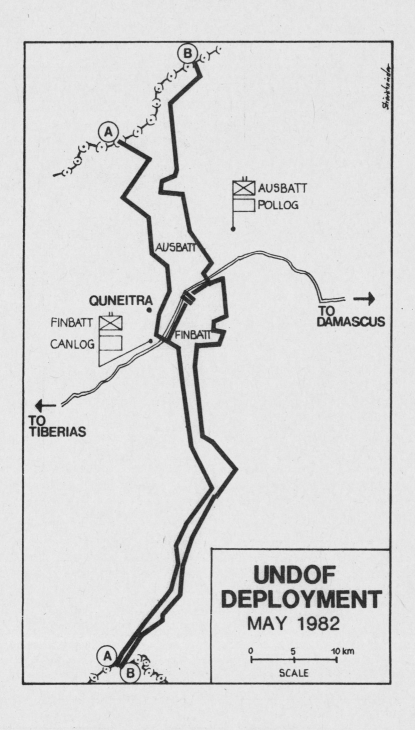

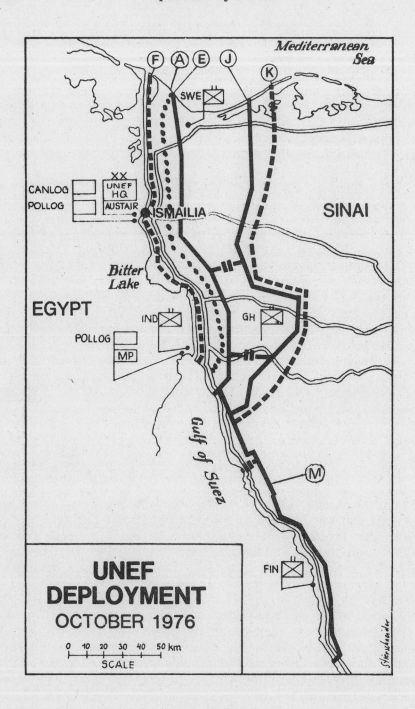

**UNEF
DEPLOYMENT**
OCTOBER 1976

0 10 20 30 40 50 km
SCALE

and Damascus continued to man selected observer posts. A forward UNDOF Headquarters was set up south of Sassa-Quneitra to facilitate liaison with the parties.

After June 26 UNDOF was redeployed — the Austrians in the northern sector with the Poles, and the Peruvians with the Canadians in the southern sector. On July 12, the Peruvians returned home without being replaced and Colonel Hannes Philipp, of Austria, was appointed Acting Commander. Until September 10, when a battalion from Iran arrived, the Austrians and UNMOs had to assume the entire responsibility for the area of separation.

Once the disengagement had been completed, UNDOF undertook the delineation and marking of lines bounding the area of separation with the co-operation of the parties. Subsequently UNDOF has maintained the ceasefire and supervised the area of separation by establishing many checkposts and observation posts, and by patrolling.

In addition to the above, UNDOF ensures the observance of the agreement concerning the limitation of forces and armaments. It carries out bi-weekly inspections of these areas by UNDOF observers and liaison officers of the party concerned. The findings of these inspections are made available to the parties. UNDOF deals with complaints and provides its good offices whenever needed.

In carrying out its mandate, UNDOF has had a few difficulties. Mines presented a major hazard and had to be cleared. The Syrian civil population has returned. The fortnightly meetings of Druze families near Majdel Shams, in the area of separation divided by the ceasefire lines, continues smoothly. Besides ensuring that there are no breaches of the ceasefire, the UN troops have to prevent civilians from straying into uncleared minefields.

After the overthrow of the Shah, the Iranian battalion was withdrawn by the Revolutionary Government, and it was replaced by a Finnish battalion. General Philipp returned to national duty in Austria and was replaced by Maj.-Gen. Guenther Greindl in 1980. With the termination of the appointment of General Siilasvuo as Chief Co-ordinator, Middle East Peacekeeping Forces, the Secretary-General re-shuffled the command arrangements and appointed Maj.-Gen. Erkki R. Kaira, of Finland, as the new Commander UNDOF.

Since UNDOF was established, both sides have kept the ceasefire. The Disengagement Agreement is not a peace agreement. Although quiet prevails along the Golan Heights, tensions remain, and dramatically dangerous crises have repeatedly occurred, e.g. the Israeli military intervention in Southern Lebanon in 1978, and the several incidents between the Israeli air force and Syrian troops of the Arab Deterrent Force near Beirut. The situation between Israel and Syria remained fundamentally unstable and potentially explosive, because little progress was made towards resolving basic conflict issues between Israel and Syria. The resumption of fighting in South Lebanon, Beirut and the Bekaa Valley involved the Syrians as well. However, the situation remains unchanged along the Golan Heights, where calm continues to prevail. Thus UNDOF continues to play a useful role between Israel and its remaining serious Arab antagonist.

By the end of November 1983, when UNDOF received another renewal from the Security Council, its total strength was 1,296, with contingents from Austria, Canada, Finland and Poland. It also had six UNMOs from UNTSO in its area of deployment. The force had not suffered any recent casualties, although mines remained a major problem and more had to be cleared. It also assisted ICRC in the exchange of prisoners. Although the force has received full co-operation from the Israelis and Syrians, restrictions in its movement continue to prejudice its effectiveness.

Because of the dangerous situation between the two states, further exacerabated by the declaration of annexation of the Golan Heights by Israel on December 14, 1981, the continuation of UNDOF remains essential. Gen. Stahl replaced Gen. Kaira as Force Commander on June 13, 1982.

Redeployment of UNEF, 1975

Having accomplished the disengagement of Egyptian and Syrian forces from the Israelis, the United States continued its diplomatic endeavours or work towards permanent peace between the Arabs and Israelis. On September 4, 1975, Dr Kissinger succeeded in bringing about an agreement between Egypt and Israel for another disengagement, and for the introduction of an Early Warning System to be provided by the United States in Sinai. In House Joint Resolution 683, the Congress on October 9 authorized the President to implement the United States proposal for the Early Warning System in Sinai with the provision that the civilian personnel assigned would be removed immediately in the event of war. On October 23 the Security Council,[14] having noted recent developments in the Middle East,[15] emphasized the implementation of its Resolution 338 (1973) and renewed the mandate of UNEF for a period of one year, until October 24, 1976. The main features of the Agreement were: (1) the Israelis were to withdraw east of lines J and M, and the Egyptians were to be deployed west of line E; (2) the areas between lines E and F and lines J and K would be limited in armament and forces; (3) UNEF was to be redeployed between lines E and J; (4) in the area south of line E and west of line M there would be no forces; (5) the parties agreed to establish a Joint Commission under the aegis of the Chief Co-ordinator of UN Peacekeeping Missions to consider any problem relating to this agreement; and (6) non-military cargoes to or from Israel would be permitted through the Suez Canal.

The annexure to the agreement provided more details regarding definition of lines and areas. The buffer zones were to be the exclusive responsibility of UNEF in accordance with procedures worked out by the Working Group. Either party was permitted to carry out aerial reconnaissance up to its own forward line and up to the middle of the buffer zone between lines E and J on an agreed schedule. The US Early Warning System was to be located between these lines with access through Egyptian or Israeli areas.

In the area south of line E and west of line M, i.e. the oil field area, UNEF had to ensure that there were no armed personnel other than Egyptian civilian police. Egyptian and other civilian workers were to be checked by UNEF at points of entry and exit to the area. Israel agreed to leave all civilian installations intact. The United States agreed to continue aerial reconnaissance missions over the area between lines F and K, making the results known to both parties. In regard to the limitations of armament and forces between lines J and K and lines E and F, both sides agreed not to construct new military defences or installations; and to keep force levels at 8,000, to include eight infantry batallions, seventy-five tanks, and seventy-two guns with a maximum calibre of 122 mm. and a range of 12 km. As to areas beyond the zones of limitation of forces and armaments, the parties agreed not to locate weapons which would have the other side within their range, or place anti-aircraft guns in the area 10 km. east of line K and west of line F. UNEF was made responsible for inspections of these areas.

The arrangements for the Early Warning System included (1) an Israeli surveillance station to remain at Mitla Pass, and a new one to be established by the Egyptians at Gidi Pass with the help of the United States, each station to have no more than 250 personnel; and (2) in support of these stations, designed to provide tactical early warning and to verify access to them, three watch stations were to be established by the United States at Mitla and Gidi Passes. The United States civilian personnel (200) would verify the functions of the Egyptian and Israeli stations and would report to UNEF any movement in the areas. The Americans would be unarmed and have freedom of movement in the area of the operations.

A joint commission under the auspices of the Chief UN Co-ordinator was established to deal with any problems. A protocol setting out all the details relating to these arrangements was signed by the Military Working Group under Siilasvuo's chairmanship at Geneva in September 22.[16]

The Secretary-General in his reports to the Security Council on October 17 explained the agreement of September 4 and the Protocol of September 22 which increased UNEF responsibilities.[17] The following day he outlined UNEF's tasks for the implementation of the new agreement and Protocol.[18] UNEF carried out the following main tasks:

(1) A new line of disengagement was marked on the ground by October 1975, as required by the Protocol. Surveyors were supplied by Sweden.

(2) Redeployment of the forces of the parties started in November 1975; the first phase, i.e. transfer of oilfields and installations from Israel to Egypt, was completed by December 1 and the second phase when the forces of the two parties redeployed in their sides of the lines with UNEF providing buffer lines.

(3) Subsequently, UNEF ensured that no military or paramilitary installations were established in the southern sector by establishing checkpoints and observation posts, and by conducting ground and air patrols. It also controlled Buffer Zones 2A and 2B by establishing checkpoints along the Buffer Zone lines as well as supervising the use of the common road sections including escorts through agreed-to sections.

(4) The functions in Buffer Zone 1 were carried out by normal means. In the Early Warning Systems area located in this zone, UNEF provided escorts to the US, Egyptian and Israeli Watch Stations personnel.

(5) It carried out bi-weekly inspections, with UNTSO observers, of the agreed limitation of forces and armaments areas.

(6) The Chief Co-ordinator acted as Chairman of the Joint Commission meeting. UNEF received a number of complaints of violations from both sides and some of them were dealt with by the Joint Commission.

(7) It continued to provide assistance to the Red Cross in its humanitarian endeavours, and facilitated family reunions and student exchanges.

In order to carry out these tasks, UNEF was redeployed as follows:

The *Swedish battalion*, with base camp at Baluza, manned three forward command posts and eighteen positions in Buffer Zone 1 in a sector that stretched from the Mediterranean Sea to a line south-east of Ismailia.

The *Ghanaian battalion*, with base camp at Mitla, manned four forward command posts and eighteen positions in Buffer Zone 1 in a sector that stretched from the southern limit of the Swedish sector to a line south of Mitla.

The *Indonesian battalion*, with base camp at Wadi Reina, manned one forward command post and eight positions in Buffer Zone 1 and one forward command post and eight positions along the Gulf of Suez in a sector that stretched from the southern limit of the Ghanaian sector to a line south-east of Ras Sudr.

The *Finnish battalion*, with base camp at Abu Rudeis, manned three forward command posts and fourteen positions along the Gulf of Suez and in Buffer Zones 2-A and 2-B in a sector that stretched from the southern limit of the Indonesian sector to Abu Durba in the south.

The *Canadian contingent* was based at El Ghala Camp in Ismailia. It provided supply, maintenance, communications and air transport support to the Force operations, including a small group of about thirty personnel deployed at the forward logistics base in El Tasa.

The *Polish contingent* was also based at El Ghala Camp in Ismailia. A group of about 115 personnel was deployed at the forward logistics base in El Tasa, and one engineering company was deployed in Suez. This company maintained small detachments in Abu Zenima (Finnish battalion area) and Checkpoint Mike (Ghanaian battalion area). The contingent provided maintenance and engineering, including mineclearing, water, supply, construction, road maintenance and transport support. It also operated the UNEF hospital in Ismailia.

The *Australian contingent* was located in Ismailia. It provided helicopter support to the Force.

The *headquarters of the Force* was located in Ismailia. In addition, liaison offices were maintained in Cairo and Suez. Other UNEF elements were located as follows:

Movement control detachments in Ismailia, Cairo, Jerusalem, Tel Aviv, Damascus and Port Said;

Military police detachments in Cairo, Port Said, Suez, Rabah, Eilat, Ofira, Tel Aviv and Jerusalem;

Ismailia airfield was the operating base for two Buffalo aircraft, a chartered Skyvan and four helicopters. In addition, UNEF had the limited use of a Fokker F-27 aircraft provided for UNTSO by the government of Switzerland.

UNTSO military observers manned six checkpoints and observation posts, provided liaison with each of the battalions, served in staff posts and carried out patrols. There were six patrol teams deployed permanently. Observer Group Sinai also had the task of conducting inspections of the limited forces and armament areas and missile restricted zones, as required by the Agreement between Egypt and Israel of Sept. 4, 1975 (S/11818/Add.1). The group was led by a Chief Military Observer attached to UNEF headquarters in Ismailia. He had representatives located at offices in Cairo and Jerusalem.

On May 25, 1979, as part of the Egyptian-Israeli Peace Treaty negotiated by President Carter at Camp David, the Israelis withdrew from northern Sinai to the east of El Arish and the Egyptians took over the vacated area. UNEF was not involved in these moves other than in permitting Egyptians access through the area of limited forces and armaments and the Buffer Zone. UNEF relinquished control of the northern part of the Buffer Zone 1, thereby reducing the area of Swedish deployment. Other contingents were not effected.

UNEF kept close contact with the parties at all levels and enjoyed their complete confidence. Contacts with the Israelis were maintained by General Siilasvuo after his appointment as Chief Co-ordinator of UN Peacekeeping Missions in the Middle East. He was replaced as UNEF Commander by the Swedish General Bengt Liljestrand, who had recently been appointed Chief of Staff UNTSO. As part of his responsibilities under the Protocol, Siilasvuo maintained high-level contacts with Egypt as well.

The appointment of a Chief Co-ordinator of UN peacekeeping missions in the Middle East was intended to meet certain essential requirements as negotiations for Israeli withdrawals and redeployment of Egyptian and Israeli forces became necessary. Essentially, the appointment was political, but it resulted in considerable controversy among the higher military command system, causing friction and to some measure affecting operational efficiency.

Unquestionably, Siilasvuo was the most experienced peacekeeper in the Middle East and had the complete confidence of his superiors, the parties and the great powers, especially the United States which emerged as the key negotiator. Therefore, his qualifications for this role were unrivalled. When UNEF II was first established and Siilasvuo was appointed its Commander, the appointment of Chief of Staff UNTSO was vacant until it was filled by General Liljestrand in April 1974. The priority at UN Headquarters was UNEF, and Siilasvuo as the former Chief of Staff UNTSO could and did take his pick in personnel and support. However, with the establishment of UNDOF, created out of UNEF with some UNTSO observers, there were three peacekeeping missions in the Middle East, and this made some co-ordination necessary.

Siilasvuo could not be appointed as an overall or a Supreme Commander (only General von Horn in the Congo had wished for such a grandiose title), as each of the peacekeeping missions has a separate mandate with the Secretary-General as the supervisor or Chief Executive, in accordance with authority given to him by the Security Council. It therefore made sense to appoint a Chief Co-ordinator during the critical early days of establishing UNDOF and redeployments of UNEF, and as such Siilasvuo played an important and effective role. However, problems relating to command interrelationship, overlapping responsibilities with the parties, and administrative support in the field remained unresolved with the promotion of Siilasvuo to Lieutenant-General by Finland and to Under Secretary-General by the United Nations. He was provided with two senior officials, viz. a Senior Staff Officer, Colonel William Callaghan (Ireland), and Chief Administrative Officer, Dennis Holland.

Certainly Siilasvuo could and did effectively co-ordinate higher policy and maintained high-level contacts. However, he lacked resources and staff to co-ordinate operational details and administration. The aircraft belonged to UNTSO and UNEF, unless special charters were arranged for the Chief Co-ordinator by Field Operations Service, New York. UNEF had the largest administrative and logistic resources under its own Chief Administrative Officer, in the shape of the Canadian and Polish contingents. The support for UNDOF came from these sources. Understandably, there were attempts by the office of the Chief Co-ordinator to co-ordinate what would normally be functions of a military theatre headquarters, but this office could really only perform in the specific area of the conduct and interpretation of higher operational tasks (excluding logistics and other military aspects).

UN peacekeeping operations are *ad hoc* by their very nature, and they often call for *ad hoc* solutions. Siilasvuo was the choice for the position of Chief Co-ordinator. A way of possibly reducing some of the difficulties that arose would have been to put him in civilian clothes and make his assignment strictly political. It is quite common practice to second military personnel to diplomatic assignments, a practice not confined to military regimes alone. In order further to avoid his being considered a military person, he could have been temporarily given an ambassador's rank. In any event, a better solution would have to be found to avoid such situations in the future.

Initially, the Secretary-General had proposed that UNEF should have a total strength of 7,000 to include thirteen contingents each of not more than 600. However, in the case of the two logistics contingents from Canada and Poland, which were to share responsibility for the support of the force, the ceiling of 600 could not be applied. Furthermore, only twelve contingents were finally selected.

By January 20, 1974, UNEF reached its authorized strength. Austria, Finland, Nepal and Sweden each had about 600; Ghana, Indonesia, Nepal, Panama, Peru and Senegal varied between 400 and 500 each; Ireland provided 271, Canada 1,907 and Poland 822. By May, the Finns, Peruvians and Swedes had been reduced and the Irish withdrawn to bring the total down to 6,374.

After the establishment of UNDOF on May 31, 1974, the Austrians, the Peruvians and elements of Canadian and Polish units were transferred to it. Therefore in June UNEF's total strength was 5,079. The Nepalese were withdrawn in August, the Panamanians in November, and the Senegalese in May-June 1976. UNEF was then left with seven contingents with a total strength of about 4,000.

During the operations there were forty-seven deaths, of which five were from firing and wounds. In addition, nine Canadian aircrew of a UNEF Buffalo aircraft were killed on a flight to UNDOF, when it was accidentally shot down by the Syrians on August 9, 1974.

The mandate of UNEF lapsed in July 1979. Subsequently, Ghanaians were transferred to UNIFIL, some Canadians and Poles were sent to UNDOF, and a Swedish guard company was retained to provide for the security of the Headquarters UNEF Liquidation Team and the depot.

Financing of UNEF and UNDOF

In establishing UNEF, the Security Council resolution 340 (1973) authorized that the costs of the Force should be considered as expenses of the organization to be borne by the members in accordance with Article 17, paragraph 2, of the Charter. The same principle was applied with UNDOF. Acting on the approval of his report to the Council, the Secretary-General authorized commitments of costs up to $1.8 million under the provisions of paragraph 1(*a*) of the General Assembly Resolution 3045 (XXVII) relating to unforeseen and extraordinary expenses for the financial year 1973. The transport of contingents was provided free by Australia, Canada, West Germany, Norway, Poland, Sweden, the Soviet Union, the United Kingdom and the United States. Japan made a voluntary cash contribution for the same purpose.

In its Resolution 3101 (XXVIII) of December 11, 1973, the Assembly appropriated $30 million for UNEF for the period from October 25, 1973, to April 24, 1974, at a rate not to exceed $5 million per month up to October 31, 1974, should the Council decide to extend the force-mandate. Furthermore, without prejudice to the positions of principle that member-states might take in financing peacekeeping operations, the Assembly reaffirmed its previous decisions regarding the fact that, 'in order to meet the expenditures caused by such operations, a different procedure is required from that applied to meet expenditures of the regular budget of the United Nations.'[19] It took into account the special responsibilities of the permanent members of the Security Council and the ability of the economically more developed countries to pay more than the economically less developed countries.

In setting up UNDOF, the Security Council authorized its financing on the same basis as UNEF. This was facilitated by integrated logistic arrangements and the fact that initially all the contingents were drawn from UNEF.

On November 28, 1974, the Assembly by its Resolution 3211B (XXIX) appropriated $30 million from April 25 to October 24, 1974, for UNEF and UNDOF, another $19.8 million from October 25, 1973, to October 24, 1974, as well as another $40 million from October 25, 1974, to April 24, 1975. It fixed a ceiling for both missions at a rate of $6,666,667 per month from April 25 to October 31, 1975. As we have seen, the mandate of UNEF lapsed in July 1979 and UNDOF continues to be operational. Although the amounts varied as changes took place in the size of the missions, a Special Account was established for the two missions pursuant to General Assembly Resolutions 3101 (XXVIII) and 3211B (XXIX).

Albania, Benin, China, Kampuchea, Democratic Yemen, Libya, Syria, Vietnam, and Yemen announced that they would not participate in the financing of these missions. Iraq paid its share for the first six months only. The Soviet Union said it would not pay any costs related to the Egypt-Israel Agreement of September 4, 1975. Byelorussia, Czechoslovakia, East Germany, Mongolia, and Ukraine expressed similar views.

A new practice for the reimbursement of troop-contributing governments was established with UNEF II, and this became a precedent for subsequent operations. The Assembly on November 29, 1974, on the basis of the Secretary-General's report on financing (A/9822) and in the Fifth Committee's recommendation (A/9825

Add. 1, para. 10), decided that the rate of payment to troop-contributing countries for pay and allowances should be standardized at $500 per person per month, and authorized an additional $150 per month as supplementary payment for specialists, not exceeding 25 per cent for the logistic units and 10 per cent for the others.

On December 2, 1977, the Assembly on the basis of the Fifth Committee's recommendation (A/32/299/Add. para. 10) and the Secretary-General's report (A/32/339 and Corr. 1 and 2), allowing for inflation, approved new rates at $680 per soldier per month, and an additional $200 for a limited number of technicians.

Earlier, in 1975, the Assembly had approved the Fifth Committee's recommendation (A/10324/Add 3 para. 40) to provide $65 per person per month for the cost of personal clothing, gear and equipment, and $5 per man per month for weapons including ammunition; provision was also made to reimburse contributing states for the cost of depreciation of heavy equipment and the cost of supplies. Provision was also made to reimburse governments for payments made by them in accordance with their national regulations for death, injuries, disability or illness.

The UN also paid a daily allowance of $1.28 per person for incidental expenses; and after completion of six months service a recreational leave allowance was given for up to seven days at $10.50 per day.

The UN assumed responsibility for logistics, local support costs including food, accommodation, medical and welfare services, and the maintenance of transport and the communications system. The UN also covered the cost of rotation of contingents and the cost of individuals repatriated for compassionate or medical reasons.

The problem of financing peacekeeping operations is far from being overcome. In fact, the UN is behind in payments to contingents, thereby creating serious difficulties for less affluent troop contributors. During 1983 UNDOF's budget was $34,979,000 and the authorization for 1984 was $2,914,916 per month. The unpaid balance for UNEF II/UNDOF at November 1983 was $79.1 million and a further shortfall of $59.6 million in a special account.

The United States Sinai Support Mission

During the negotiation for the withdrawal of the Israelis from the general line of the Mitla and Gidi Passes in Sinai, Israel was not prepared to abandon its electronic surveillance system set up on these strategic passes. Dr Kissinger broke this impasse and obtained an agreement for the Israeli system to remain, with the United States providing a system to the Egyptians to be built near Gidi Pass and for the United States, at the specific request of the two parties, to provide tactical electronic surveillance of the two passes. The United States station was to be staffed by US civilian volunteers and to be located in a demilitarized buffer zone separating the two belligerents.

The Sinai Support Mission (SSM) and the role of the unit in Sinai — Sinai Field Mission (SFM) — were established in January 1976, following its authorization by a Joint Resolution (Public Law 94–110) and implemented by President Ford through an Executive Order signed on January 13, 1976.

First a temporary camp was established in Sinai to enable the SSM and its American contractor to vest all the early warning systems, to be operational by February 22, 1976. The more permanent facilities were built by July 1976. The early warning system remained effective until the withdrawal of the IDF on January 25, 1980, in compliance with the Egyptian-Israeli peace treaty.

The SFM operated independently and yet collaborated with UNEF II. The UN peacekeeping force and the UNTSO observers attached to it were responsible for this buffer zone and the limited forces zones. The SFM monitored access to the critical Gidi and Mitla Passes. This visual and electronic surveillance was backed up by aerial photo reconnaissance along the median line of the buffer zone by the United States based on the results made available to the two sides and to the UN.

The SFM was responsible for monitoring both the Passes and the Egyptian and the Israeli surveillance stations. The monitoring of the Passes was done by the US liaison personnel, who checked all movement in and out of the stations and conducted periodic inspections to check the number of personnel vehicles, weapons etc. They also checked whether there was any variance from the visual or electronic roles permitted to both parties. Sensor fields and watch stations were used, the purpose being to report to the two parties and the UN any movement of armed forces by either side. The surveillance system included unattended ground sensors and visual coverage by watch stations. Depending on the terrain, seismic, infra-red or strain-sensitive sensors were used, and in a few instances seismically-operated microphones proved effective. At Gidi west, which could not be physically observed, a remote-control TV camera was installed. Each watchtower was equipped with high-power wide-angle binoculars, a terrestrial telescope for daytime use and a high-power, wide-angle image intensifier for night use. This permitted vehicles to be identified at distances of up to 20 km. by day under average conditions and 5 km. by night.

The SFM reported a number of ground and air violations, more by the Israelis than the Egyptians, but none serious. Adding to the watchfulness by the UN, the SFM provided a number of guarantees, including an American commitment to place its nationals between Egypt and Israel. The deployment of an early warning system significantly contributed to confidence-building.

Many in the UN are convinced that peacekeeping operations could be made more effective and observation capability enhanced significantly by the use of improved optical instruments and by using sensors to provide early warning. The Dutch and the Norwegians, learning from this experience, have improved their observation capability. While budgetary considerations remain important, understanding of the characteristics of electronic surveillance, and especially of its benefits, has to be sufficiently realized to make its use more readily accepted.

In July 1979 the Security Council did not extend the tenure of UNEF II, which was to expire that month. At the request of the two parties, the United States agreed to alter the role of SFM to verify Egyptian forces and armament levels in Zone A and part of Zone B, and the nature of the operations of the four Israeli technical sites within the Interim Buffer Zones, specified in Annex I of the Peace Treaty. The results of these inspections were reported to both parties and to the Joint Commission to deal with violations. The SFM added a small number of aircraft to carry out this new role while the responsibilities in the two Passes had been overcome by events. The above-described role of SFMs ended on April 25, 1982, when Israel withdrew east of the International Frontier and a multinational force organized by the United States with the consent of Egypt and Israel assumed responsibility in Sinai.

The Sinai multinational force

The Camp David accords of September 17, 1978, in Annex 1 to the Peace Treaty between Egypt and Israel, contain a Protocol concerning the Israeli withdrawal and security arrangements. This Annex defines the terms of Israel's phased withdrawal from Sinai and establishes the post-withdrawal levels of military personnel and equipment to be allowed in Sinai and in Israel along the international border. Also, it established the principle that 'the Parties will request the United Nations to provide forces and observers to supervise the implementation of this Annex and employ their best efforts to prevent any violations of the terms.'

This mandate of UNEF II in Sinai was due to expire in July 1979 and therefore the participation of these troops to implement the Camp David accords needed a final resolution. Because the Soviets had been isolated from the Middle East peacemaking process, it was evident that they were unlikely to support a UN peacekeeping force, and therefore the parties to the Camp David accord agreed to establish a multinational force outside the UN framework. Such a force was to be responsible to Egypt, Israel, the United States and troop-contributing nations.

The task of establishing a multinational peacekeeping force outside the framework of the United Nations had not been attempted before. The parties were to lay the foundations of an organizational and administrative structure unlike any of its predecessors in international peacekeeping.

There were a number of novelties. Egypt and Israel had signed a peace treaty and were no longer combatants, which thereby eliminated the need for a Buffer Zone, ceasefire or armistice lines; the new force was to operate on the territories of the two states who were in effective control of their lands. The treaty provided specific and complete arrangements for both states' military forces limitations, there was to be a naval component and the United States was to act as a guarantor.

The main tasks assigned to the force were:

1. Operation of checkpoints, reconnaissance patrols, and observation posts along the international boundry (line A) and a small zone running parallel to it (line B) as also in Zone C (starting from Rafah on the Mediterranean running parallel to the international frontier, then southwest of the Gulf of Aqaba at a distance of 20–40 kms.).

2. Periodic verification of the arrangements, not less than twice a month, unless otherwise agreed upon by the parties.

3. Additional verifications within 48 hours after the receipt of a request by either party.

4. Ensuring the freedom of navigation in the Straits of Tiran.

Sinai was divided into four zones: A — east of the Suez Canal, B — in the Centre, and C — adjacent to the Israeli Zone, as described above and the forth Zone D, a line just east of the international frontier inside Israel. In Zone A, Egypt may maintain one mechanised infantry division with its installations and fortifications; in Zone B four border units are permitted; and in Zone C only civilian police armed with light weapons may be deployed.

According to the provisions of the treaty, Leamon R. Hunt, a US Foreign Service officer, was appointed Director-General, and he in turn appointed Lt.-Gen. Fredrik V. Bull-Hansen of Norway to the post of Force Commander.

By March 1982, the assembling of the Multinational Force and Observers (MFO) in Sinai had begun, and it assumed its responsibility as required by the Camp David agreement by April 25. The force consisted of 2,500 men from eleven countries, composed as follows:

United States	1,250 (800 paratroopers, 400 military and civilian personnel for support and observer duties)
Colombia/Fiji	500 (an infantry batallion)
Netherlands	100 (signals corps and military police)
Australia/New Zealand	140 (helicopter crew and ground personnel)
Uruguay	74 (transport unit)
United Kingdom	35 (headquarters personnel)

France, Norway and *Italy* provide the remaining personnel for transport aircraft, flying and ground crew

The US contingent is responsible for the southern sector of the Egyptian-Israeli border and for safe passage through the Straits of Tiran; the United States Observer Force headquarters is at Eitan. The Colombian and Fijian battalions are responsible for the northern sector, and the other contingents have provided support personnel.

The cost of the force is estimated as over $225 million for the first year, as offices and residential buildings are being constructed. This will be met by contributions of 60 per cent from the United States and 20 per cent each from Egypt and Israel.

The fact that little has been said about this force after its deployment in Sinai can be attributed to its success. Some critics view the organization of a peacekeeping operation outside the framework of the UN as another notable sign of the weakness of the world organization, but doing so they fail to consider that the parties to the Camp David accord were determined to exclude the Soviet Union from these negotiations and that therefore they were compelled to settle for an arrangement outside the UN, even though that was not their preferred choice.

However, the UN can take pride in the fact that the Sinai force has been entirely organised on the basis of the UN experience in peacekeeping, that its commander is an old UN hand, and that the force was prepared, assembled and deployed with the advice of a former senior UN administrator.

The MFO does operate as a peacekeeping force along the lines first evolved and subsequently developed by the UN. However, there are a number of notable differences. (1) Hitherto, international peacekeeping has preceded a final accord like the Egyptian-Israeli Peace Treaty. Such forces have usually been withdrawn either just before or at the moment when a final accord is concluded, because by then they have concluded their task. In this case the task of the MFO began after a peace treaty. (2) The United States has provided the major support and is the guarantor. The early practice of excluding permanent members of the Security Council from international peacekeeping changed when troops from the United Kingdom were included in UNFICYP. Later the French contributed troops to UNIFIL. The participation in peacekeeping by the United States, a superpower, is unique.

The states represented in the MFO are either members of NATO or friends of the United States. Therefore, the multinational participation has been viewed by some states as an attempt to reduce the impact of an American presence in Sinai, a part of Egypt. The fact that the United States is the guarantor has also raised the question of whether the MFO is truly a peacekeeping force as developed by the international system. However, MFO deserves credit for promoting peace

between Egypt and Israel, and it has proved a useful confidence-
building measure between the people of these countries, where
tensions remain.

Multinational forces for Beirut

In 1982, fighting in Lebanon escalated. The Israelis encircled the PLO
positions and camps in West Beirut, and simultaneously blocked
Syrian troops to prevent any possibility of their providing direct aid to
the PLO. The house-to-house fighting in the streets caused heavy
civilian casualties, leading to a universal demand for an end to the
war. Many Third World nations, supported by the Soviet Union,
urged that a UN force be introduced to end the impasse in Beirut, but
this was not acceptable to Israel. A series of ceasefire arrangements
were negotiated by the American mediator, Ambassador Philip
Habib, only to be violated by one or the other party. By early August,
the Israelis had captured Beirut airport and surrounded key
Palestinian camps.

On August 1 the Security Council authorised the UN Secretary-
General to deploy, at the request of the Lebanese government, the UN
Observers to monitor the situation in and around Beirut.[20] Two days
later, Pérez de Cuéllar reported to the Council that Israeli military
authorities had told the Commander of the UN Observers that no co-
operation would be extended to any monitors until a decision had been
taken on this question by the Israeli government. In another meeting,
the Security Council voted unanimously on August 12 to demand the
immediate lifting of all restrictions on the city of Beirut to permit free
entry of supplies for the civilians and that Israel co-operate in securing
effective deployment of UN Observers.[14] Already ten observers had
arrived in Beirut and another eighty were ready to take up positions as
soon as permitted to do so by Israel. These observers were drawn from
UNTSO, representing many nationalities, including the United States
and the Soviet Union.

The UN Observers were finally allowed entry as part of an overall
agreement. These negotiations by the United States dealt with a ceasefire that would be established in Lebanon to be supervised by UN
Observers, the withdrawal of the Palestinian forces from West Beirut
and the establishment of a multinational force. None of the military
forces, Lebanese and foreign, would in any way impede the departure
of the PLO, with guarantees provided by the Lebanese and United
States governments. The mission of the UN Observer Group in Beirut
was authorized by the Security Council in its resolution No. 521 and
implied five main tasks: (1) to maintain a UN presence in and around
Beirut; (2) to monitor deployment and activities of all forces in the
area; (3) to patrol the Damascus Highway, since it is a route for
resupply of the UN observers and for evacuation if necessary; (4) to

monitor and report breaches of human rights in the area; and (5) to maintain liaison with the legal forces in Lebanon. Fifty unarmed military observers, representing several nations, are continuing with these vital and arduous tasks up to the time of going to press.

The multinational force, set up on a temporary basis, consisting of contingents from France, Italy and the United States at the request of the Lebanese government, was to assist the Lebanese armed forces in (1) assuring the safety of departing PLO personnel, (2) assuring the safety of other persons in the Beirut area, and (3) restoring Lebanese sovereign authority over the Beirut area.

The multinational force entered Beirut on August 25, 1982, and on the completion of its tasks withdrew from Lebanon on September 10. On September 14, Bashir Gemayel, the President-elect of Lebanon, was assassinated; his assassins were suspected of being from the opposition Christians. Fearing anarchy and loss of control of the capital by Gemayel's Phalangists, the Israelis re-entered Beirut on September 15. The following day, when the Israelis were supposed to be providing security for civilians, Phalangists and other Christian Lebanese troops, who have been Israel's allies in recent years in their invasion of Southern Lebanon, went through the Shatila and Sabra refugee camps in West Beirut, killing the Palestinians, most of them women, children and older men. This terrible massacre shocked the world and persuaded the Lebanese to invite the multinational force back.

On September 20, 1982, the Lebanese government requested the governments of France, Italy and the United States to contribute forces to serve as a temporary multinational force, whose presence would facilitate the restoration of Lebanese sovereignty and authority and thereby further the efforts of the Lebanese government to assure the safety of persons in the area and end the recurring violence.[21]

The French were the first to arrive, but they were obliged to remain in the area of Beirut port and their own embassy until the Israelis vacated East and West Beirut. About 1,100 French legionnaires were deployed across the Green Line which divided the Muslim part of the city from the Christians. The French area included the port, the main shopping areas and the Shatila and Sabra camps. About 1,100 Italians were in the south and were responsible for a zone that included another Palestinian camp, Brajnib. Some 1,200 US Marines took over positions in the area of the airport, south of the Italians. The deployment of the Americans was delayed, since the Israelis were reluctant to vacate the airport, and were only eventually persuaded to do so by American diplomacy. The multinational force was not designed to engage in combat. It was, however, empowered to act in self-defence and was equipped accordingly.

President Reagan's spokesman said on September 29: 'We fully expect all foreign forces to be out of Lebanon by the time we have reached the goal of restoring the stability of the Government of Lebanon.' Similarly, the French and Italian foreign ministers declared in press statements at the UN, where they were attending the General Assembly session, that their joint force with the United States was likely to stay in Beirut until other foreign troops left Lebanon.

The remaining months of 1982 and the early months of 1983 witnessed little peace in this strife-torn country. There was fighting between various factions, with the Israelis on the one side mostly in the Shouf and with the Syrians in the Bekaa Valley. There was intermittent firing in Beirut, with continuing casualties among both civilians and the fighters. There were repeated incidents involving the MNF with factions, including some ugly exchanges between the US Marines and the IDF.

In the meanwhile, US negotiators persevered with their efforts to obtain the withdrawal of foreign forces, and the United States introduced a programme to train and equip the Lebanese forces. However, the basic Lebanese weaknesses remained, making national unity an illusion. President Amin Gemayel could only establish central authority with an effective Lebanese army. After eight years of anarchy, they needed an army to protect its borders, ensure its sovereignty and security; become a national unifying factor by bringing soldiers of many factions into a single melting pot; and be strong enough to disarm all autonomous militias. All efforts to unify the army had so far failed. The Lebanese army is largely based on the Phalangists, who support Gemayel. Since the United States and France support President Gemayel, their troops in Beirut were seen by the opposing factions as friends of their enemies. This had led to a series of incidents including the tragic blowing up of the US Marine barracks and French quarters, resulting in very heavy casualties, by what was generally reported as a pro-Iranian Shiite faction.

The United States had provided support with the naval guns and aircraft of the Sixth Fleet to the Lebanese forces fighting in the hills south-east of Beirut. Similarly, the French had been drawn in to help the Lebanese army. Such actions were viewed by the opposing factions as hostile, and resulted in retaliation against the US and the French troops, which in turn invited counter-retaliation. Thus the peacekeeping functions of these two contingents had been seriously compromised. The Italian troops had remained cautious and avoided open hostility against any Lebanese faction. A small contingent of British troops had joined MNF too by May 1983 but had confined its role to peacekeeping patrolling.

On May 17 Israel and Lebanon signed an agreement, a step which came short of a peace treaty. It ended the state of war between the two countries, respected the sovereignty and political independence of each, and required a withdrawal by the Israelis when certain conditions were met. In an Annex, the security arrangements were defined. A security region was established in southern Lebanon along a line north of Sidon running due east to the Syrian border. Only the Lebanese army, police and auxiliary forces (Ansar) would operate in this area and they would be responsible for security. A joint liaison committee, including a security arrangements committee, would be established, composed of an equal number of senior Israeli and Lebanese officers. A US representative would participate at the request of either party. The withdrawal of Israeli forces was contingent on withdrawal by Syria and the PLO.

The Agreement also had an understanding that the Lebanese government might request the UN Security Council for one unit of UNIFIL to be stationed in the Sidon area to supplement the Lebanese forces in the Palestinian camps in that region. This unit could also send teams to survey and observe the Palestinian refugee camps in the vicinity of Sidon and Tyre, if so authorized by the arrangements contained in the protocol.

The Agreement was to go into effect after the Israelis had withdrawn. Thereafter, negotiations were to resume within six months to normalise relations. It was signed by a retired Lebanese diplomat, Antoine Fattal, representing President Gemayel, and by David Kimche, Director General of Israel's Ministry of Foreign Affairs. It was witnessed by Morris Draper, a US Special Envoy. Much of the groundwork had been done by Israel's Defence Minister Ariel Sharon.

Syria and most of the Arab states denounced the Agreement. US attempts to persuade Syria to withdraw proved futile. Meanwhile, Israeli forces remained committed in the Shouf and in their confrontation with the Syrians in the southern Bekaa Valley. IDF losses in these areas and from Lebanese factions in southern Lebanon continued to increase, causing concern in Israel. Finally, Israel arranged unilateral withdrawal to the general line of the Awali river to reduce its force in Lebanon as well as its exposure to many hazards. US efforts to prevent this action failed, and with that, the leverage which the offer of Israeli withdrawal might have provided in negotiations with Syria.

Backed by Saudi Arabia, US negotiating efforts finally led to a meeting of Lebanese leaders in Geneva in November 1983. The rival groups agreed to end the fighting and create a unified army and government. They decided on equal representation for Christian and Muslims, yet leaving the top positions as before. However, leaders opposing Gemayel insisted on the cancellation of the Israeli-Lebanese Agreement. The talks were interrupted to allow time for Gemayel to negotiate new arrangements. Meanwhile the other leaders returned home to sell the agreement reached in Geneva to their respective factions. Despite all this, fighting in Lebanon continued uninterrupted. As 1983 was about to end, there were renewed efforts by the Reagan Administration to seek a solution.

The mission of the MNF was one of peace, the improvement of

stability and the establishment of conditions under which Lebanon could have recovered its full independence and integrity. The main priorities of the four countries supplying troops were national reconciliation in Lebanon and withdrawal of foreign forces, and all the four countries did their utmost to promote this. Since the tragic bombing of the US and French quarters, this role had been under consideration.

Early in December 1983 at a NATO meeting, the foreign ministers of the contributing countries met and renewed their intention to maintain MNF. However, there were indications that every effort was being made to train the Lebanese security forces to assume more and more responsibility. Also, renewed efforts were under way to support Gemayel and to promote reconciliation with the opposition leaders. In whatever solution finally emerges, there is likely to be a role for UN peacekeeping.

Amid all these events, Yassir Arafat arrived in Tripoli, in northern Lebanon, to strengthen his remaining fighters, who were surrounded by pro-Syrian PLO groups, and to shore up his own diminishing political power base. After several weeks of intensive fighting, Arafat was persuaded to leave for Tunisia with his supporters. So ended another chapter in the saga of the Palestinians.

President Gemayel failed to persuade the opposition to join him. Early in February the Druse and Shiia troops opened a major offensive against the Lebanese Army which splintered along factional lines. The advancing opposition forces created a serious threat to the MNF. The British and the Italians pulled out, leaving the French in West Beirut and the US Marines at the Beirut airport. However, when the opposition troops reached the Mediterranean coast and opened a road link from there to the Bekaa, the US Marines were withdrawn to their ships, less 300 left behind to guard the US Embassy and to provide instructors for the Lebanese Army.

The French troops remained behind, and their government tried in vain to obtain a Security Council approval for a UN peacekeeping operation in which their contingent would participate. For all purposes, the MNF does not exist anymore.

Returning to the principles relating to the operations of the MNF, it is questionable whether they could correctly be called 'peacekeepers'. Each of the four contingents was in Beirut under a bilateral arrangement between its own country and President Gemayel's government. Since Gemayel's Lebanese army, despite its legitimacy, had only limited control of Beirut and the surrounding area, it was in effect but one faction in the labyrinth of Lebanese politics. The contingents of MNF were committed to support Gemayel. So their role was hardly that of 'peacekeepers'.

NOTES

1. UN General Assembly Resolution 1001 (ES-1), Nov. 7, 1956.
2. UN General Assembly Resolution 1124 (XI), Feb. 2, 1957.
3. (*a*) Introduction to the annual report of the work of the UN, 1960.
   (*b*) UN General Assembly A/6672, July 12, 1967, UNEF Report of the Secretary-General.
4. I.J. Rikhye, *The Sinai Blunder* (New Delhi: Oxford & IBH, 1979; London: Frank Cass, 1980).
5. UN Security Council Resolution 242, Nov. 22, 1967.
6. UN Security Council Resolution 338, Oct. 21, 1973.
7. *Ibid*.
8. UN Security Council Resolution 340, Oct. 25, 1973.
9. Secretary-General's Report, S/1102/Rev. 1, Oct. 26, 1973. (The Organization's expenses should be borne by the members as apportioned by the General Assembly.)
10. UN Security Council Resolution 341, Oct. 27, 1973.
11. UN Document Annexure to S/11056/Add. 6, Nov. 21, 1973.
12. UN Document S-11198, Jan. 18, 1974.
13. UN Security Council Resolution 350, May 31, 1974.
14. UN Security Council Resolution 378, Oct. 23, 1975.
15. UN Secretary General's Report, S/11849.
16. UN Document S/11818, Sept. 2, 1975.
17. UN Document S/11849, Oct. 17, 1975.
18. UN Document S/12212, Oct. 18, 1976.
19. UN Document S/11052/Rev. 1, Oct. 27, 1973.
20. UN Security Council Resolution 516, Aug. 1, 1982.
21. Text of President Reagan's letter of Sept. 29 to Congress as published by the *New York Times*, Sept. 30, 1982.

4

MAINTAINING PEACE

General

By the end of the 1950s, the UN had gained experience in observer missions for fact-finding, armistice and ceasefire observation; and in mounting peacekeeping forces to separate combatants, observe a ceasefire and provide certain measures of security. The outbreak of the civil war in the Congo (now Zaire) after it gained independence from Belgium on June 30, 1960, called for the UN to progress a number of steps forward in developing a collective security capability. The West wanted a peaceful transfer of power and, once civil war had broken out, a speedy end to internal fighting and the prevention of external interference that could have kindled and East-West conflict. The Soviets, supporting decolonization, wanted early departure by the Belgians, especially the Belgian metropolitan troops which had been flown in after the mutiny of the Congolese security forces. For once, both sides agreed on an international peacekeeping action, although this accord proved short-lived.

The Africans and the nonaligned agreed with the superpowers, but had major differences with both. They wanted the Belgians and the Western commercial interests out quickly, and the Soviets to remain out. Thus UN action received universal support.

The secession of Katanga, the row between President Kasavubu and Prime Minister Lumumba and the subsequent removal of the latter, later the coup by the army Chief of Staff Colonel Mobutu, and the splintering of the Congo created enormous problems for the UN peacekeeping force. As it attempted to keep law and order, maintain peace between warring ethnic groups representing splinter groups, and control the divided Congolese security forces which opted to fight on one or the other side or went on the rampage, these already formidable difficulties were further exacerbated by foreign military aid with equipment, advisers and mercenaries. It was an unenviable task that the UN had to work its way through, and mistakes were not avoided because of the lack of past experience and because of the unexpected nature of the task. Yet the operation ended in success.

Operations in aid of one's own national government are difficult enough. The tragic shooting of four students on the campus at Kent State University, Ohio, USA, during rioting against the Vietnam war is an example of failure by the US National Guard. Yet aid to a foreign civil power is far more complex. The United States decided to support the junta in Santo Domingo in the 1965 civil war in the Dominican Republic, and supported other dubious governments established by military coups; but what the United States, or for that matter any other great power, has done in the past and may do in the future does not provide a suitable example for the UN to follow. The UN may only deal with a legitimate government, and in the absence of such a government has to be guided by the UN organs, i.e. the Security Council or the General Assembly. In a civil war, a distinct authority with which the UN can and should deal has scarcely ever been present.

The Congo operation was followed by the UN operation in Cyprus. Here the Greek and Turkish Cypriots had divided the central authority, presenting the UN with problems somewhat similar to those it had experienced in the Congo. Whichever side the UN supported was wrong for the other side. The Greeks held the Turks responsible for breaking the law, and the Turks accused the Greeks of violence. The civil police was split, the Turks withdrew from the government and all civil authority was left in Greek hands. Such a situation left the UN with few choices, and those very difficult ones. In Cyprus too there was illegal arms traffic, and both sides brought military personnel surreptitiously from mainland Greece and Turkey respectively.

The UN evolved some guidelines from these experiences, namely non-interference in internal affairs and the need to support the legitimate authority or, when this is lacking in an area, to operate under a strict framework in order not to influence the political outcome. Furthermore, the UN must do everything in its power to maintain peace, provide humanitarian assistance and protect life and property. It must support efforts to end the internal fighting and to keep the country isolated from harmful external influences.

Congo

The peacekeeping operation in the Congo presented the first serious challenge to the UN to prove its capability for collective action in a complex situation. As the nation moved towards its independence date of June 30, 1960, law and order were already breaking down. Within a week of independence the Force Publique, the Congolese security force, mutinied, and civil war broke out throughout the land. To appease the soldiers, Patrice Lumumba, the Prime Minister, appointed Victor Lundula, a former medical non-comissioned officer, as the new force commander, with Joseph Mobutu, a journalist who had served as a civilian quartermaster's clerk, as Chief of Staff. He then allowed the soldiers to elect their own officers.

Dissatisfied with these developments, Moise Tshombe, President of the copper-rich province of Katanga, proclaimed Katanga's own independence on July 11. Belgian troops, who had remained in the bases permitted them under a Treaty of Friendship, were joined by metropolitan forces from Belgium, and together they intervened to protect life and property. Fearing that the Belgians intended to re-occupy the country, the Congolese government sought the help from the United States, which advised them that UN endorsement was essential. On July 13 Lumumba requested Dag Hammarskjöld, the UN Secretary-General, for military assistance, and in the mean time asked Ghana for help.

The transfer of power in the Congo turned out very differently from the way the Belgians had envisaged it. Like the British and the French in their former colonies, especially the latter, the Belgians hoped that they would be asked to resume an important role in the newly-independent state. But the Belgians had not created any indigenous leadership, as the British had done in their colonies; nor had they established a cadre of *évolués* (highly educated Africans), as the French had done. Within a few days of independence the whole administrative infrastructure had disappeared amid chaos and bloodshed. Thus the UN was needed to provide massive technical assistance as well as direct military action to restore law and order.

On July 14 the Security Council called upon the Belgians to withdraw their forces from the Congo, and authorized the Secretary-General to provide the Congolese government with what military assistance might be necessary until the national security forces were capable of fulfilling their tasks.[1] Then on July 22, in addition to calling upon Belgians to withdraw speedily, it requested all states to refrain from action that might impede the restoration of law and order or in any way prejudice the Congolese government's authority.[2] It also invited the UN agencies to render such assistance to the Secretary-General as he might require.

The UN quickly established ONUC, the peacekeeping force, and troops from several nations were airlifted and despatched to the national capital, Leopoldville (now Kinshasa) and the provinces to deal with the disorders. The Force Publique, lacking proper leadership, was out of control and had in fact become a positive force of disorder. Determined to protect their economic interests in the mineral-rich province of Katanga, the Belgians increased their military intervention and actively supported Tshombe's secession. The UN operations were further hampered by a dispute over the disarming of the Congolese army on a personal initiative of the British Chief of Defence Staff of Ghana, Maj.-Gen. Henry Alexander, who had arrived in Leopoldville with his troops to serve with ONUC. When the Secretary-General's Special Representative in the Congo, Ralph Bunche, failed to arrange the entry of UN troops into Katanga, the Security Council met again and resolved on August 9, 1960, that such action by UN troops was necessary to implement the mandate; called upon the Belgians to withdraw from Katanga; and reaffirmed that ONUC would not be a party to, or in any way intervene in, the Congo's internal affairs.[3]

Three days after the passage of the resolution, Hammarskjöld arrived in Elisabethville, the provincial capital of Katanga, with the advance elements of the UN's Swedish contingent, which took over security duties from the Belgians there and in Jadotville, a mining centre. However, the Belgians still remained in the province; the secession of Katanga had by no means ended; and Hammarskjöld's relations with the Congolese government, tenuous from the start, now worsened because he had refused Lumumba's demand to include Congolese representatives and their military along with the UN advance elements in Katanga. This caused the Secretary-General to be criticised by the Soviet Union. The Soviets also tried to get the Council to accept that Hammarskjöld's implementation of its resolution should be subject to agreement by the troop-contributing states. They failed; but later Hammarskjöld had this suggestion in mind when he established a Congo Advisory Committee along the lines already adopted in the Advisory Committee for UNEF.

By early September, a serious constitutional crisis had developed. Lumumba, frustrated by the UN's refusal to quell the Katanga secession by force, decided to do so himself. He launched the Congolese army with the aid of Soviet aircraft and ground transport which had initially been made available for the civilian administration. His ill-prepared force, lacking access to airfields in Katanga, landed in the neighbouring Kasai province and immediately became embroiled in internecine fighting with Baluba tribes. Many Balubas were killed; others were made homeless and became refugees, further adding to the critical problems facing the UN aid agencies. The Congolese President, Joseph Kasavubu, had opposed Lumumba's action; as the differences between their views widened, Kasavubu dismissed him under the authority given him by the *loi fondamentale*. Nothing daunted, Lumumba in turn 'dismissed' the President. Kasavubu replaced him as Prime Minister with Joseph Ileo, the Senate President, who proved ineffective in the face of political squabbling and the collapse of all Congolese authority. While a divided UN debated the problem on September 16, Colonel Mobutu, the army Chief of Staff, staged a coup, neutralizing Kasavubu and Lumumba and dismissing Ileo's government.

Two days earlier the Soviets, bitterly critical of Hammarskjöld, had introduced a resolution in the Security Council requiring the Secretary-General to remove the Commander of ONUC. After a number of further attempts by the Soviets and others to obtain similar Council resolutions, the United States gained approval for a Special Session of the General Assembly under the Uniting for Peace Resolution.[4] Because of the importance they attached to the UN role in the Congo, many heads of state and government attended this session. The ensuing debate was tumultuous. Hammarskjöld was severely attacked by the Soviets in a campaign personally led by Chairman

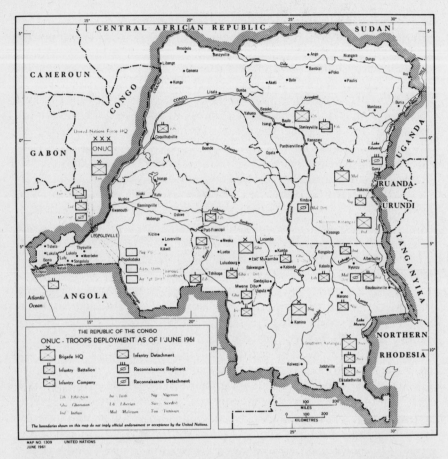

THE REPUBLIC OF THE CONGO
ONUC - TROOPS DEPLOYMENT AS OF 1 JUNE 1961

Khrushchev; they called for his removal as Secretary-General and his replacement by a 'troika' of three men. Hammarskjöld survived this attack with the help of the middle powers and Third World countries, and far from being dismissed, he was requested by the Special Session to continue his efforts to implement previous Resolutions,[5] and appoint a conciliation commission; he recognized Kasavubu as the constitutionally-elected President of the Congo by accepting the credentials of his delegation.[6] However, having failed in the attempt to oust Hammarskjöld, the Soviets thereafter opposed his every move, making his task ever more difficult.

Lumumba meanwhile had not been inactive. He enjoyed considerable political influence at home, and his seditious utterances soon led to his arrest by Mobutu. This caused a furore among the UN membership, making it well-nigh impossible to get them to agree on any future course of action. Nor did it settle anything, for even in gaol Lumumba was a problem. Mobutu had him removed from Leopoldville because of his popularity there, but his presence was equally influential among the soldiers at the prison. Mobutu transferred him again, this time to Tshombe's custody in Katanga. On February 13, 1961, Lumumba was killed by his captors.

At the UN, the pro-Lumumba states in Africa, such as Ghana and Egypt, many non-aligned states and the Socialist bloc had wanted Mobutu's ouster by ONUC and the restoration of Lumumba to his elected office. The West and many African states were sympathetic towards Mobutu. The Council Resolution that was finally adopted followed Hammarskjöld's suggestions and became the major mandate for future actions. This Resolution specifically authorized ONUC 'to prevent the occurrence of civil war,' and to use force if necessary in the last resort for this purpose, and not only in self-defence, as in the past; it called for the withdrawal of Belgian and all other foreign military and para-military personnel, political advisers and mercenaries; urged the convening of the Congolese parliament and the reorganization of the Congolese Army (ANC) and an end to its interference in the country's political life.[7]

Lumumba's death led to the splintering of the fledgling nation and the outbreak of civil war. For this the UN was blamed, and Hammarskjöld came under attack for his failure to protect Congolese leaders and cope with lawlessness. After careful consultation, Hammarskjöld advocated eight measures.[8] The first five were: an investigation into Lumumba's death; protection of the civil population against armed attack; containment of clashes between armed units by introducing ceasefire arrangements, neutral zones etc.; reactivation of the UN's attempt to reorganize the ANC; and elimination of the Belgian political element. He argued that these five tasks could be pursued within a flexible interpretation of the existing mandate outlined above. But a new mandate would be needed for the last three measures: the UN's right to inspect trains and aircraft for arms; the control of funds and capital; and the compulsory convening of the Congolese parliament.[9]

With a strengthened mandate, ONUC launched a major initiative to deal with the civil war, restore the basic economy, and help the Conciliation Commission to start the negotiating process leading to the convening of parliament. Though impatient with the pace of developments, the African nations became hopelessly divided. Many had contingents in ONUC. Of these Egypt, Libya, Morocco, Guinea and Ghana, joined by Ceylon and Indonesia (the two Asian countries with troops in ONUC), met at Casablanca in April, and decided that insufficient progress was being made to implement S/4741 of February 21. They wanted a time-limit to be met, after which enforcement action should follow. By contrast, the French-speaking states (less Guinea and Mali) with some other governments met at Tananarive and supported the more cautious approach of the Conciliation Commission.

A similar division developed between non-African troop-contributing countries. Several of them had little faith in the Conciliation Commission, and all member-states felt that Moise Tshombe and his Belgian advisers had manipulated the conference at Tananarive. Others supported the proposals of the Conciliation Commission on the grounds that they only reflected the reality of Congolese politics. In the face of this diversity, the General Assembly on April 15[10] was able only to agree to call on Belgium to comply with UN resolutions, and to demand that Belgian and other foreign military, para-military and political personnel not under the UN command, including all mercenaries, should be withdrawn.

In another resolution[11] the Assembly called on the Congolese to desist from seeking a military solution to their problems and to prevent the introduction of military hardware into the country. They were to release members of parliament and the provincial assemblies who had been detained and convene parliament. Lastly, the Assembly decided to appoint a second Conciliation Commission to end the political crisis.

ONUC then succeeded in negotiating an agreement between Kasavubu and Gizenga, who had assumed the leadership of Lumumba's followers. Under the UN protective agreements the parliamentarians met at Lovanium University, outside Leopoldville. Cyrille Adoula emerged as the Prime Minister of the new government with Gizenga as the first Deputy Prime Minister. The new arrangements covered the whole country except Katanga. To this problem ONUC now turned its attention. In August it started rounding up mercenaries; but in the absence of full co-operation by some of the consulates of Western European countries from which the mercenaries had been recruited, the ONUC operation turned into a military action. This had historic consequences for the UN. On a flight to meet Tshombe, who had fled to neighbouring Northern Rhodesia (now Zambia), Hammarskjöld was killed in a plane crash.

A ceasefire was arranged, but Katanga remained in a state of embattled rebellion. Disappointed with the UN, Gizenga returned to Stanleyville to reorganise his troops for an operation against Katanga. The Central Government also launched an offensive against Tshombe's forces along the Kasai-Katanga border. Soon Kivu, Northern and Western Katanga and Eastern Kasai all became areas of renewed fighting. The Security Council, while deprecating the secessionist activities of Katanga, as well as attacks on ONUC personnel, now authorized 'the Secretary-General to take vigorous action, including the use of the requisite means of force, for the immediate apprehension, detention pending legal action and/or deportation of all foreign military and para-military personnel and political advisers . . . and mercenaries. . . .'[12]

In the face of attacks by the Katanga gendarmerie, ONUC launched another offensive, and this time established a strong position throughout the province. On December 21, 1961, Tshombe signed an agreement terminating Katanga's secession. ONUC still had to deal with Gizenga and troops loyal to him in the Stanleyville area. But after some resistance by Gizenga forces, it succeeded in gaining control, and Gizenga was brought back to Leopoldville, where he was wanted by the central government.

In the months that followed, ONUC was occupied with helping Adoula's government restore law and order. While it provided some help in reorganizing and training the ANC, Adoula and Mobutu preferred to make bilateral arrangements. Meanwhile, attempts were being made to reconcile Adoula and Tshombe and provide for an amicable reunification. In August 1962 Hammarskjöld's successor, U Thant, proposed a Plan of National Reconciliation,[13] and by the first week of September he had the acceptance of both Adoula and Tshombe. The plan provided for a federal constitution; the regulation of currency; the sharing of revenues and earnings; the integration of the army and security forces; a proclamation of amnesty; and the reservation of foreign relations to the central government. However, acceptance was not the same as implementation. Tshombe dragged his feet, and on December 10, ONUC announced that because Katanga had not made any serious effort to carry out the plan, it would proceed to implement UN resolutions to end the secession, using force in self-defence if attacked.

Meanwhile, Katanganese harassment of ONUC continued. On December 24 the Katanga gendarmerie opened fire on ONUC positions, force-landed an unarmed ONUC helicopter, blocked ONUC movement, and fired at ONUC positions in Elisabethville and other places, causing casualties. Only after ONUC representatives failed to persuade Tshombe to order that his gendarmerie desist from attacking ONUC and to remove roadblocks did the UN troops act. Soon ONUC was in control of Elisabethville, and by January 3, 1963 it had secured the mining installations at Jadotville. On that day, representatives of the central government assumed control in Elisabethville. At a meeting with ONUC representatives on January 17, Tshombe at last formally agreed to end the secession, and ONUC entered Kolwezi on January 21.

By now ONUC had carried out most of its mandate. The Congo had been unified; foreign military and para-military personnel and political advisers had been removed; and progress had been made in coping with the revenues from foreign economic interests, i.e. the central government assumed responsibility but agreed to share them with Katanga. In the months that followed, ONUC was engaged in restoring the central government's authority throughout the country and assisting in the maintenance of law and order. It was time to reduce the UN's enormous financial burden, and to start a gradual withdrawal. The last of ONUC left by the end of June 1964.

ONUC had been charged with many responsibilities. On the peace-keeping side it was a totally new experience for the UN whose activities had previously been confined to peace observation and, with the intro-duction of UNEF, the separation of forces by agreement. In the Congo it was plunged into the middle of a civil war. This entailed involvement in the civil affairs of the Congo as well as a highly delicate military mission. Throughout this period, ONUC never received a precise definition of its functions, because the international commu-nity was as divided as the Congo itself. A tremendous responsibility was thus placed on the UN Secretary-General, and by him, in turn, on his political representative and the military commanders in the field.

Hopeful of the support of the Third World, Hammarskjöld accepted this herculean task with the confidence born of his experience with UNEF after the Suez war, which turned out to be a misleading precedent. That operation had been authorized by the General Assembly, which lacked the executive·machinery possessed by the Security Council and was therefore happy to follow the formula of 'Leave it to Dag'. ONUC, on the other hand, was set up by the Security Council, and as Hammarskjöld ran into political difficulties in New York, its voice changed. Katanga's secession became a fester-ing sore, soon to be followed by the worsening of Hammarskjöld's relations with Lumumba and the consequent hostility of the Soviet Union. The Western powers, as NATO partners of Belgium, were not enamoured of Hammarskjöld's independence, still less of the support that he enjoyed in the Third World, including several nations which had only recently achieved independence from France and Britain. A further complication was the division within Africa, where the franco-phone community gave generous support to Tshombe, while the rest of the continent mostly backed Lumumba.

It was inevitable that these cross-currents would have an impact on ONUC. The direction of this large and multifarious force reflected the changing and stormy political winds in New York and the conflicting interests of the embassies in Leopoldville. After Lumumba's assas-sination the Congo splintered into four regions. The central govern-ment retained tenuous control of Leopoldville and of the Equatorial and Western Kasai provinces. Gizenga gained control over Oriental and Kivu provinces and the border area of Kasai and Katanga. In Bakwanga, the diamond state, Munongo declared himself king. Tshombe continued to control most of Katanga.

The Security Council peacekeeping mandate given to the UN Force in 1960 included these responsibilities: to provide such military assistance as might be necessary, and technical assistance for the Congolese internal security forces; to supervise the withdrawal of the Belgian forces; to assist in the maintenance of law and order and in the exercise of Congolese authority; and to assist in preserving the territorial integrity and political independence of the Congo. Later, in 1961, the Council authorized ONUC to take vigorous action, including the use of force, to deal with the foreign mercenaries and to take measures to exclude arms and material supplies.

Like UNEF, the UN force in the Congo supervised the withdrawal of foreign (i.e. Belgian) troops; but that was only one of its tasks. On a number of occasions, ONUC had to separate rival ANC groups. Troops loyal to Lumumba, and later to Gizenga, were separated from those loyal to Mobutu. Lumumba forces and/or Mobutu's troops had to be separated from the Katanga gendarmerie. On such occasions, the separation of rival forces followed a pattern already established by the creation of ceasefire lines and by neutral or limited armed zones. ONUC either interposed troops or established observers to supervise the ceasefire arrangements.

It was the responsibility of ONUC to assist the Congolese in the maintenance of law and order and related responsibilities, i.e. to help reunify the country, remove foreign personnel not under UN command, prevent the flow of unauthorized weapons and military personnel, and secure the country from outside interference. These tasks were not only novel but also highly complex and sensitive. They were made even more difficult after the removal of Lumumba as Prime Minister, because ONUC had no central authority to deal with until the formation of the Adoula government in 1962. Several months passed before President Kasavubu was accepted by the 1960 General Assembly as the head of the central authority, and even then effective power remained in the hands of Colonel Mobutu to the extent of his control over elements of ANC. In the absence of established and effective civic authority, ONUC Commanders exercised their own judgment in responding to requests for assistance which, without exception, were politically or tribally motivated.

After the splintering of the Congo, ONUC was the only effective unifying force in the country. At significant human and financial cost, it was ONUC which achieved eventual reunification. In a variety of ways, every move it made had an important policy impact on the future of the Congo. Thus, for the first time in history, a multinational force, free of colonial or other national interests, operated for the benefit of a sovereign people, and to serve the interests of global peace. In spite of the difficulties and limitations, international peacekeeping not only survived the challenge but established beyond any doubt that, without its involvement, the Congo would have ceased to survive as a unified nation and could easily have become a battleground of economic and ideological warfare.

Cyprus

The role of the United Nations Force in Cyprus, until the Turkish military intervention in 1974, is another example of maintaining peace within a community. But after 1974, UNFICYP's role changed to separating the Greek and Turkish Cypriots from each other.

Cyprus, with its strategic location in the eastern Mediterranen, has been ruled by many foreign invaders. The Greeks, who came to the island some 3,300 years ago, had the longest occupation, and their culture and heritage pervades it. The Turks were in occupation between the sixteenth and nineteenth centuries, and the British acquired the island from the Turks in 1878.

The great majority of the population of about 600,000 is of Greek origin, some 18 per cent Turkish. At the end of the Second World War the Cypriots, caught by the winds of change, began to press for political change. The Greek-led national organization of Cypriot fighters — EOKA — started to wage a guerrilla campaign against the British to obtain self-determination and union with Greece, known as *Enosis*; at the same time the Turkish Cypriots formed their own underground groups and looked towards Turkey for ultimate help and security. After some years of bitter fighting and debates in the UN, the London and Zurich Agreements were signed in 1959 by the British, Greek and Turkish governments. These laid down the provisions of the constitution, the main points of which were: (1) the President was to be elected from the Greek community and the Vice-President from the Turkish community; (2) the Civil Service was to be 70 per cent Greek and 30 per cent Turkish; (3) the Police and Army ratios were to be Greek 60 per cent and Turkish 40 per cent; (4) the Turkish Vice-President was given veto power in defence and foreign policy; (5) on financial matters the concurrence of the Turkish deputies was essential.

Immediately after independence, difficulties arose between Archbishop Makarios, the President, and Mustafa Fazil Kütchük, the Vice-President, over financial, police and defence matters. The administration and election of local bodies became another point of conflict. The Greek Cypriot leaders concluded that the constitution was unworkable and should be revised. But the Turkish leaders were determined to protect their minority interests and built-in safcguards. They therefore prepared themselves against the possibility of the Greeks using force to achieve their ends.

An exchange of firing in Nicosia on December 21, 1963, signalled the start of intercommunal fighting. The Greek leadership called for majority control as the only effective way to govern the island, ignoring the Treaty of Guarantee providing the right to Britain, Greek and Turkey to intervene if the constitution were voided. The Turkish leadership insisted on partition to ensure their survival. When efforts to deal with the conflict by negotiations between the Guarantor Powers failed, the two communities agreed to the establishment of a peacekeeping force consisting of troops already on the island: the British under the Treaty of Guarantee, and Greek and Turkish troops under the Treaty of Alliance. The force was placed under British command.

On December 26, 1963, the Government of Cyprus asked for a meeting of the Security Council,[14] alleging that the Government of Turkey was committing acts of aggression by violating air space and territorial waters, and was intervening in the internal affairs of Cyprus by the threat and use of force against its territorial integrity and political independence. The next day the Council duly met, but no resolution emerged.

On the same day, British troops from the Sovereign Base Areas, under the command of Maj.-Gen. Peter Young, moved into Nicosia and other communities to keep the peace. Owing to the intensity of the emotions surrounding the Greek and Turkish garrisons in Nicosia, these contingents were not deployed for peacekeeping. Early in January 1964, on a joint request by Britain, Greece, Turkey and Cyprus, the UN Secretary-General appointed Lt.-Gen. Prem Singh Gyani of India, then serving as Commander UNEF in Gaza, as a UN Observer in Cyprus.

Meanwhile, as fighting between the two communities continued unabated, the British government was able to arrange a meeting of the four powers in London, which started on January 15, 1964. U Thant nominated his Deputy *Chef de Cabinet*, José Rolz-Bennet (Guatemala), as his representative. Britain, having only recently granted independence, did not think it desirable to carry the main burden of peacekeeping in Cyprus alone, and wished to enlarge the process. In February an agreement was reached to set up an international peacekeeping force under the UN. At about the same time Britain sent additional troops under Maj.-Gen. Michael Carver, who replaced Maj.-Gen. A.E. Younger.

On March 4, the Security Council approved a draft Resolution by its members, submitted by five of the non-permanent members of the Council, establishing a UN peacekeeping force in Cyprus (UNFICYP). The Resolution noted that the situation there, which threatened international peace and security, required prompt measures, and took note of the treaties which led to the independence of Cyprus without questioning the views of the two communities or compromising their legal validity.

UNFICYP was to be the first major peacekeeping operation at a force level since ONUC, which had bitterly divided the permanent members of the Council as well as other UN member-states. The Resolution had therefore to be carefully worded to avoid a veto by any of the five permanent members. The main points of the operative paragraph were as follows: (1) the composition and size of the force would be established by the Secretary-General in consultation with the four Governments; (2) the Commander of the force would be appointed by the Secretary-General; (3) the force would be stationed for a period of three months, the costs to be met by governments providing the contingents and by Cyprus itself. The Secretary-General could also accept voluntary contributions; and (4) the Secretary-General was to report periodically on the operation.

As prior consultations had taken place, the two main opponents of the conduct of ONUC — France and the Soviet Union — did not veto the proposal despite their reservations. The Soviet Union could not accept that the Secretary-General should appoint the Force Commander, which it contended was the Council's prerogative. It therefore asked that a separate vote be called for on this paragraph, and then abstained in the vote. The Soviets noted the method of financing and the period for stationing the troops, adding that any period beyond three months should have the Council's approval. The French expressed their reservations concerning the principle of intervention by the UN military means, and over the authority given to the Secretary-General. The separate vote on the paragraph relating to the authority given to the Secretary-General was eight in favour with Czechoslavakia, France and the Soviet Union abstaining. The Resolution as a whole was adopted unanimously.[15] The importance of this Resolution was that, although every one of the major issues concerning peacekeeping remained unresolved, the Security Council did agree to establish this operation.

The mandate given to UNFICYP was to use its best efforts to prevent a recurrence of fighting; to contribute to the maintenance and restoration of law and order; and to promote a return to normal conditions. The Council had also authorized the Secretary-General to appoint a mediator to promote a peaceful solution.

The character of the fighting between the Greek and Turkish communities was almost that of a civil war, and the British troops under General Carver were reluctant to impose peace; that, after all, had been their function in the decade before independence. Frustrated by the complexity of the task, they hoped for an early internationalization of the mission, and looked to the UN to facilitate this task. However, this left the Secretary-General with many difficulties. Although a number of contributing countries expressed interest in participating in UNFICYP, they were apprehensive about becoming embroiled in a Congo-type operation. Most Third World nations felt that Cyprus was a responsibility of NATO, because all three Guarantor Powers were NATO members, and Cyprus was part of Europe. Some member-states could not afford to pay the cost of contributing troops. U Thant was able to deal with the apprehensions of likely contributing states by agreeing to inform them of the substance of the instructions and directives to the Commander.

The Canadians offered a composite contingent, but required more information on the role it would have to play so as to ensure parliamentary approval. The Irish agreed to provide and pay for a 500-man infantry unit provided that the operation was not expected to impose a settlement; in particular, they insisted that there should be no attempt to solve the problem by partition while the Irish troops remained on the island. The Finns and the Swedes also made offers, the Swedes insisting that they would only agree if Finland and Ireland, two other neutral nations, participated. By the end of March, U Thant had resolved all the major issues. UNFICYP became operational on March 27 with the appointment of the Indian Lt.-Gen. P.S. Gyani as Commander. Some 950 Canadian troops, advance parties of the Finnish and Swedish contingents, and about 6,000 British soldiers came under the UN flag. The advance party of the Irish contingent was on its way, and its main body was due in April, by which time it was hoped that parliamentary approval would be obtained. The British troops were to be reduced to 3,500 as they were replaced by other UN contingents.

Along with obtaining troop contingents the Secretary-General dealt with a host of logistic, administrative and budgetary matters. The force level was fixed at a maximum of 7,000. Canada and Britain would pay entirely for their troops. The Irish government would bear the cost of pay and allowances for theirs; and the UN would reimburse such costs for the remaining contingents. The UN did not procure any aircraft or vehicles since these were held to be part of troop contributions. The UN agreed to pay all local costs except for those of the British. There would be no reimbursements for any special flights (for welfare or national purposes) for contingents, e.g. the Canadians and the Swedish. The United States agreed to provide the first airlift at no cost to the UN.

At the Secretary-General's request, Austria agreed to provide a medical unit at UN cost. The UN also agreed to pay for some 200 UN-recruited civilian police, and to keep the international civil staff to sixty-five. As time went by, UNFICYP costs exceeded contributions, and large sums are still owed to some of the troop-contributing states, most notably Canada. Later in the operation, the Canadians and the Irish negotiated some increase in their reimbursements by the UN. Economies were also effected by reducing the international civilian and local staff.

The main guiding principles for the operation of UNFICYP were as follows. (1) In performance of their stated responsibilities, the troops could employ arms in self-defence should this become necessary, but they must act with restraint and complete impartiality. (2) The principle of 'self-defence' included the defence of the UN posts, premises, vehicles and other UNFICYP personnel. The Commander on the spot would decide when force was to be used. (3) Force could be used in self-defence if there were attempts to compel the troops to withdraw from a position; attempts by force to disarm them; or attempts by force to prevent them from carrying out their responsibilities.

The UNFICYP civilian police responsibilities included: (1) establishing liaison with the Cypriot police; (2) accompanying Cypriot police patrols to check traffic and other offences; (3) establishing UN police posts in sensitive areas; (4) observing searches at road blocks; and (5) investigating incidents where Greek or Turkish Cypriots were involved with the opposite community.

By mid-June 1964 UNFICYP had made good progress. Its troops were deployed mainly between the armed elements of the two communities, at vulnerable points and around UN installations. A recurrence of fighting was prevented not only by the interposition of troops, but by negotiation with the leaders of the two communities on co-operation to end hostilities. A number of fixed posts were established on the ceasefire line, and frequent patrols were sent along it. The Force assisted civilians and tried to deal with their security problems. It also had two other important functions to perform: to observe the rotation of the Turkish troops, and to check the importation of arms and equipment by the Cypriot government.

At the end of the first three months, in June, the Force was extended for another three-month period up to September 1964.[16]

During the second week of August 1964 fighting erupted in the Tylliria area, and Turkish aircraft intervened. The Security Council called for an end to hostilities.[17] The Secretary-General reported to the Council on August 10 that both sides had agreed to cease fighting and that all concerned would co-operate with the Force Commander. The Secretary-General had reported to the Council that the presence of UNFICYP was essential to prevent resumption of the civil war and to enable mediation and negotiations to continue. Accordingly, three-month extensions were successively given till the end of 1966, when the Council approved an extension for six months,[18] and further six-month extensions were continued in the express hope that by the end of the next period, sufficient progress would have been made for a withdrawal, or at least a substantial reduction, of the Force to be possible.

In November 1967 an outbreak of fighting at Ayios Theodhoros caused a serious political crisis. A proposal by UNFICYP to extend the functions of the Force was not acted upon. The Secretary-General urged the three parties to agree on a staged reduction and withdrawal of non-Cypriot armed forces other than those of the UN. The Security Council endorsed U Thant's appeal.[19] The parties agreed to withdraw their non-Cypriot personnel by January 16, 1968.

UNFICYP instituted a number of procedures to promote a return to normal conditions on the island and to find a political solution. Besides providing security, it concerned itself with humanitarian and relief assistance. A number of *ad hoc* measures were also undertaken to save lives, e.g. escorts for essential civilians and supplies, escorts and patrols to protect harvesting and to guard government property in each community-controlled area, procedures to ensure regularity of postal services, payment of social benefits and the re-employment of Turkish Cypriot civil servants, and co-operation with the Red Cross and the Cyprus Joint Relief Commission. In October-November 1964, UNFICYP tried to persuade both sides to withdraw economic and security restrictions in respect of movement of personnel. But despite these efforts, inter-communal talks made little progress because of basic political differences.

On July 15, 1974, a *coup d'état* against President Makarios radically changed the situation for UNFICYP. The *coup* leaders announced their wish for early *enosis,* and called for military assistance from Greece. Fearing Greek military intervention, the Turkish government decided to invade Cyprus, and began landing forces on July 20. The situation that now developed had not been envisaged when UNFICYP was first established. The UN Force had to establish and observe a ceasefire between Turkish forces, who were joined by Turkish Cypriots, and the Cypriot National Guard reinforced by Greek military cadres. Equally there had been a large infusion of weapons to both sides. The Security Council called for a ceasefire and requested all parties to co-operate fully with UNFICYP to enable it to carry out its mandate.

UNFICYP endeavoured to arrange local ceasefires to protect life and property, and played a major role in the safe evacuation of foreign nationals while the Secretary-General and members of the Council were attempting to end the full-scale fighting. When the ceasefire came into effect on July 22, UNFICYP sought to assist the parties in making it effective by delineating the positions at 1600 hours. However, the next day fighting again broke out. With the consent of both sides the UN troops, at great risk to themselves, temporarily took over the Nicosia international airport and declared it a UN-protected area.

On July 30, the Foreign Ministers of Greece, Turkey and Britain agreed in Geneva to establish a UN-controlled security zone, at the limit of Turkish military-occupied territory, which would be for the exclusive use of UNFICYP. All the Turkish enclaves occupied by the Greek or Greek Cypriot forces would be vacated. UNFICYP would assume security and police responsibility for mixed villages. Military and civilian personnel detained during the fighting would be exchanged or released under the auspices of the International Committee of the Red Cross (ICRC). The Security Council approved the above functions for UNFICYP on July 31.[20] However, the Geneva talks broke down and fighting resumed on August 14. UNFICYP continued its vigorous efforts and a partial ceasefire was restored. This finally became a full ceasefire on August 16.

Throughout this period, as already indicated, UNFICYP had assumed important humanitarian responsibilities in co-operation with the ICRC. A special humanitarian branch had been set up at Head-quarters UNFICYP; and on August 20, the Secretary-General desig-nated the High Commissioner for Refugees as Co-ordinator of the UN Humanitarian Assistance in Cyprus. In recognizing the dire need and the importance of this role, the Secretary-General declared that 'it is one of the foremost purposes of the UN to lend humanitarian assis-tance in situations such as the one currently prevailing in Cyprus.'[21] With the available manpower, transport and aircraft, UNFICYP was able to assist the Co-ordinator in a variety of tasks related to aid to civilians, which included protection of human rights, tracing and accounting for missing persons, and so on.

Since the ceasefire was established on August 16. 1974, the role of UNFICYP has remained the same up till the time of writing. The Turkish intervention led to a division of the island, with an area between the two ceasefire lines under UNFICYP control. In the area under the control of the Cyprus government (Greek), UNFICYP initially remained interposed between the National Guard and the Turkish Cypriots, much as it had done from the time the operation had first been established.[22] This responsibility ended when the great majority of Turkish Cypriots departed to the Turkish-controlled area in September 1975. In the northern area under Turkish Cypriot control, and occupied by the Turkish Army, there have remained many Greek Cypriots, to whom UNFICYP has had difficulty in gaining access. In 1976 a large number of them were evacuated to the government-controlled area, but the UN could not verify the circum-stances of this exodus. In 1977 there were some improvements, and the UN was provided with free and normal acess. In 1980, 1,286 Greek Cypriots were reported to be living in the north.

UNFICYP maintains some 135 posts within the buffer zone, but the number of these occupied at any one time varies. Temporary standing patrols, mobile patrols and round-the-clock surveillance are maintained along the two ceasefire lines.

Headquarters UNFICYP includes political and military personnel. Galo Plaza of Ecuador was the first and last Mediator; after his departure, mediation responsibilities remained with the Secretary-General, and the political head of the mission is called the Officer-in-Charge. This post has always been filled from Latin America, with the exception of two in acting positions for brief periods. Bibiano F. Osorio-Tafall, the last Officer-in-Charge ONUC, served the longest in Cyprus, between February 1967 and June 1974.

The first Commander, General Gyani, was replaced by General K.S. Thimayya, former Chief of Staff, Indian Army, who had also served with the Neutral Nations Repatriation Commission in Korea. Thimayya, an able and popular man, died in Cyprus; and after a brief acting command by the then Chief of Staff, Brigadier A.J. Wilson of the United Kingdom,[23] he was replaced by a former Military Adviser to the Secretary-General and a distinguished soldier from Finland, Lt.-Gen. I.A.E. Martola. In December 1969 Martola was in turn replaced by Lt.-Gen. Prem Chand of India, who had commanded the ONUC troops in Katanga. He served for seven years, including the critical period of the Turkish intervention and the redeployment of UNFICYP in a new role, and was succeeded by Maj.-Gen. J.J. Quinn of Ireland who had previous UN experience. In 1981 Maj.-Gen. Günther Greindl of Austria, formerly Commander UNDOF, assumed command. Thus the experience and level of Cyprus Commanders has been very high by comparison with any other UN Command. They have included Carver who became a Field-Marshal; Thimayya who was idolised in India (much to the concern of his national political superiors); Martola, a national hero in Finland; and Prem Chand, with his outstanding record in leading the UN troops who ended the secession of Katanga.

The Special Representative — or the Officer-in-Charge — and the Force Commander held parallel positions in UNFICYP. The fact that they have always worked well together testifies to their outstanding capability and tact. Several other notable features have contributed to the smooth and successful functioning of the Cyprus operation. The Chief of Staff position is alternately held by British and Canadian officers, as is the post of Deputy Chief of Staff, thus providing continuity. There is an Economics Section and a Police Adviser.

The number of contingents and the size of the Force have varied. Eight nations contributed military and police in 1964, when the strength of the Force was 6,411. As tensions were reduced, the Force shrank to 3,708 by the end of 1968. In 1973 it was down to 3,150. In October-November 1973 Austrian, Finnish and Swedish personnel were despatched to become the advance elements of UNEF II in Egypt. But when hostilities broke out in Cyprus in 1974, the Force level was increased again and had reached 4,444 on August 14. By June 1980, it had been reduced again to 2,491; its contingents were from Austria, Canada, Denmark, Finland, Ireland and Sweden. The civilian police came from Australia and Sweden. Up to June 1980, 111 personnel had died in Cyprus, including twelve killed in action and two missing in action, presumed dead.

An exceptional feature of this operation is that logistic support is provided by the British forces from their sovereign bases in the island. The role of the UN Field Service is therefore on a reduced scale. UNFICYP ranks as the best logistic-supported of all peacekeeping operations; for the first time a UN peacekeeping operation has had the logistic support of a major power. Exclusive dependence on a single nation for this important service has its risks; but where undue influence does not occur, as in Cyprus, it has proved ideal. However, the operation of the force was frequently hampered by actions of the Cyprus National Guard or Police, and sometimes, in the period before

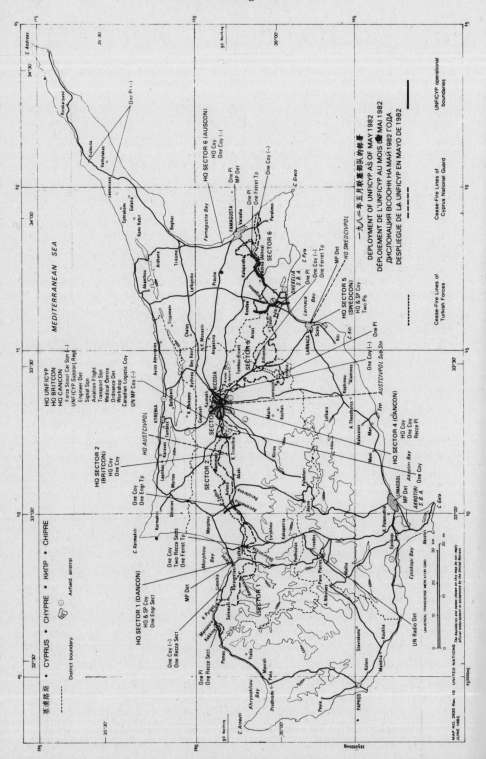

DEPLOYMENT OF UNFICYP AS OF MAY 1982
DÉPLOIEMENT DE L'UNFICYP AU MOIS DE MAI 1982
ДИСЛОКАЦИЯ ВСООНК НА МАЙ 1982 ГОДА
DESPLIEGUE DE LA UNFICYP EN MAYO DE 1982
一九八二年五月联塞部队的部署

the Turkish intervention, by the Turkish Cypriots. The situation has changed for the better since then.

The financing of UNFICYP continues to cause concern. From June 1980 the deficit has reached $99.8 million. The money owed to troop-contributing countries for reimbursement of extra and extraordinary costs had only been met up till March 1976. The disproportionate burden shouldered by these governments has caused some of them to convey to the Secretary-General their serious concern, and to have second thoughts about their participation in UNFICYP. The Secretary-General sent a Secretariat team to review the entire operation and it recommended some improvements and cost-reducing measures. But it is understood the team established that although some cuts could be made here and there, costs cannot be appreciably reduced without basically altering UNFICYP's mandate.

Since it was first established UNFICYP has, as we have seen, under-gone several reductions, from about 7,000 in 1964, when it was first formed, to about 2,100 by July 1974. Had the *coup* against Makarios and the Turkish intervention not occurred, it was likely that improv-ing conditions would have led to further reduction and perhaps reorganization of the force to 'observer status'.

There are two main questions to be considered in contemplating reductions. First, if the Force is to be reduced, will its mission/man-date be changed accordingly? The views of many delegates in New York indicate that such an action by the Security Council is most unlikely. The second question follows the first: failing a change in mission, will the parties to the dispute give the Secretary-General assurances that they will increase co-operation with UNFICYP forces, as regards its freedom of movement or access to areas which it con-siders require its attention? Will they implement more stringent controls over the actions of their own forces in maintaining the cease-fire? And will they reduce their own forces significantly?

It is likely that some assurances will be given to the UN, since both sides would wish to appear to be co-operating with it. Hence, the Secretariat review committee rightly related any further reductions to a change in the mandate, which will only be possible if the whole question of Cyprus is dealt with, a step which is likely to be counter-productive.

Despite repeated efforts, the inter-communal talks have made little progress. The Cyprus government remains anxious to continue UNFICYP; and the Turkish Cypriots, secure under the protection of a sizeable Turkish army and in occupation of almost half the island, still realize the usefulness of the UN troops. The periodic extensions of UNFICYP placed some pressure on the two communities to resume talks; but this limitation has not significantly influenced the political process. The crucial fact remains that if UNFICYP were withdrawn or its capability reduced, daily occurrences of minor incidents could detonate a resumption of fighting.

On November 15, 1983, the Turkish Cypriot leadship announced its independence as the Turkish Cypriot Federation of the North. Dr Rauf Denktash, named President of this entity, declared that this move enhanced Turkish Cypriot capability to negotiate a federation with Greek Cypriots, and improved opportunities to reach an agreement. The Cyprus government, represented by the Greek Cypriots, brought the case to the UN Security Council, which condemned the Turkish community's unilateral declaration of independence and urged the two communities to enter into talks to be arranged by the UN Secretary-General.

The Turkish Cypriot leader, Dr Denktash, in a public statement to the press (*N.Y. Times*, Nov. 27, 1983) stated that when the question of renewal of UNFICYP came up at the end of 1983 the Turkish community would call for a review. He indicated that he intended to raise the question of the participation in UNFICYP of contingents whose countries had voted in support of the Greek Cypriot government of the Republic of Cyprus.

The Turkish community's move makes the presence of UNFICYP all the more essential. If the force were to be withdrawn in face of it, a *de facto* partition of Cyprus would be perpetuated and new tensions would arise that could escalate with a high probability that fighting would be renewed.

UNIFIL

The United Nations Interim Force in Lebanon (UNIFIL) was established by the Security Council at Lebanon's request on March 19, 1978, following Israeli military intervention in the south of the country.[24] The conflict had deep roots. As a consequence of fighting between Jordanian forces and the PLO in the early 1970s, the Arabs agreed to the removal of Palestinian fighters from Jordan, and Lebanon provided a haven (Fatahland) for them in Southern Lebanon. Since the Cairo Agreement (1969), the Chief of Staff, Lebanese Army, had given the PLO authority to use southern Lebanon as a base of operations against Israel.

UNRWA camps containing large numbers of Palestinian refugees already existed in and around Beirut; now the bulk of el Fatah, the liberation fighters, were moved to the territory south of the Litani river. It was not long before the PLO started raids across the Israeli-Lebanese armistice line, which in the past had been traditionally quiet, and these resulted in Israeli retaliatory attacks.

In 1975 civil war broke out between Christian factions and leftist Muslim Lebanese, assisted by the PLO. With the increase in the intensity of fighting, the Lebanese administration collapsed and its security forces were divided. An Arab League peacekeeping force (the Arab Deterrent Force), predominantly Syrian with token representation from Kuwait, Libya and Saudi Arabia, was brought in to end the civil war and keep the peace. The other Arabs soon withdrew their contingents, and thereafter only the Syrians, some 25,000 in number, remained. The deployment of this force in Lebanon, specially in the Bekaa Valley, positioned these troops on the flank of UNDOF, which separated the Israelis from the Syrians, and this provided the Syrians with access to sensitive approaches to Israel. Realizing this new danger to their security, the Israelis insisted that Syrian troops remain north of the Litani River (the Red Line). In order further to safeguard the approaches from the Bekaa Valley, the Israelis decided to assist the Christian forces under the command of Major Haddad in southern Lebanon.

UNTSO observers were helpless as PLO raids and Israeli counter-raids increased. The Christians, Muslims and PLO elements, frustrated by the presence of UNMOs in their midst, rough-handled and humiliated UN personnel until the situation became intolerable. Unable to check PLO infiltrations, the Israelis resorted to large-scale military operations into southern Lebanon with a view to clearing the area of the PLO. These actions seriously threatened international peace and security, and it was in response to this danger that the Council decided to call for an Israeli withdrawal, and to establish a UN peacekeeping force to separate the warring parties.[25] The terms of reference of the force were as follows:

(1) to confirm the withdrawal of Israeli forces, restore international peace and security and assist the Government of Lebanon in ensuring the return of its effective authority in the area;

(2) to establish and maintain an area to be defined in the light of para. 2 of the relevant UN Resolution;[26]

(3) to use its best efforts to prevent recurrence of fighting and to ensure that its area of operation is not utilized for hostile activities of any kind;

(4) to take all measures deemed necessary to ensure the effective restoration of Lebanese sovereignty and authority;

(5) the force would have the co-operation of UNTSO observers who would continue to function along the ADL after the termination of UNIFIL's mandate.

There were several armed elements[27] in the area, armed with modern and powerful weapons, who were not under any effective control. A peacekeeping force could only use force in self-defence. Therefore, in deciding the force level and its weapons, a careful balance had to be achieved so that it should be strong enough to deter attacks by uncontrolled elements. The Secretary-General had initially decided on 4,000 as the force ceiling; but it was soon apparent that more would be needed. On the recommendation of the Force Commander,

MAP NO. 3201 UNITED NATIONS
SEPTEMBER 1982

Maj.-Gen. Emmanuel Erskine of Ghana, formerly Chief of Staff UNTSO, the Council increased the strength to 6,000.

From the outset the UN headquarters and General Erskine, who had established his headquarters in Jerusalem, had to cope with the difficulties relating to the different interpretations by the parties to the conflict. Israel expected UNIFIL to control the entire area south of the Litani river, including Tyre and the Kasmeya bridge, but excluding the southern enclave under Lebanese Christian control. Israel wanted UNIFIL to occupy Nabatiye and Hasbaye, and urged that it should clear those areas of Palestinians and ensure that the PLO would not strike against Israel.

The PLO felt that Resolution 425 favoured Israeli interests. Yassir Arafat suspected that Israel would not withdraw completely from the area and therefore demanded that it should do so immediately and unconditionally. The PLO felt that it had a legitimate right to operate freely in southern Lebanon — a right accorded to it under the Cairo Agreement. Therefore it should be allowed to keep its men in the UNIFIL areas of Tyre, Qasmiye and sixteen other settlements. The Lebanese, for their part, hoped that UNIFIL would deploy every-where and help restore their government's authority.

After consultations with the parties and due consideration by the Secretary-General and Siilasvuo and Erskine, UN Headquarters decided that all areas held or used by the Israeli Defence Force (IDF) would become UNIFIL's area of operations, i.e. all the area south of the Litani except the Tyre pocket. UNIFIL was also required to control the movement of arms and personnel in order to prevent a resumption of fighting. This was to be achieved by admitting only unarmed and un-uniformed personnel in possession of Lebanese identity cards. All others would be denied entry. These tasks proved more formidable in their execution than in their planning.

The advance troops were made available on a temporary basis. The first to arrive on March 22, 1979, were a strong company of the Iran battalion from UNDOF, another company of Swedes from UNEF II, and Canadian Logistics and Movement Control units and a detach-ment of Signals from UNEF II. UNTSO personnel with the Israeli-Lebanese Mixed Armistice Commission (ILMAC) met the troops, guided them to their positions, and helped liaise with the parties involved. The advance party of the contingent from France, another major power participating in UN peacekeeping for the first time, arrived a short time afterwards.

The initial phase of the Israeli withdrawal proceeded smoothly. However, by the end of April, many difficulties arose from the IDF and from Christian forces which enjoyed Israeli support. There was no precise delineation of the UN's operational area. UNIFIL's attempts to patrol towards Qasmiye bridge and the Tyre Palestinian pocket were resisted by armed elements. It turned out that the Israelis had not entirely succeeded in removing all PLO and leftist Muslim groups from the area south of the Litani river, as they claimed to have done. In fact they had met strong pockets of resistance which, in their hurry to reach the river, they had by-passed and left alone.

The worst was yet to come for UNIFIL, when the IDF handed over the entire sector along the Israel-Lebanon ADL to the Christian forces of Major Haddad, thereby leaving the UN troops sandwiched between the PLO in the north and north-west and the Christians, with several pockets of resistance amid the UN's area of deployment. After two months' negotiation with the parties, UNIFIL was able to occupy fourteen positions and another ten in September. These positions were more symbolic than tactical; all approaches were controlled by the Christians, and harassment was never brought to an end.

In spite of earlier impressions, Israel never intended to turn over the Christian enclave to UNIFIL, because it intended to keep control over an area which it considered vital to its security. The UN was apparently lured into this situation by the fact that various parties held the view that UN troops should only move into areas after withdrawal by the parties; and where there were no forces of the parties, those areas should be left vacant. Having been required to deploy UNIFIL troops with the agreement of the parties, Commander UNIFIL had no choice but to accept this situation. Therefore, once the IDF withdrew from southern Lebanon (having never been in the Christian belt), UNIFIL was obliged to report that Israel had complied with the mandate, whereas in fact it had left its surrogates behind.

Thereafter the UN was left to pursue gradual deployment by negotiation and persuasion. While the attempt to control the area as required by the Council Resolution was not abandoned, it remained far from being fully implemented. The Council reiterated and reinforced its resolution (425) by further decisions, e.g. Resolutions 434 of September 18, 1978, and 444 of January 19, 1979; but no progress had been made in that regard. In fact the IDF/Haddad position became even more rigid and brazen. Israel had stressed the 'security belt' concept in supporting the Christian militia, and had exaggerated the PLO infiltration which, it argued, UNIFIL was unable or unwilling to check.

Ranged in opposition to Israel were many diverse groups under the PLO umbrella, united only by their hatred of Israel. Earlier UN relations with these groups had been difficult, but with great effort and skill, the UN Secretariat and UNIFIL established a working relationship which facilitated its operations.

Headquarters UNIFIL was located at Naqoura, the other options having been Tyre and Zaharani. Naqoura consisted of a Lebanese customs compound used by ILMAC, and was within the Christian pocket. It offered no other accommodation. Tyre was a congested town containing a heavy PLO concentration. Zaharani, further up the road to Beirut, was offered by an oil company. It was the best location, but troops of the Arab Deterrent Force occupied part of the building and refused to leave despite personal intervention by Dr Waldheim with President Sarkis of Lebanon. Apparently the Syrians disregarded Sarkis's communication on the subject. So with little choice in the matter, UNIFIL had its headquarters located at Naqoura — a decision for which it had to pay a heavy cost. The Christian militia blocked the approaches at will, shelled and damaged buildings and material, destroyed helicopters and inflicted casualties.

A more serious effort should have been made to locate the headquarters at Zaharani, with an advanced HQ closer to one of the contingents for its own safety, and near good roads. The effectiveness of any army Commander is reduced if he is unable to operate from safety, and in unable to visit his troops at will.

The entire UNIFIL operation was beset with problems. The deployment of troops was made to suit the circumstances and availability of equipment with each of the contingents. Shia Muslim Iranians were deployed in the Shia Muslim Lebanese area; French and Irish were allotted Christian areas. A number of the contingents arrived ill-equipped for the mission; some lacked transport, others had inadequate radio sets. Such inadequacies are not abnormal when a peacekeeping force is being put together with a wide geographical representation; the standard of equipment and training from different acceptable countries naturally varies.

The build-up of the force took several months, requiring some six redeployments. The advance elements of Iranians were placed near Akiya bridge, the French south of the Litani and the Swedes in the north-east, all these positions being occupied by March 26. On April 11 the IDF completed its first phase of withdrawal. By then the Norwegian contingent had replaced the Swedes, the latter being moved to the west-central sector. On April 14, the IDF vacated the Akiya bridge area which (with Khardala bridge) was taken over by the Nepalese contingent. The Senegalese, who had also arrived, were deployed east of Tyre. By May 12 the Nigerian troops had arrived. The redeployment, they replaced the Swedes, who left the area and took over some positions from the Senegalese in the central sector; the Irish were deployed in the south-eastern sector; the Fijian battalion, which had also joined, replaced the French on the Litani, the latter being switched to the central sector; the Iranians returned to UNDOF; the Nepalese and the Norwegians remained in the north-eastern sector. On June 13, when the IDF finally withdrew, its positions were taken over by UNIFIL execpt for the Christian enclave, where it handed over to Haddad's troops.

The French logistics unit, less the engineer unit, was located near Headquarters UNIFIL and the engineers at Jwaya, and later moved to Ras al Lawzah. The Norwegians, in addition to the infantry battalion,

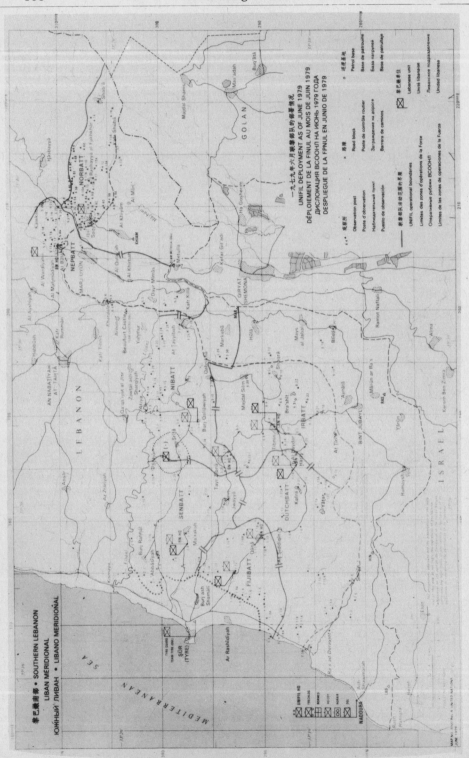

provided a maintenance company located near Tibin, as well as a medical company and helicopters at Naqoura. UNTSO observers manned two of the former ILMAC observation posts and were employed for liaison duties with the parties. On March 1, 1977, the French infantry battalion was withdrawn and replaced by a Dutch battalion. But when the Iranians finally left, after the overthrow of the Shah, no replacement battalion was available for them. However, Fiji and Nigeria agreed to increase the size of their battalions.

When the IDF withdrawal was completed, UNIFIL sought to restore normality and Lebanese sovereignty, both formidable tasks considering the conflicting interests of the parties and the general lack of co-operation. At one time or another, each party had restricted or blocked UNIFIL's movements, which had created operational and logistical problems, sometimes sufficiently serious to jeopardize the UNIFIL mandate. The Tyre pocket controlled the road to Beirut, which was an important supply base for the UN. The crossing of the Israel-Lebanon border involved delays, searches, harrassment and frustration. Only lieutenant-colonels and equivalent UN civilian ranks could cross freely on principle. All helicopter flights had to be cleared with the IDF. The Haddad forces and the PLO prohibited over-flying of their camps.

The number of shooting incidents against UN troops was comparable to the worst of the Congo experience. In fact 'low-level war' against the UN seemed to be almost uninterrupted: never since the Katanga operation had such disregard been shown for the UN flag. The parties occasionally fired at strategic UNIFIL positions and patrols, presumably to reduce their effectiveness. The number of deaths of UNIFIL personnel directly attributable to these shooting incidents up to February 2, 1984, was forty-three. Some 120 persons were wounded in armed clashes, shellings and mine explosions.

UNIFIL's administrative and logistic problems in the early stages were enormous. Since Canadian troops were not to be part of the force, the advance Canadian logistic team was withdrawn, and several weeks elapsed before the French logistic team could operate effectively. It was a typical UN peacekeeping operation, in that the basic infrastructure for effective command, control and logistics did not exist and everything had to be *ad hoc*, which had an adverse effect on the performance of the force in the early stages. The political environment in which it had to operate made its functions no easier.

The PLO challenged UNIFIL's authority from the start, when it prevented French troops from taking positions at Qasmiye bridge. Otherwise relations with the PLO were generally good, though subject to fluctuations in its internal politics. Chairman ILMAC and the UN liaison officer in Beirut maintained contact with Yassir Arafat and the Lebanese authorities. Contacts in the field were kept by Headquarters UNIFIL and UNMOs. Relations with Major Haddad were far less easy. To facilitate contacts between him and UNIFIL, the Lebanese government agreed to recognise him as the *de facto* Commander of the Lebanese forces in the area. Two liaison officers were to be appointed to UNIFIL, an arrangement which was never implemented. However, a proper relationship had been frustrated by the IDF handing over some of its areas to Haddad. These included places which the IDF had taken from the PLO during its military operation.

A serious incident on March 29, 1979, left a permanent mark. The Christians had asked for unrestricted access through the UNIFIL headquarters compound in Naqoura, but while negotiations were in progress, the Christians opened fire, killing a French soldier and damaging UN property.

This frustrating, unrewarding and costly UN operation could only have succeeded if a number of changes had taken place in Lebanon: first, if Lebanese had been able to place a credible army and police force in the area to assume law and order responsibility; secondly, if the parties had shown confidence in the UN and co-operated with it, and thirdly, if the Lebanese government had proved administratively and politically effective enough to influence UNIFIL's task. But developments in Lebanon showed no evidence that any of these conditions might be met. Thus the continuation of UNIFIL became extremely questionable. It was generally agreed that if it were terminated, fighting between the PLO and Haddad would resume, and that even PLO raids across the Israel-Lebanon border would intensify, if not immediately. Such a situation would inevitably have led to another IDF action, possibly drawing in the Syrians, with the possibility of a new Arab-Israeli war. The problem of southern Lebanon was intertwined with the Lebanese question as well as with the future of the Palestinians. But as long as no political solution was in sight, and in spite of the cost and the frustrations, UNIFIL served an important function in the area.

The fighting in southern Lebanon in 1978 and the number of incidents, regardless of UNIFIL's presence, had taken a heavy toll of civilian life and property. The women and children had suffered most. UNIFIL had kept some control, although of a somewhat tenuous nature as far as protecting life and property was concerned.

When UNIFIL first moved into southern Lebanon, the area had been almost bereft of people. Villages were heaps of stone and rubble. Agriculture had come to a halt. UN troops cleared the debris, buried the dead and helped to rebuild the villages. Gradually people returned, and it became a haven for the victims of the civil war and of Syrian and Israeli actions. Civilian services were restored, schools were opened and medical facilities provided. UNIFIL could take great pride in its humanitarian activities.

In June 1982 Israel reinvaded Lebanon. UNIFIL, given about half an hour's notice by the IDF, was in no position to prevent the Israelis from advancing through their lines and moving north towards Beirut and the Bekaa Valley. The UN troops have remained in the area continuing with their humanitarian tasks, and the Security Council has authorized extensions for them in the hope that there will be a role for them at the end of the negotiations being conducted by the United States between the parties to the conflict. The United States and Lebanon, the PLO and other Arabs want the UN to play a role in future peacekeeping.

UNIFIL has some successes to its credit, although it is popularly regarded as a failed mission. This operation was carried out at the insistence of the United States, who felt it was essential to persuade the Israelis to withdraw from southeast Lebanon; in other words, it was to be a face-saving device to effect Israeli withdrawal. The Israelis were reluctant at first to accept a UN force because they did not expect it to further their goals. They had entered Lebanon to remove the PLO as a military threat and to open up an opportunity for it to negotiate with a second Arab country (Egypt being the first). In Israeli eyes, the UN was pro-PLO, and its troops, who were usually from neutral and non-aligned states, would naturally favour the PLO cause. Therefore, in responding to American pressure, the Israelis assured their own security by helping to enlarge the area under the control of their sponsored Lebanese Christian forces commanded by Major Haddad. Accordingly, the Israelis handed over the entire frontier sector to Haddad from the junction point of the borders of Lebanon, Syria and Israel to the Mediterranean.

Senior UN officials in New York and in the field — as, for example, General Siilasvuo, the Middle East UN Coordinator — were reluctant for the UN to assume a role in South Lebanon because of Haddad's presence there, and because elements of the PLO had remained south of the Litani river despite the Israeli operations. The Security Council, faced with the daunting task of arranging Israeli withdrawal, decided to establish UNIFIL, knowing that the force would be like 'salami in a sandwich'. The early return of the displaced persons brought PLO elements back into abandoned villages, resulting in exchanges of fire and UN casualties. As to Haddad's forces, their character remained unchanged; they co-operated with UNIFIL even less than they had done with UNTSO officers in the past. The UN mandate did not include the removal of PLO already present, nor did it include the removal of the Christian forces from along the Israeli frontier. There were gaps between UN troop deployment areas: a large one was adjacent to the Litani river controlled by Haddad in the Merj'Uyum area. Both sides were free to move and continue fighting, which they did ceaselessly; thus it was only a question of when fighting would resume. In the mean time, while the

UN kept a fragile peace, the United States pressed forward with its negotiations, which proved to be a hopeless task.

There are some aspects of the conduct of the operations which demand a critical review. The media in the West and some governments have reflected Israeli accusations that UNIFIL has failed in particular to resist violations. Of course. Israelis only charge the UN with its failure to control PLO infiltration whereas the PLO and the Arabs blame the UN for allowing pro-Israeli Christian forces to remain in South Lebanon and operate at will. However, there were a number of occasions when UN troups sustained punishment and did not resist violations — when, in other words, it proved its weakness.

The mandate of the UN troops included the right of self-defence and authority to use minimum force when it was prevented from carrying out its task. In fact, the behaviour of contingents has varied. Generally, all have avoided the use of force, except when under fire and gravely threatened. A number of observers have said that UNIFIL showed great reluctance to resist violations by either side — an attitude which stemmed from the determination of the troop-contributing countries to avoid combat and not to be put in a situation when their troops had to fight one or the other side in the performance of their legitimate responsibilities. These troops have avoided involvement and therefore have not repeated the example of the UN's role in the Congo. The Force Commander, General William Callaghan, has denied this and has pointed to the number of casualties incurred in performance of the Force's responsibilities. Anyway, in political terms cautious behaviour was justified; the conditions under which UNIFIL was first introduced were not conducive to an effective peace-keeping role. It could not assume a law and order role, since it was never intended to fight for Lebanon. Given the circumstances, they performed extraordinarily well.

However, from 1981 onwards there was a gradual escalation in incidents between the PLO and the leftist groups against Haddad's forces and the Israelis. During July 1981 the situation became so serious that an Israeli military retaliatory reaction was expected. President Reagan sent his special envoy, Philip C. Habib, who was assisted by Saudi Arabia and the UN Secretary-General Dr Waldheim, to seek to restore the ceasefire. These developments made the presence of UNIFIL vital to promote the diplomatic efforts to maintain peace in the area. The situation again worsened in the early part of 1982, leading to large-scale military intervention in southern Lebanon.

The financial arrangements of the force were authorised by Security Council Resolution 426 (1978) to conform with Article 17 (2) of the Charter. After initial financing under the terms of General Assembly Resolution 32/214, the Assembly approved $54 million by its Resolution S-8/2 of April 21, 1978, for a period from March 19 to September 18, 1978. It authorized $6 million per month for subsequent periods of extension beyond the initial period of six months. The apportioning of the costs among member-states was done on an *ad hoc* basis without prejudicing the position of the members in the Special Committee on Peacekeeping, i.e. 'in order to meet the expenditure caused by the operations, a different procedure is required from the one applied to meeting expenditure from the regular budget.' It took into account the fact that the more developed countries were better placed to make relatively large contributions than the less developed ones; and it bore in mind the special responsibility of the permanent members of the Security Council in the financing of peacekeeping operations as indicated in Resolution 1874 (S-IV) of June 27, 1963.

When in May 3, 1978 the manpower of the force was raised from 4,000 to 6,000,[28] the budget was proportionately increased by another $6.9 million for six months. In its Resolution 33/14, the Assembly provided $44,568,000 for the period September 19, 1978 to January 18, 1979; and from then to October 31, 1979, the expenses were not to exceed $11,142,000 per month. In the subsequent months the figure was around $10 million per month.

Twenty-one member-states announced their disinclination to finance UNIFIL.[29] On December 17, 1979, the Assembly by its Resolution 34/9 C decided that at the end of the twelve-month period provided in Financial Regulations 4.3, any unliquidated obligations for which claims had been received should be transferred to accounts payable, and remain recorded in the Special Account until payments were effected. As to obligations for which claims had not been received, another five years would be permitted for submission of claims. The same General Assembly session, noting the additional burden of costs on troop-contributing states and the continuation of the important principle of equitable geographical distribution, appealed to member-states for voluntary contributions, in cash and kind, to meet about a quarter of the costs of the twenty-one states which would not finance the operation. The response to this and the Secretary-General's appeals was not promising. On June 18, 1980, the deficit was about $70.5 million out of the total budget costs of $281.9 million. The reimbursement to troop-contributing countries was established along the same lines as for UNEF II.

The size of UNIFIL was somewhat reduced from 6,286 in January 1983 to 5,780 in October. There had also been some changes in contingents. The Nepalese left in November 1982, resulting in an adjustment in deployment of other contingents. The Nigerian troops left about this time, and the French infantry unit strength was reduced to enable the main part to join the French troops in MNF. A Finnish battalion arrived in December 1982. The French provide the logistics unit together with Norway and Sweden. The Italians provide the helicopters. On October 12, 1983, the national composition of the force was as follows: Fiji 625, Finland 495, France 940, Ghana 704, Ireland

655, Italy 41, Netherlands 731, Norway 804, Senegal 559, Sweden 143. There are 73 UNMOs maintaining five OPs along the Israel-Lebanon Armistice Demarcation Line and with teams at Tyre, Mettula and Beaufort castle.

A number of incidents of high-handedness in the UNIFIL area by the *de facto* Christian force and the IDF battalion were reported. Otherwise, the area remained quiet. The fighting in Beirut led to more refugees seeking shelter in the area. The force mans checkpoints and patrols to keep order and maintain the security of the local population. There is good co-operation with the Lebanese authorities and UN agencies in extending humanitarian assistance to the population. The fighting in Aley and the Shuf region between the Lebanese army on the one side and the Druze and other Muslim factions on the other did not affect UNIFIL operations. Despite Israel's re-invasion and continued occupation of southern Lebanon, as well as the intransigence of the *de facto* forces of Major Haddad (who left the area for medical treatment in the United States where he later died), UNIFIL continues to fulfil most of its interim tasks.

On October 10, 1983, the Lebanese government again requested the Security Council to extend the force. In his letter to the Secretary-General requesting an extension for another six months, the Permanent Representative of Lebanon at the UN said: 'UNIFIL, in its present roles, has provided all possible support to enable the Lebanese Government to restore its legitimate support in southern Lebanon, and security to the Lebanese population and, above all, an international commitment to the sovereignty and independence of Lebanon. Furthermore, UNIFIL has performed its role with courage and distinction under very difficult circumstances.'

Although the Israeli invasion of June 1982 had radically changed the conditions which had led to the creation of UNIFIL, the force continues to perform an essential role. It has provided an increase of stability and humanitarian assistance in southern Lebanon, and most of all it represents the commitment of the UN to support the independence, sovereignty and territorial integrity of Lebanon and to help bring about the withdrawal of Israeli forces from the country. It is particularly important for UNIFIL to remain just when the Lebanese are trying to achieve national unity. The conditions under which UNIFIL is asked to operate are most unsatisfactory, but its presence, which is like a holding operation pending further developments and negotiations, is vital to the future of Lebanon.

In his report to the Security Council on the Force's operations, the Secretary-General on October 12, 1983 (S/16036), reported that the shortfall in the UNIFIL special account was then $173.9 million. This had placed an increasingly heavy burden on the troop-contributing countries, particularly the less wealthy ones. He appealed to the developed nations voluntarily to contribute funds to meet these costs.

The Security Council on October 18 decided to extend UNIFIL for another interim period of six months, that is, until April 19, 1984. A budget of $70,446,000 was authorized for a force of 5,200 troops.

Namibia

Namibia, formerly known as South West Africa, was incorporated by Germany within its colonial empire in the late nineteenth century when the scramble for colonial acquisitions in Africa was in its final stages. During the First World War, troops of South Africa, then a British Dominion, occupied the territory, and in 1920 South Africa was authorized to administer it under a 'C' mandate of the League of Nations on behalf of Britain. The prefix 'German' was dropped from the name, and it continued to be called South West Africa until June 1968, when the UN General Assembly formally changed its name to Namibia.[30]

Estimates of Namibia's population range from a South African supplied figure of 852,000 to 1,500,000 from the office of the UN Commissioner for Namibia.[31] These numbers include the Europeans, Coloureds and Africans. Whether one is considering the original Namibians (the San or Bushmen), the Hereros, the Namas, the Damaras or the Ovambos, one attribute that is present in all these groups is their fierce resistance to colonization. Although they were subjugated because of their military weakness, and subsequently entered into agreements in the form of 'treaties of protection', it cannot be said that they were ever pacified to the extent of losing the conviction that their ultimate goal would be freedom from foreign settler rule and control.

When South African troops invaded German South West Africa in 1915, the inhabitants saw one form of foreign control being replaced by another, and this new control was too close for comfort. What they witnessed in effect after South Africa was given a 'C' mandate for their administration was a creeping strategy of annexation by close proximity. The practice of apartheid was extended within the territory.

With the growing independence movements from the 1940s onwards and the pervasive mood in the international community at that time to encourage the process of decolonization, the South African campaign to have South West Africa incorporated into the Union did not succeed. Ever since then, the strategy of planning for a *fait accompli* has been a feature of South African policy in relation to its perceived interests in Namibia. However, since the late 1970s, South Africa has repeatedly pledged that it would grant independence to Namibia — under certain conditions.

Attempts to define the status and determine responsibility for the territory of South West Africa constituted one of the major preoccu-

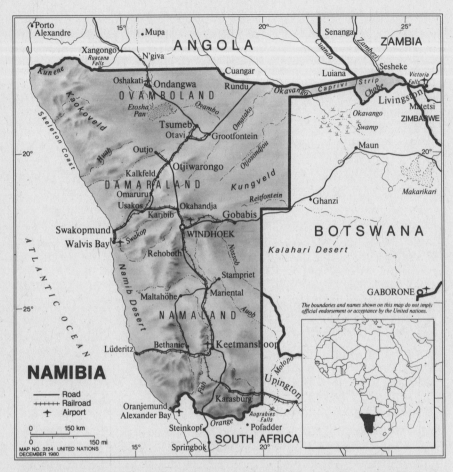

NAMIBIA

— Road
+++++ Railroad
+ Airport

0   150 km
0   150 mi
MAP NO. 3124 UNITED NATIONS
DECEMBER 1980

*The boundaries and names shown on this map do not imply
official endorsement or acceptance by the United nations.*

pations of the international community at the birth of the United
Nations systems in 1945. The trusteeship system came into being with
the UN, and countries administering League of Nations mandates
agreed to enter into trusteeship agreements with the UN. Indeed,
a majority of the governments of member-states pressed for the
inclusion of South West Africa into the trusteeship system so that
the territory would ultimately become a 'self-governing' or an
'independent' territory[32] as by Article 76 of the UN Charter.

In 1946, South Africa requested the General Assembly to terminate
the mandate established under the League of Nations and incorporate
the territory as a province of the Union.[33] It also announced plans to
consult the population of South West Africa on the issue. The General
Assembly rejected this request and recommended the conclusion of a
trusteeship agreement to replace the mandate,[34] which South Africa
did not accept. The *status quo* remained unchanged.[35] Thus began the
moves to seek legal interpretations of the status of the territory and
statements on the obligations of states under the system. In December

the General Assembly requested the International Court of Justice (ICJ) to define South Africa's status. The first of the advisory opinions, handed down by the ICJ in July 1950, pronounced that the League's mandate still continued in force with supervision to be exercised by the UN General Assembly. It also ruled that South Africa was under no obligation to conclude a trusteeship agreement, although it had to make an effort to this end. This judgement sought to achieve a solution by compromise.[36]

Meanwhile, in December 1960 the UN General Assembly passed a resolution containing the 'Declaration of the Granting of Independence to all Colonial Countries and Peoples'.[37] As the years went by, a *de facto* annexation was becoming discernible in the relationship between South Africa and the South West African territory. In reaction to the 1966 ICJ ruling, the South West African People's Organization (SWAPO), which had first been formed in 1959 as the Ovambo People's Organization, decided from August 1966 to launch an armed struggle for self-determination. On October 27, 1966, the General Assembly adopted Resolution 2145 (XX1), terminating South Africa's Mandate and placing Namibia under direct UN control. A long and fruitless period of discussion inside and outside the UN followed. In 1975 the Ambassadors of the United States, Britain and France met the South African Foreign Minister in Cape Town to discuss the Namibian question.

In January 1976, an International Conference on Namibia and Human Rights was held in Dakar, Senegal. At the end of that month, the Council unanimously adopted Resolution 385, calling for the transfer of Namibia to the UN and the holding of free elections under UN supervision and control. South Africa meanwhile had been working hard towards an internal settlement which it expected would be acceptable to the international community. On August 20, 1976, the UN Council on Namibia rejected proposals made by the Turnhalle (Constitutional) Committee.

The disappointment of the majority of member-states with ongoing developments led to new attempts to impose a mandatory arms embargo on South Africa, denounce the Turnhalle conference and condemn all attempts by South Africa to evade the UN's clear demand for free elections in Namibia under its supervision. This again was opposed by the three Western permanent members of the Council who were of the view that they as well as Canada and West Germany — the five together were now referred to as the 'Contact Group' — should continue negotiations.

The Africans persisted in their demands for the imposition of full economic sanctions and an arms embargo on South Africa. These were further suggested in draft resolutions discussed by the African states in March 1977. So as to avoid the embarrassment of having to use the veto once again, the 'Contact Group' offered to help negotiate terms for the independence of Namibia on the basis of free territory-wide elections under the aegis of the UN.[38] Thus began the new Western initiative.

The 'Contact Group', also known as the Western Five, submitted its settlement plan in Namibia to the UN on April 5, 1978, which eventually became a Security Council proposal.[39] The proposal included provisions for holding elections in the territory under the supervision and control of the UN. The plan was accepted by the South African government on April 25 and by SWAPO on July 12, 1978.[40] In a report dated August 29, 1978,[41] which the Security Council approved by its Resolution 435 of September 29, 1978, the UN Secretary-General made a number of recommendations for implementing the proposal. The South African government then agreed in December 1978 to co-operate in the implementation of Security Council Resolution 435 (1978) on the basis of certain understandings.[42] It was followed by other reports dated February 26,[43] and early March[44] 1979 by the Secretary-General.

South Africa objected particularly to the absence of a specific provision for the UN Transition Assistance Group (UNTAG), established by Security Council Resolution 435 (1978) to monitor SWAPO bases in neighbouring African states, and to the Secretary-General's recommendation that any SWAPO forces in Namibia at the time of a cease-fire should be restricted to base at designated locations in the territory. In a letter to the Secretary-General dated March 5, 1979, Mr Botha, the South African Foreign Minister, affirmed that his government interpreted the settlement proposal to mean that 'SWAPO would have no right to create bases or be designated bases in South West Africa.'

In July 1979, in an effort to break the stalemate with South Africa, the late President Agostinho Neto of Angola put forward proposals for the establishment of a demilitarized zone extending to a depth of 50 km. on each side of Namibia's borders with Angola and Zambia. The demilitarized zone would prevent both SWAPO attacks on Namibia and South African invasions into Angola during the transitional and electoral periods. Those proposals, as subsequently elaborated by the Western members of the Security Council, together with officials of the UN Secretariat, were the subject of high-level consultations held at Geneva on November 12–16, 1979, under the aegis of the Secretary-General.[45]

The principal features of the proposal for a demilitarized zone were
(1) the provisions of Security Council Resolution 435 (1978) would continue to bind the parties in all their terms;
(2) in addition, the Governments of Angola, South Africa and Zambia would agree to the establishment of a demilitarized zone to facilitate the implementation of the original five-power settlement proposal;
(3) the purpose of the zone, which would be free of the military forces

of the parties and of SWAPO, would be to assist UNTAG in its monitoring and border surveillance functions;

(4) SWAPO would co-operate with Angola and Zambia in implementing the agreement;

(5) each government concerned would be responsible for the demilitarization of its portion of the zone and within the zone UNTAG would operate freely to carry out its responsibilities;

(6) the zone would be established fourteen days after the ceasefire for the duration of the transition period;

(7) selected locations, generally including a military base, its supporting airfield, population centre and immediate environment, would be excluded from the demilitarized zone;

(8) the provisions of the five-power settlement proposal for the phased withdrawal of the South African Defence Forces (SADF) would also apply to the selected locations; i.e. SADF within such selected locations on the Namibian side of the border would be restricted to base and withdrawn by the twelfth week after a ceasefire;

(9) UNTAG would monitor the bases, logistic resupply and authorized movement of military personnel by land and air;

(10) SWAPO forces would be excluded from the selected locations.[46]

The concept of the demilitarized zone and the broad outlines of the proposal were accepted at the close of the consultations by the frontline states (Angola, Botswana, Mozambique, Tanzania and Zambia) and by SWAPO. The South African Foreign Minister stated that his government accepted the concept also, provided that agreement was reached in further discussions on a number of points. Among other things, South Africa would require confirmation that 'the claim for SWAPO bases inside South West Africa/Namibia . . . will not be revived.'

In view of South Africa's provisional acceptance of the concept, the Secretary-General informed the Security Council on January 9, 1980, that he proposed to proceed with detailed technical discussions on the demilitarized zone with the parties concerned, and that in order to facilitate those discussions and with a view to the implementation of Security Council Resolution 435 (1978), he intended to propose Lt.-Gen. Prem Chand of India as Commander-designate and later as Commander of the military component of UNTAG.[47] In February General Chand, accompanied by advisers, visited Angola, Zambia and Botswana, and in Luanda and Lusaka met representatives of SWAPO. He also held discussions inside Namibia with senior SADF personnel and visited the forward areas on the territory's northern borders. In Cape Town, Prem Chand was joined by other senior members of the UN Secretariat for talks with the South Africans.

On March 31, the Secretary-General reported on Prem Chand's discussions to the Security Council. The governments of Angola and Zambia had informed Chand that they would require a total of seven selected locations in their sectors of the demilitarized zone. The Botswana government confirmed that there was no need for a demilitarized zone in its country because SWAPO did not operate there and would have no bases there during the transitional period. SWAPO confirmed its acceptance of the concept of the demilitarized zone and that it would respect the wishes of Angola and Zambia over its implementation in their respective territories. However, SWAPO expressed opposition to South Africa having selected locations in the demilitarized zone. In that connection, the UN mission indicated the terms of the settlement proposal, which provided for the total withdrawal of the SADF from the proposed demilitarized zone by the end of the twelfth week after the ceasefire.

The discussions with the South African government were principally concerned with practical issues related to the demilitarized zone. The South African delegation requested further clarifications from the UN as to how UNTAG would meet its responsibilities in the zone and how the Angolan and Zambian governments would insure the fulfilment of their commitments under the UN plan, including the arrangements they envisaged for the restriction and monitoring of SWAPO in their respective territories. The South African delegation also informed the UN mission that the SADF was currently located in approximately forty bases in the proposed demilitarized zone area, and suggested that it be allowed to retain twenty bases before vacating the demilitarized zone entirely twelve weeks from the start of the transitional period.

In the course of the discussions, the UN mission informed the South African delegation that the military component of UNTAG would need to be deployed at the authorized upper limit of 7,500 men. It also confirmed that the settlement proposal, as reflected in Security Council Resolution 435 (1978), remained unchanged, the demilitarized zone proposal having been conceived to facilitate the implementation of that Resolution. At the end of the talks, the South African delegation reaffirmed its government's acceptance of the settlement proposal and its decision to co-operate in implementing Security Council Resolution 435 (1978). The government's conclusions regarding the feasibility of the demilitarized zone proposal would be transmitted as soon as possible.

The South African Foreign Minister Botha affirmed that his government had accepted the concept of a demilitarized zone on the understanding that certain issues would be satisfactorily resolved; it still wished to be informed whether the introduction of the zone would mean (*a*) that its 'offer' to reduce its bases inside the zone to twenty selected locations had been accepted; (*b*) that a substantially larger percentage of UNTAG would be deployed in the proposed zone in order to increase its effectiveness; (*c*) that acceptable arrangements would be made for the disarming of SWAPO personnel once the

SWAPO bases were closed (i.e. seven days after the certification of elections); and (*d*) that 'the claim by SWAPO to bases inside the Territory would not be revived.'

The Foreign Minister also stated that South Africa would consider it desirable that all elements present or operating in the demilitarized zone, including the Angolan UNITA, co-operate to make the settlement proposal effective. He stressed that South Africa had been pressing for urgent implementation of the settlement plan since accepting it on April 25, 1978, but that various opportunities had been frustrated 'as a result of deviations condoned by the United Nations at the insistence of SWAPO'. The successful implementation of the settlement plan or of any proposal designed to achieve a peaceful solution would continue to be seriously jeopardized unless all the parties were treated equally, including the various political parties operating in Namibia. Accordingly, the South African government wished to be informed whether (*a*) the Secretary-General and the Secretariat would refrain from giving effect to General Assembly resolutions recognizing SWAPO as the 'sole and authentic representative of the people of Namibia'; (*b*) the Secretariat would refrain from giving effect to those elements of General Assembly resolutions, and resolutions of subordinate bodies, which 'single out SWAPO for preferential treatment not accorded to other political parties'; and (*c*) the Secretary-General would refrain from applying funds from the regular UN budget for the exclusive use of SWAPO. As soon as those issues had been resolved, South Africa would co-operate in implementing Resolution 435 (1978).

On June 20, the Secretary-General addressed a reply to the Foreign Minister[48] in which he confirmed that, in the interest of obtaining a final settlement, the front-line states and SWAPO would agree to allow South Africa to retain a total of twenty bases in the Namibian sector of the demilitarized zone during the first twelve weeks after ceasefire. Also, the Angolan and Zambian governments had reassured him that no infiltration of armed SWAPO personnel would take place from their territory into Namibia after the ceasefire. As to the question of SWAPO bases in Namibia, the Secretary-General recalled that the front-line states and SWAPO had decided in August 1979 that on South Africa's acceptance of the demilitarized zone and the implementation of Security Council Resolution 435 (1978), the question would no longer arise. On the subject of equal treatment for all political parties in the Territory, the Secretary-General said that the UN would continue to deal only with the parties envisaged in the settlement plan and the demilitarized zone proposal, and that the principle of impartiality had been, and would be, consistently followed. He also noted, in reference to South Africa's concern over various General Assembly Resolutions, that the implementation of Security Council Resolution 435 (1978) was being undertaken specifically under the authority of the Security Council in the context of the provisions of the UN Charter. In conclusion, the Secretary-General expressed the view that his letter should resolve all outstanding issues and suggested that dates for a ceasefire and the implementation of Security Council Resolution 435 (1978) shall be established as soon as possible.

In a reply to the Secretary-General, Botha made several 'assumptions' on the Secretary-General's clarifications regarding military and technical subjects. He then dealt at length with the question of impartiality, charging that the greatest obstacle to the implementation of the settlement plan was a lack of good faith and mutual trust 'directly attributable to SWAPO's actions and attitudes, together with United Nations bias in favour of SWAPO'. He further declared that the South African government welcomed the Secretary-General's statement that the implementation of the settlement proposals was being undertaken specifically under the authority of the Security Council in the context of Charter's provisions. It was therefore assumed that no action contrary to those provisions would be initiated by the General Assembly or by UN officials. In closing, Botha said that on the basis of the assumptions he had enunciated and the Secretary-General's confirmation, the South African government was ready to discuss the composition of UNTAG, the status of forces agreement and the setting in motion of the implementation of Security Council Resolution 435 (1978). The successful implementation of the settlement proposal would, however, be seriously jeopardized if all the parties were not treated on an equal basis. The South African Government accordingly considered it essential that the Secretary-General thenceforth include 'the leadership in the Territory' in all future considerations.

In a statement made on his behalf on August 30, Waldheim rejected the accusations contained in Botha's letter and said that he would continue to carry out his duties with strict impartiality on the basis of the Charter of the UN and of the relevant decisions of the Organization.

A UN mission headed by Brian Urquhart, Under Secretary-General for Special Political Affairs, held discussions with the South African government in Pretoria on October 20–25. Urquhart emphasized that the outstanding matters for discussion occupied a very narrow spectrum and that consensus had been reached on virtually all the technical aspects of Resolution 435 (1978) and the demilitarized zone. While the mission was willing to discuss the various matters raised by Botha, many of the questions raised concerning implementation could be definitively dealt with only in the context of a firm time-frame for a ceasefire and the emplacement of UNTAG in Namibia.

Brand Fourie, South African Director-General for Foreign Affairs, responded by stating that his government also saw the need for a time-frame for implementation but believed that that could not be achieved without resolving the remaining issues, particularly the question of impartiality and equal treatment of the parties. He stressed that the Namibian people were deeply suspicious that the UN was not impartial and therefore could not enjoy their confidence in supervising and controlling the free and fair elections to which all parties were committed. Urquhart replied that the establishment of trust and confidence was a subjective and imprecise criterion and that if any party sought to use it as a pretext for delay, the implementation of Resolution 435 (1978) would be seriously undermined. Urquhart noted that impartiality had two aspects: undertakings which the UN might reasonably require of the South African administration so as to ensure the impartial discharge of its responsibilities under the settlement proposal; and those which the UN would wish to adopt so that its impartiality as the supervisor of free and fair elections would be manifest. As to agreement on implementation, including an early date for a ceasefire and emplacement of UNTAG, appropriate measures would need to be taken to support and ensure such an approach by both the UN and South Africa.

The discussions also covered the composition of the UNTAG military component, the draft status of forces agreement and other matters.

The conclusions contained in the Secretary-General's report to the Security Council were as follows:

(1) The independence of Namibia should be achieved in 1981, in accordance with Security Council Resolution 435 (1978).

(2) One of the main obstacles to progress in the negotiations thus far had been acute mutual mistrust and lack of confidence.

(3) A means of facilitating agreement and of creating the necessary climate of confidence and understanding would be a pre-implementation multiparty meeting, under the auspices of the Secretary-General, in which all the parties concerned in the envisaged election would be included.

(4) Such a meeting could facilitate the implementation of Resolution 435 (1978) by discussing relevant aspects of implementation with the purpose of securing the co-operation of all concerned. In that connection it was recalled that, under the settlement proposal, the task of drawing up and adopting a constitution would be the function of a constituent assembly to be elected by the populace.

(5) The proposed meeting would be held in the context of an agreed time-frame, with a view to the parties themselves assisting in resolving difficulties created by distrust and lack of confidence, South Africa having reaffirmed its continuing role as the interlocutor under Resolution 435 (1978).

(6) In the expectation that the problem of confidence could be overcome, and subject to a satisfactory arrangement concerning the composition of UNTAG, the Secretary-General would propose March

1981 for the start of implementation of Resolution 435 (1978).

(7) The intention would be to hold a pre-implementation meeting from January 7 to 14, 1981, under the auspices and chairmanship of the UN, the basis of which would conform to a formula agreed upon earlier during bilateral discussions. South Africa and SWAPO had been contacted concerning the composition of the respective delegations; the Secretary-General had also contacted the front-line states, Nigeria, the OAU and the five Western members of the Security Council about sending observers.

The proposed pre-implementation meeting was in fact held in Geneva on the dates suggested. The participants were a SWAPO delegation headed by Sam Nujoma, that organization's President, and a South African delegation headed by Danie Hough, the Administrator-General of Namibia. Observers representing the front-line states, Nigeria, the OAU and the five Western members of the Security Council also attended. The opening sessions were chaired by the Secretary-General, and the working sessions that followed by Brian Urquhart. Dr Waldheim's opening statement reiterated that the meeting's main aim was to obtain a firm agreement on a ceasefire date and the start of implementation of the settlement proposal, to allow for Namibian independence to be achieved before the end of 1981. He also made it clear that basic agreement on the settlement proposal and the demilitarized zone had already been reached and that there could be no question of renegotiating those fundamental arrangements.

Representatives of the so-called 'internal' Namibian parties in the South African delegation protested that the Secretary-General had taken no specific note of their presence, and demanded that they be identified as parties rather than only as members of the South African delegation. The demand reflected South Africa's position that South Africa, as such, was not participating in the meeting, and that the internal parties must be given equal status with SWAPO. Those represented in the South African delegation included the Democratic Turnhalle Alliance (DTA) and the Action Front for the Retention of Turnhalle Principles (AKTUR), successor to the all-white National Party.

Starting the working sessions on January 8, Urquhart described the wide area of agreement that had been reached with South Africa during more than two years of consultation and stated that the UN believed that no technical issues existed that could justify any failure to decide to go forward. Urquhart stressed that not only the future of Namibia was at stake, but also that of the entire region and the prospects for peace and progress in the whole of Africa. Later, senior UN officials made detailed presentations dealing with the overall structure and functions of UNTAG and the duties of the Secretary-General's Special Representative for Namibia; the functions of the Office of the UN High Commissioner for Refugees (UNHCR); the election supervisory role of UNTAG; the tasks and deployment of UNTAG police monitors; and the tasks and deployment of the UNTAG military component.

The South African delegation asserted that the UN had disqualified itself from supervising free and fair elections in Namibia, in particular by recognizing SWAPO as the sole and authentic representative of the people of Namibia and by its attitute towards other political parties in the territory. Consequently, a definite date for implementing Security Council Resolution 435 (1978) would be acceptable only after an unspecified period in which the UN would have to demonstrate its impartiality. Anxiety was also expressed regarding the nature of the laws and related arrangements under which the territory would be governed in the future. Urquhart said that the matter of trust and confidence was a two-way street and that what was sought was a definite agreement to proceed on a specific date with the implementation of Resolution 435 (1978). At that date, a number of things would have to change because there would be a completely different situation. Both South Africa and the UN would need to make the necessary arrangements for the impartial discharge of their respective responsibilities under the settlement proposal.

After the session, there was a discussion of a course of action designed to lead to a declaration of intent by the parties to the provisional establishment of an early ceasefire (March 30) to be confirmed in writing by February 10. It was also suggested that in the meantime specific measures could be taken to ensure — and reflect in public decisions — the impartiality of the UN, as well as South Africa, from the time of agreement on the implementation date. However, the Administrator-General stated that it would not be possible to achieve a declaration of intent at the meeting in Geneva; he affirmed that from the proceedings thus far it was clear that the issue of mutual distrust and lack of confidence had not been resolved, and it would therefore be premature to discuss the fixing of a date for implementation. Sam Nujoma reiterated that SWAPO was ready to sign a ceasefire agreement and to set a target date for the arrival of UNTAG in Namibia, but that since South Africa had not agreed, SWAPO had no alternative but to continue its liberation struggle.

Urquhart, on behalf of the Secretary-General, appealed to those who had thus far been unable to assent to the Secretary-General's proposals to reconsider their position as early as possible so that means could soon be found to proceed to the early implementation of Resolution 435 (1978). The UN would not relax its efforts to ensure for the people of Namibia their right to self-determination and independence through free and fair elections under UN supervision and control. When the Secretary-General reported on the Geneva meeting to the Security Council, he said that the outcome of the meeting must cause the most serious international concern, and he urgently appealed to the South African government to review the meeting's implications with the utmost care and reconsider its position on the implementation of Resolution 435 (1978).

During 1980, while participating in UN-sponsored negotiations for an internationally acceptable settlement to the Namibia question, the South African government persisted in defying the organization and the international community by taking further steps to impose an internal settlement under a puppet government dominated by the DTA. The most significant of those steps was the establishment of a so-called Council of Ministers with executive powers. Thus almost all legislative and executive powers with the exception of foreign affairs, constitutional development, defence and railways and harbours became nominally vested in the local authorities, laying the groundwork for an eventual unilateral declaration of independence. In addition, through the establishment by the Administrator-General of so-called second-tier authorities, apartheid institutions were made the cornerstone of future constitutional developments. South Africa also continued to strengthen its military presence in Namibia and intensified its efforts to annihilate SWAPO politically and militarily.

At the Ministerial Conference of Non-Aligned Countries, held in New Delhi on February 9–12, 1981, South Africa was condemned for its persistent refusal to withdraw from Namibia, and was held responsible for the failure of the pre-implementation meeting held in Geneva. The Conference called on the UN Security Council urgently to impose mandatory economic sanctions on South Africa under Chapter VII of the the UN Charter and so compel it to terminate its illegal occupation of Namibia. On March 16, 1981, the General Assembly adopted a resolution calling on the international community to continue not to recognise or co-operate with any regime that the 'illegal' South African government might impose on the Namibian people in disregard of Security Council Resolutions 385, 435 and 439, and other relevant UN resolutions. The resolution also called on the Security Council to impose comprehensive mandatory sanctions against South Africa, as provided for under Chapter VII of the UN Charter.

At an Extraordinary Ministerial Meeting of the Co-ordinating Bureau of the Non-Aligned Countries on the Namibia question at Algiers in April 1981, to evaluate the situation in Namibia and take measures for strengthening all forms of aid in support of the Namibian people, approval was given to a demand that the UN plan be implemented without delay. It too called for a Special Security Council Session in April 1981 to demand economic sanctions against South Africa. The United States, Britain and France vetoed four Security Council Resolutions aimed at halting all trade with South Africa.

A meeting of senior officials from the Western Five, held in London on April 22–23, agreed that it was of the utmost importance to bring Namibia to independence at the earliest date. It also noted that Security Council Resolution 435 still provided a solid basis for Namibia's transition to independence. Following a meeting in Rome on May 3, 1981, the Foreign Ministers of the Western Five issued a joint communiqué on Namibia, reiterating their governments' commitment to an internationally acceptable settlement to the Namibia issue. They also affirmed that the close co-operation of all the parties concerned was essential in order to bring about a negotiated solution, and that the search for a settlement should be intensified and ways of strengthening the existing plan considered.

The Paris Declaration on Sanctions against South Africa and the Special Declaration on Namibia were adopted by the International Conference on Sanctions against South Africa held on May 20–27, 1981. The Conference recommended sanctions (arms and oil embargoes and economic sanctions) that would force South Africa partly to abandon its apartheid policies and end its illegal occupation of Namibia.

The Special Committee of the General Assembly on the Situation with Regard to the Implementation of the Declaration on the Granting of Independence to Colonial Countries and Peoples in August 1981 adopted resolutions that reiterating the call for the immediate implementation of Security Council Resolution 435 without any prevarication, qualification or modification and not later than December 1981.

Meanwhile, the Foreign Ministers of the Western Five 'Contact Group' issued a statement indicating that recent exchanges with the parties concerned had made it possible to identify more clearly the issues involved and a process for their resolution, which could lead to the implementation of the UN Plan for Namibia. They indicated that they had completed an initial consideration of possible constitutional principles for the Constituent Assembly, and that this would be likely to 'secure the confidence of all concerned'. The constitutional principles included provisions for a bill of rights; separation of powers; fair representation for all groups, including the 11 per cent whites; ratification of the constitution by a two-thirds majority of the Assembly, who had to be elected on a one-man, one-vote basis; and a designated process for changing the constitution either by the legislature and/or by referendum.

Towards the end of January 1982 the South Africans assented to the proposals of the 'Contact Group'. The Africans met on January 23, 1982, and gave qualified approval, questioning the voting formula, notably the provision that half the members of the Assembly be elected on a proportional basis, the other half being on a single-member constituency basis — what came to be known as the one-man-two-vote proposal. Negotiations continued in the hope of getting the Africans to respond positively. The 'Contact Group' met on a number of occasions between February and April. Chester A. Crocker, Assistant US Secretary of State for African Affairs, then travelled to Luanda in April to try to persuade Sam Nujoma, the SWAPO leader, to accept the proposals as they stood. But early in May, the Africans formally rejected the proposed voting formula — they had earlier accepted all the other constitutional guidelines. The Foreign Ministers of the 'Contact Group' met in Luxembourg on May 17, and decided to shelve temporarily the question of the voting formula, since it was felt that this had held up the negotiations that were supposed to have reached the phase of UN involvement. The new proposals put forward concentrated on two issues that were worrying South Africa: the question of UN impartiality and the composition and size of UNTAG.

Early in June, President Reagan's Special Envoy, General Vernon Walters, went to Dar-es-Salaam in Tanzania to submit the new proposals. By June 15, SWAPO and the 'Front Line States' had agreed to put aside temporarily the political issues and to concentrate on the military ones: namely, a ceasefire and the size of UN peacekeeping forces. Washington seemed to be optimistic that the negotiations would be successfully concluded by the end of 1982. The differences had been narrowed, and the negotiations were in an active or critical phase. On June 23, the 'Contact Group' met in Washington amid what a US official called 'controlled optimism'.

A problem that could delay further progress is South Africa's insistence on linking Namibia with the withdrawal of Cuban troops from Angola. On June 25, Angola formally rejected any attempt to link these questions. There was already agreement between Cuba and Angola that Cuban troops would be withdrawn when so requested by the legitimate Angolan government, and Angola felt that the determination of how and when the Cuban troops should pull out was its own sovereign right. The demand for changes in Angolan defence and security arrangements presupposes an aggressive intent on Angola's part to use the Cuban troops on its territory in destabilization manoeuvres via an independent Namibia. Angola and the Africans consistently pointed to the fact that since its independence Angola had been subjected to repeated invasions and occupations by the South African armed forces, and their Cuban troops had never been put into the field on any of those occasions as they were restricted to a perimeter just south of the capital, Luanda. Hence there was no evidence that they might pose a threat to South Africa after Namibian independence. If there were other motives behind the demand, they were obviously not in pursuance of UN Security Council Resolution 435. Angola reiterated its firm rejection of any such link on July 25, 1982.

On July 6, 1982, negotiations began between the 'Contact Group' and the Africans, including SWAPO, and by July 12, the former was able to present to the Security Council a text of principles concerning the Constituent Assembly and the Constitution for an independent Namibia which had been agreed to by all the parties involved.[49] During August 1982, a number of meetings were held at different locations. In Washington, the US administration and South African officials held a series of discussions. The talks in Angola between the US and Angolan authorities centred on the proposed withdrawal of South African troops from Angola and a pullback deeper into Angola by Cuban and SWAPO forces. One round of talks in New York was held between the 'Contact Group' and the Africans, including SWAPO, on the details of the UN plan; an outstanding problem was South Africa's non-commitment towards an electoral system (constituency-based as opposed to proportional). Other problems seemed to have been resolved, since the UN Secretariat was engaged in discussion with the South Africans on issues related to UNTAG and its deployment.

Angola's role in allowing its territory to be used by SWAPO to launch armed attacks on the South African Defence Forces had provided another basis for concern expressed by the South Africans during the continuing phases of the negotiations. Partly to assuage South African fears, the Africans agreed during the latest series of negotiations that the UN would be allowed to monitor SWAPO bases in Angola and Zambia to prevent infiltration and other ceasefire violations. By September, the enthusiasm that had been generated by increased momentum in the negotiating process had once again fizzled out.

Although negotiations continued at the UN, there were no signs of progress. South Africa remained in direct control of Namibia. The heads of the Front Line States and SWAPO rejected the attempts by the United States to link the independence of Namibia with the withdrawal of Cuban troops from Angola, which constituted interference in Angola's internal affairs. The leaders of the non-aligned states and a meeting of African leaders at Tripoli in November 1982 also rejected this 'linkage'. The UN General Assembly session in 1982 reaffirmed Security Council Resolution 435 and called for immediate and unconditional implementation without qualification and modification. In spite of this, the United States stepped up its efforts to gain acceptance for it.

In persistently attempting to link the Namibia question with extraneous issues such as the presence of Cuban forces in Angola, South Africa and the United States have not only prevented progress but have also sought to give the Namibia question a character quite different from its essential one of decolonisation.

On March 31, 1983, the Security Council condemned the illegal occupation of Namibia in violation of the Assembly and Security Council Resolutions, and called upon South Africa to meet its commitments under Resolution 435. In May the Security Council again devoted its attention to the question, as had been decided in the spring meeting of the heads of the non-aligned states in New Delhi. On May 31 the Council, among other decisions, mandated the UN Secretary-General to undertake consultations with the parties to the proposed ceasefire, with a view to securing speedy implementation of its Resolution 435.

In his report (S/15943 of August 29, 1983) the Secretary-General informed the Security Council that while South Africa accepted Resolution 435, her Foreign Minister had insisted that 'the one major issue still to be resolved was the withdrawal of the Cubans from Angola.' He said that other outstanding issues, e.g. the electoral system, should be addressed and resolved within the framework of the understandings reached with the United States and the Western Contact Group. Because of the 'linkage' Pérez de Cuéllar stated that it was important to launch the UN plan. In October 1983, the Council condemned South Africa's illegal occupation of Namibia in defiance of UN Resolutions and called on her to co-operate. It asked the Secretary-General to report again before the end of the year.

The General Assembly has since been seized with the Namibian issue. It strongly condemned South Africa for blocking independence for Namibia and called for the Security Council to apply comprehensive sanctions. At the time of going to press, there are no signs of a change on the part of the United States and South Africa on the 'linkage' question, although the other Western Contact Group members have expressed opposing views.

General Prem Chand, Commander-designate UNTAG, has returned to India, and visits New York and Namibia only when required. Martti Ahtissaari, the Secretary-General's Special Representative on Namibia, has also returned to his own country, Finland while retaining his UN position. Thus neither Attiasari nor Prem Chand is needed in New York by the Secretary-General, indicating that the implementation of the UN plan for Namibia, if not entirely dead, is at best in a state of suspended animation. This is indeed an unexpected turn of events for what has been the best planned UN peacekeeping operation.

NOTES

1. UN Security Council Resolution S/4387, July 14, 1960.
2. UN Security Council Resolution S/4405, Jully 22, 1960.
3. UN Security Council Resolution S/4426 of Aug. 9, 1960.
4. UN Security Council Resolution S/4526, Sept. 17, 1960.
5. UN General Assembly Resolution 1474 (XV) Sept. 20, 1960.
6. UN General Assembly Resolution 1498 (XV), Nov. 22, 1960.
7. UN Seccurity Council Resolution S/4741, Feb. 21, 1961.
8. UN General Assembly Resolution 1600 (XV), April 15, 1961.

9. Rosalyn Higgins, *United Nations Peacekeeping 1946–1967: Documents and Commentary*, vol. 3: *Africa* (Oxford University Press, 1980).
10. UN General Assembly Resolution 1599 (XV), April 15, 1961.
11. UN General Assembly Resolution 1600 (XV), April 15, 1961.
12. UN Security Council Resolution S/5002 of Nov. 24, 1961, and related amendments.
13. The main points of the Plan of National Conciliation were; agreement of the central government and Katanga authorities; freedom of movement for ONUC in Katanga; the central government to exercise control and to regulate imports and exports; the central government and Katanga authorities to declare publicly their acceptance of the Plan; the central government to negotiate with the Belgian government arrangements to collect duties on export of foods to the Congo and Katanga; UN to provide some military equipment to the ANC, and reduce its activity in South Katanga; the central government to establish controls over foreign exchange; the United States to provide additional aid and ask Belgium and other states to do likewise; neighbouring and other states to stop movement of arms and military personnel; the UN to invite Belgium and the Union Minière du Haut Katanga to discuss questions relating to protection of their personnel and installations.
14. UN Security Council Resolution S/5488, Dec. 26, 1963.
15. UN Security Council Resolution S/5575, March 4, 1964.
16. UN Security Council Resolution 192, June 20, 1964.
17. UN Security Council Resolution 193, Aug. 9, 1964.
18. UN Security Council Resolution 231, Dec. 15, 1964.
19. UN Security Council Resolution 353, July 20, 1974.
20. UN Security Council Resolution 355, July 31, 1974.
21. UN Security Council Resolution 361, Aug. 30, 1974.
22. UN Security Council Resolution 186 (1964).
23. He retired as a lieutenant-general after a distinguished career in the British Army.
24. UN Security Council Resolutions 425 and 426, March 19, 1978.
25. UNIFIL was authorized by UN Security Council Resolution 425, March 19, 1978.
26. Security Council Resolution 425 called for the Secretary-General to submit a report within twenty-four hours, which he did. This report was approved by the Council in its Resolution 426, March 19, 1978.
27. Lebanese National Movement (LNM); AMAL (meaning 'hope' in Arabic); a militia representative of Shiite Muslims (60 per cent of the population of Lebanon).
28. UN Security Council Resolution 427 (1978).
29. Albania, Algeria, Benin, Bulgaria, Byelorussia, China, Cuba, Czechoslovakia, South Yemen, East Germany, Hungary, Iraq, Laos, Libya, Mongolia, Poland, South Africa, Syria, Ukraine, Vietnam, the Soviet Union.
30. UN General Assembly Resolution 2372 (XX11).
31. International Defence and Aid Fund for Southern Africa, *Namibia: the Facts*, London, 1980; UN General Assembly Document A/AC.109/699 of June 18, 1982.
32. Franz Ansprenger, 'Namibia and Apartheid' in R. and A.-M. Jutte (eds). *The Future of International Organizations*, London: Frances Pinter, 1981, p. 185.
33. UN Document A/123.
34. UN General Assembly Resolution 65(1), Dec. 14, 1946.
35. Ansprenger, *op. cit.*, p. 199.
36. UNICJ (05) R3, 1950.
37. UN General Assembly Resolution 1514 (XV), Dec. 14, 1960.
38. *Namibia: The Facts*, p. 61.
39. UN Doc. S/12636, April 10, 1978.
40. Official Records of the UN General Assembly, 33rd Session, Supplement 23 (A/33/23/Rev.1), vol. 11, chap. V111, annex, paras. 80–90, 96.

41. Official Records of the Security Council, 33rd Year, Supplement for July, August and September 1978, Document S/12827.

42. *Ibid.*, Supplement for Oct., Nov. and Dec. 1978, Document S/12983, annex 1.

43. *Ibid.*, 34th Year, Supplement for Jan., Feb. and March 1979, Document S/13120.

44. Official Records of the UN General Assembly, 34th Session, Supplement no. 23 (A/34/23/Rev.1), vol. 11, chap. IX, annex, paras. 88–94.

45. A/Ac.109/604, paras. 21–26.

46. Official Records of the UN Security Council, 35th Year, Supplement for Jan., Feb. and March 1980, Document S/13862, para.2.

47. *Ibid.*, 35th Year, Supplement for Jan., Feb. and March 1980, Document S/13740.

48. *Ibid.*, Document S/14011, June 20, 1980.

49. UN Document S/15287, July 12, 1982.

5

REGIONAL ORGANIZATIONS

General

The evolution of an international political system and attempts to develop a global security arrangement encouraged regionalism. The Arabs, with their common language, culture and religion, were the first to recognize this by setting up the League of Arab States in 1946, just as they were beginning to shed colonialism. Latin America, isolated from the rest of the world with the exception of North America, was determined to keep the influence of other powers, most notably the Soviet Union, out of its region. Both the Roman Catholic religion and the structure of their society were threatened by socialism in any guise, communism being from their point of view by far the worst. The regional great power, the United States, concurred in this view, and this led to the establishment of an Organization of American States in 1948.

Europe, divided by a rising East-West conflict, witnessed the establishment of NATO (the North Atlantic Tready Organization) and the Warsaw Pact. Although these arrangements primarily signify regional military pacts, they also provide the machinery for regional cooperation. Also NATO became the first step to the development of a Council of Europe intended for free democracies.

The end of the colonial era in Africa and emergence of many newly independent states in Asia and Africa led to considerations as to how to shed dominance by the former colonial masters and to prevent interference by the great powers. Because of past rivalries and its diversity, Asia has been slow in developing its regional systems, whereas such a need was strongly felt in Africa. The Maghreb Arabs north of the Sahara and black Africa to its south, anxious to settle their own disputes, were quick to establish an Organization of African Unity in 1963 on the basis that Africans should be the first to deal with African disputes.

In Asia, an attempt by the United States to create a southern tier of defence against communism (the People's Republic of China and the Soviet Union) in the shape of SEATO (Southeast Asia Treaty Organization) did not prove successful. Its members, representing a diversity of nations ranging from Turkey in the eastern Mediterranean to the Philippines in the Pacific, had different reasons for joining the organization. Of course, they were opposed to communism, but mostly their worst enemies were their immediate neighbours, i.e. Greece in the case of Turkey and India in the case of Pakistan. The war in Vietnam and the restoration of relations between the United States

131

and the People's Republic of China hastened the demise of SEATO.

ASEAN, the Association of South-East Asian Nations, has emerged as a social and economic organization. A Gulf Co-operation Council was established by the Arab Gulf states to guard against the ominous threat of Islamic fundamentalism and the consequences of war between Iraq and Iran. Even the South Asian nations, hitherto kept divided by the Indo-Pakistan conflict and by the apparently dominant position of India, have joined together to strengthen their economic and social ties. Although Soviet intervention in Afghanistan has caused them concern, they have so far excluded security considerations from their agenda.

The regional system authorized by the UN Charter (Chapter 8) provides an institutional arrangement to strengthen co-operation and deal with conflicts before they become internationalized. Even when conflicts have broader involvements, their solutions may sometimes be easier in a regional context. The following description and analysis of regional systems examines their capabilities and interrelationship with the UN.

The League of Arab States

General. The League of Arab States was established in 1945 for the primary purpose of resolving regional disputes. The League's Council has played a prominent role in coping with issues. The Council is not only the principal organ, but it may meet at different levels — e.g. as a political committee or as a meeting of either heads of state, foreign ministers or of permanent members.

The League has dealt with conflicts through conciliation, mediation, good offices and arbitration. Although fact-finding was not specified in its Charter, it has assumed the power to fulfil that role under its broad functions of mediation (Article 5) and of adopting measures to counter aggression (Article 6), to justify the establishment of the necessary organs for that purpose.

The League's Secretary-General has been entrusted with much more responsibility than was envisaged in the treaty signed at Cairo on March 22, 1950, and has often been called on to play a significant role, e.g. in the Algerian-Moroccan conflict in 1963, Yemen in 1948, 1962 and 1972, and Lebanon in 1958.

In its relations with the UN, the League has dealt with strictly local disputes. Inter-state problems, such as the crisis in Jordan in 1950, the dispute of 1961 between Syria and the United Arab Republic (Egypt), and the Yemen situation in 1948 did not influence the international environment and were dealt with by the League. However, in the cases of Lebanon in 1958 and Yemen in 1962, which had serious international overtones, the Security Council retained a supervisory function, leaving the League to resolve the main issues. In both of these cases, UN peacekeeping operations were established, leaving agreement to be reached by the League's good offices. In the case of the crisis in 1961 concerning Bizerte (which Tunisia had allowed the French to keep as a military base under a post-independence agreement) and the Arab-Israeli conflict, the UN Security Council played a prominent role, as it was clear that international peace and security were being seriously threatened.

The collective security function of the League was established in the 1950 Collective Security Pact, which authorizes it to act in resolving disputes between members and when it involves a member or members with a third party. The League's approach has basically been one of conciliation. However, the first instance of this system coming into use was the dispute between Iraq and Kuwait in 1961. An Arab League Security Force in Kuwait was established. In the case of Bizerte, the League adopted measures to support Tunisia, including the provision of military assistance, but they were not actually put into effect. When civil war broke out in Lebanon, an Arab Deterrent Force was established to separate the PLO from Lebanese factions that opposed it and the warring factions from each other. However, when there has been a threat from third parties, certain arrangements have been utilized, e.g. an Arab high command in the 1960s to deal with the 'Israeli threat' through reliance on self-defence arrangements. Since it is not our purpose to deal with military alliances, an analysis follows of the two Arab peacekeeping forces that have been mounted.

On gaining its independence, Kuwait, threatened by Iraq, invited the outgoing British to dispatch troops in defence of their territory. Kuwait also raised the issue with the League, which called on the British to withdraw and decided to replace them with an Arab League peacekeeping force. Although not happy with the idea of losing a British guarantee of sovereignty, Kuwait agreed. The Arab League Security Force in Kuwait, consisting of 1,000 Egyptians, 1,700 Saudis, 400 Sudanese, 950 Jordanians and 200 Tunisians, was established on July 20, 1961. The Supreme Command was entrusted to Maj-Gen. Abdullah Al-Isa of Saudi Arabia, whose country had the largest contingent. The force was of a temporary nature; it was introduced into Kuwait with the consent of the host-party, and would withdraw when Kuwait so requested in accordance with an agreed procedure.

The League's Secretary-General, in an exchange of letters with Kuwait, established a status of forces[1] somewhat along the lines established by the UN. In fact, the entire operation followed the UN precedent. However, the arrangement for withdrawal of the forces was clearer than that established for UNEF I.

It took the League almost two months to organize the force, during which period the British troops deterred a possible Iraqi attack. Because the League's regular budget was small, Kuwait agreed to bear most of the costs. The League Secretariat is also much smaller than that of the UN and therefore would not have been able to support a large force in the field. On the other hand, the League had less problems than the UN and the OAS in agreeing on plans for peace-keeping, including training, standardization of equipment and policies. As quiet returned to the area, the Force was withdrawn in February 1963.

In 1979, when North Yemen and South Yemen accused each other of armed aggression, the Arab League dispatched a military commission consisting of officers from Iraq, Syria, Algeria, Kuwait, the Emirates and the PLO. The Commission arranged a ceasefire, and Kuwait was able to reconcile the two parties so that they could end the conflict.

The Arab Deterrent Force. As we have seen in another context, the delicate balance between the Christians and Muslims in Lebanon, already disturbed by the presence of large numbers of Palestinian refugees, was finally destroyed when a further influx of Palestinians, notably fighters expelled from Jordan in 1970, heightened inter-communal tensions to the point where they exploded into full-scale civil war. After earlier attempts to end the fighting had proved unsuccessful, a six-party Arab summit was held in Riyadh on October 18, 1976, under the aegis of the League of Arab States and decided on a ceasefire to be effective from October 21. The Syrian troops already in the Arab security force were to become part of an enlarged Arab Deterrent Force (ADF) that would operate under the orders of the President of Lebanon.

The main points of the Riyadh resolutions were: (1) that the Cairo agreement, referring to the PLO presence in southern Lebanon, be implemented; (2) that a ceasefire, with armed personnel and weapons being withdrawn to locations prior to April 13, 1975, be supervised; (3) that internal security be safeguarded; (4) that Lebanese authority be restored; (5) that the PLO affirm its respect for Lebanon's sovereignty and security and its agreement not to interfere in domestic affairs; and (6) that the conferring Arab states (which included Syria) pledge to respect Lebanese sovereignty.

In an appendix on the implementation of the Riyadh resolutions, (1) a ceasefire was declared to be effective 0600 hours on October 21, 1976; (2) observation posts to be established along the buffer zone; (3) armed personnel and weapons to be removed in accordance to a set timetable; (4) international highways to be reopened; (5) the legal Lebanese authorities to take over public services, institutions and establishments both civilian and military; (6) the formation of the forces required to strengthen the Arab security force to take place in agreement with the Lebanese President; those forces to arrive within two weeks; and (7) the Cairo agreement and its appendices to be implemented as a second stage, especially with regard to the presence of weapons and ammunition in the refugee camps, and with regard to the departure of the armed Palestinian forces which entered after the events began; this co-ordination to be completed forty-five days from the date of the formation of the deterrent Arab security force.

At a Cairo summit meeting on October 26, 1976, the heads of state approved the Riyadh resolutions. Furthermore, they decided on the financing of the ADF by establishing a special fund with each Arab state participating with a percentage that was to be determined by each state according to its capability. The fund was renewable by the decision of the Arab League Council at the request of the President of the Lebanese Republic. The fund for the first six months was fixed at $90 million, a figure which has varied since that time.

Initially 30,000 troops were provided: 22,000 from Syria, 700 from the United Arab Emirates, and contingents from Saudi Arabia and Sudan. Libya and South Yemen agreed to contribute but did not in fact send any troops. After the first period, only Syrian troops remained and the brunt of responsibility was borne by them. While the Lebanese were not happy with only Syrian forces, the fact remains that they would be helpless without them.

At a meeting of Arab states supporting the ADF, held at the invitation of President Sarkis of Lebanon at Beiteddin on October 15–17, 1978, it was agreed that reaching a comprehensive solution to the Lebanese crisis on the basis of the Riyadh agreement was extremely important. Furthermore, it was agreed that Lebanon should be unified under its sovereign authority and a timetable should be laid down for rebuilding the army on a national and balanced basis, to enable it to carry out its role in realizing national security and undertaking the missions now being assumed by the ADF on Lebanese territory.

The Beiteddin declaration was seen as a triumph for Syria. The Christians in Lebanon expressed reservations. The People's Socialist Party leader Walid Jumblatt said that the recommendations provided what could form the framework for a 'final solution.' The Palestinians also expressed some reservations. While they intended to co-operate with the Lebanese government, they felt that the demand for the removal of their positions in areas outside ADF control between the Litani and Zaharani rivers was unfair.

The command and control of the ADF was vested in the President of Lebanon who in turn appointed a Lebanese military commander. The Commander in fact operated merely as the representative of the Lebanese head of state, while a Syrian General remained in charge.

The ADF was mainly deployed in and around Beirut, in the Bekaa valley and in the north. It maintained law and order, and managed to keep the parties apart. Its presence remained vital in the prevailing political and strategic environment in Lebanon. However, its attempts to improve its positions caused concern to the Israelis who remained determined to maintain the position of Haddad's Christian forces in southern Lebanon.

The Organization of American States

General. The origins of the inter-American system go back to the initiative of Simon Bolivar, which led to the convening of the Panama Conference in 1826. Although no agreement emerged, the Bolivarian concept remained alive, and by the end of the nineteenth century the United States had joined in the efforts to promote an inter-American system. In 1890 the International Union of American Republics, with a permanent office in Washington, and the Commercial Bureau of the American Republics were established, later to become the Pan-American Union.

Following the Spanish-American war of 1898, the United States unilaterally assumed policing responsibilities in the Caribbean and Central America, an interventionist policy which angered the Latin Americans. This policy only changed under President Franklin D. Roosevelt. However, United States non-military intervention remained a fact of life in the region; for example, President Lyndon Johnson's intervention during the civil war in the Dominican Republic in 1965 was started unilaterally. It was with this background that the Latin Americans preferred to exclude politico-security matters from their discussions.

The experience of the League of Nations had not endeared this world organization to the Latin Americans. The ineffectiveness of the League in resolving conflicts through peaceful means was highlighted during conflicts like the Chaco war between Bolivia and Paraguay. However, the good neighbour policy of President Roosevelt and the collaboration between Latin America and the United States in economic and defence matters during and after the Second World War encouraged interest in strengthening an inter-American system.

In developing a new international system for peace and security after 1945, the United States had prepared a global arrangement, with the big five powers of the wartime Grand Alliance assuming primary responsibility. At the same time there was serious concern in the Americas over the growing power of the Soviet Union. The discussion at the UN Charter Conference at San Francisco of the dominant role of the Security Council in the maintenance of peace and security worldwide could lead — so some Americans thought — to interference from outside in hemispheric matters, from which they particularly wished to exclude the Soviets. The Latin Americans were determined to win recognition for regional arrangements at the UN Charter Conference. The Charter eventually emerged reflecting various interests, and there is not unanimity in the interpretation of those parts of it that concern the relationship between the Security Council and regional systems.

The Security Council was given the primary responsibility for the maintenance of international peace and security.[2] However in dealing with conflicts, the Council has to function under Chapters VI, VII, VIII and XII.[3] Chapter VI, in requiring pacific settlement of disputes, states: 'The parties . . . shall, first of all seek a solution by negotiation, enquiry, mediation, conciliation, arbitration, judicial settlement, resort to regional agencies or arrangements, or other peaceful means of their choice.'

Chapter VIII provides for regional arrangements. For example, 'nothing in the Charter precludes the existence of regional arrangements or agencies dealing with such matters relating to the maintenance of international peace and security'.[4] The Security Council shall, when appropriate, utilize such regional arrangements or agencies for enforcement action under the authority.[5] However, the Charter added the reservation that 'no enforcement action shall be taken under regional arrangements or by regional agencies without the authorization of the Security Council with the exception of any measure against any enemy state.'[6]

Finally the Charter requires the Security Council to be kept fully informed at all time 'of activities undertaken or in contemplation under regional arrangements or by regional agencies'.[7] Thus the Security Council was intended to have primary authority for the maintenance of peace and security anywhere and a monopoly in the use of force except when an armed attack has to be fought off. The regional organizations were subordinated to the global system. This concept could be effective for as long as there was agreement among the permanent members of the Security Council. Yet from its very beginning the inter-American system envisaged exclusion from Western Hemisphere affairs of Soviet influence and the power of its veto. Thus globalism and regionalism, which were intended to be complementary, have resulted in some conflict of interests between the UN and the regional systems, more so in the case of the Organization of American States (OAS) than any other.

The Latin American states include a few medium powers (including two major oil-producers, Mexico and Venezuela) and several very small states. Their immediate neighbour to the north, the United States, has not hesitated in the past to use its economic and military power for the advancement or protection of its interests, while Canada is a medium but industrial power which has its own problems with the United States, yet has maintained friendly relations with the other states in the Americas, has proved to be a good trading partner, and has come forward with help to the needy countries.

The immense power of the United States, and historical factors, led the Latin American states, in choosing an inter-American system, to place particular reliance on the juridical arrangements to limit intervention by the United States. Thus the evolution of the OAS leads it to rely especially on pacific means in the settlement of disputes and to shy away from the use of military means because such means would inevitably be dominated by the United States. Their hesitant acceptance of an Inter-American Peace Force, even though it was under a Brazilian general, could not conceal the obvious predominance of the United States in the force and its strong influence in all the force's operational and logistics aspects. Therefore the Latin Americans remain extremely sensitive to any suggestions regarding the introduction of peacekeeping.

The inter-American system is quite comprehensive in establishing procedures for peaceful settlement of disputes. A collective security treaty (the Rio Treaty of 1947), a Treaty on Pacific Settlement (Bogota, 1948) and the Charter (Bogota, 1948) all have the intention of finding peaceful solutions to conflicts. There is a strong commitment to non-intervention (mainly with the United States in mind), and the military part of the system, namely the Inter-American Defence Board (IADB), has not only been kept but with a few minor exceptions has been excluded from playing a role. Thus the emphasis within the OAS is on peacemaking rather than peacekeeping.

The evolution of the OAS has been based on the three key factors referred to above: (1) the Inter-American Treaty of Reciprocal Assistance, or Rio Treaty, signed in 1947; (2) the various pre-existing treaties which were consolidated into the American Treaty of Pacific Settlement at the Bogota Conference in 1948; and (3) the OAS Charter, which was drafted at the same Conference in 1948.[8]

The Treaty of Pacific Settlement proved impractical because it was too legalistic, seemed to infringe national sovereignty, and made no provision for third-party roles in peaceful settlement of disputes. The treaty failed to come into effect because there were not enough states, including the United States, which ratified it. On the other hand the Rio Treaty proved flexible enough to be employed as a useful instrument to permit peace observation or peacekeeping. The Treaty provides a framework for a defensive alliance in the face of external threats, and a collective security system to impose sanctions against an aggressor in the case of an inter-hemispheric dispute; it also provides for the calling of a meeting of Consultation to consider measures to maintain peace and security.

Unlike other military alliance systems, the Rio Treaty lacks a military infrastructure and in any event does not have UN support; the availability of troops is on a voluntary basis just as it is in the UN peacekeeping system. Only in the Cuban missile crisis in 1962 was Article 8, providing for armed force, invoked. However, sanctions were imposed in the Dominican Republic in 1960 and in Cuba in 1962, 1964 and 1967.

The OAS Charter has established a Permanent Council (Article 81) empowered to act as a provisional Organ of Consultation for peaceful settlement of disputes. The Council has available to it the successor to the Inter-American Peace Committee, the Inter-American Committee on Peaceful Settlement. The OAS has been able to use this Committee for peace observation/peacekeeping because it provides for consent of the parties and a degree of flexibility. The Council has been used liked the Rio Treaty, to make up for the failure of the Treaty of Pacific Settlement.

The OAS has two permanent military organs, the Inter-American Defence Board (IADB) and the Advisory Defence Committee (Articles 64–67). The IADB has not usually been consulted by the OAS since it came into existence in 1942 and has no operational or support functions. Its activities are confined to making recommendations and planning for collective defence. However its educational arm, the Inter-American Defence College (IADC), has an important role as a senior-level inter-American institution for military studies.

The Advisory Defence Committee has never been called into being. The theory is that if the Organ of Consultation so decides, it may be called upon to play a role in peacekeeping.

Peacekeeping operations. The first peacekeeping operation in Latin America was over the Leticia Trapezium in 1932 following a clash between Colombia and Peru. The League of Nations administered Leticia for about a year and some seventy-five Colombian soldiers were employed, bearing international armbands.

The first OAS peace observation effort followed a border dispute between Costa Rica and Nicaragua. An *ad hoc* Committee of Information was established which in turn created an Inter-American Commission of military experts. Since then the OAS has established a number of peace missions to deal with conflicts, e.g. concerning Guatemala in 1954, Costa Rica and Nicaragua in 1955 (when a buffer-zone manned by some twenty military personnel was established for the first time), Ecuador and Peru in 1955, Honduras and Nicaragua in 1957, Panama in 1959, the Dominican Republic in 1959, and so on.

Later, the Latin Americans participated in a combined Inter-American Naval Quarantine Force during the Cuban missile crisis in 1962, and dealt with the supply of arms by Cuba to Venezuela in 1963. On the latter occasion, it used IADB experts for the first time and therefore categorized the mission under 'Collective Security' rather than peace observation.

The OAS established its first peacekeeping force in the Dominican Republic following the civil war in 1965–6. This will be dealt with below in more detail.

In 1969–71 and again in 1976, when armed clashes erupted between Honduras and El Salvador, ceasefires were arranged, demilitarized

zones established and military observers made responsible for supervision — all under the Rio Treaty. This operation was larger than any
earlier undertaking. There were thirty-three observers from seven
countries represented on the OAS committee. The United States
provided aircraft, including helicopters, and logistic support.

Shortly before the crisis in Guatemala in 1954, the OAS created an
Inter-American Emergency Fund. After fighting broke out, the OAS
Council appealed for disaster relief assistance, and member-states'
contributions, including a large donation by the United States, were
received. About 140 civilian staff members of the OAS Secretariat,
responsible for disaster relief assistance, were later made responsible
for supervising the guarantees obtained from both sides for protection
of nationals of either country residing in the other. The administrative
responsibility for distributing disaster aid and observation responsibilities placed a heavy burden on the OAS staff.

The OAS Secretary-General, Galo Plaza, with his past experience
with the UN in Cyprus, wished to avoid getting 'locked in', for, apart
from the need to obtain an early resolution of the conflict, the OAS
could ill afford a prolonged operation, and efforts were made to bring
the parties to terms and to assume more responsibility on their own.
By the end of 1969, most civilians had been withdrawn, and only two
military observers remained with one helicopter. In 1972, when
Guatemala accused the United Kingdom of reinforcing its troops in
Belize, the OAS, acting under a resolution of the UN General Assembly (a procedure never adopted before), sent a lawyer from the OAS
Secretariat and a General officer from the Colombian delegation to
the IADB to check on the complaint. However, the IADB was not
involved in this mission.

The Guatemalan case[9] in 1954 and the Bay of Pigs[10] in 1962 had
already brought a difference between the OAS and the UN into the
open. The Dominican crisis was to bring the issue to a critical stage.

The Dominican Republic. After the assassination of Generalisimo
Rafael Trujillo, the country had returned to democratic rule, but
the administration of Juan Bosch of the *Partido Revolucionario
Dominicano* (PRD), a noted historian, was more visionary than pragmatic. In 1946 Donald Reid Cabral overthrew Bosch with the assistance of the military. When Reid introduced a strict economic regime
and curtailed the privileges of the élite class, including the military, the
latter, suspecting that Reid would rig the coming elections in his own
favour, set aside their differences and, deposing Reid, established the
Council President José Molina Urena as provisional President on
April 25, 1965. It was not long before the officers themselves began to
disagree on the future of the government. A rebel group, calling themselves 'Constitutionalists' and headed by Colonel Francisco Com-
maño Deño, demanding Bosch's return, seized two military camps,

the government palace, the radio and the Duarte bridge over the Ozama River, and established a new government.

The United States became alarmed at these developments. The US embassy's immediate evaluation was that Reid would regain power and that the pro-Bosch uprising was Communist-inspired — an assessment that later had to be revised. However, the 'Constitutionalists' had freely handed out rifles and machine-guns to several thousand civilians, and petrol bombs were being made.

Attacks by pro-Urena armoured units under General Wessin y Wessin, commander of the élite San Isidro troops, against pro-Bosch forces failed to cut the Duarte bridge despite air attacks ordered by General Juan de los Santos against the rebel forces. The first attempt to arrange a ceasefire by the Dominican Archbishop Beras and the diplomatic corps proved unsuccessful. Concerned at the danger to American citizens, the US embassy requested the US Navy's Caribbean Amphibious Task Force to move closer to Santo Domingo and to evacuate those citizens who wished to leave. The Task Force's helicopter-carrier *Boxer* landed a detachment at the polo ground near the Hotel Embajador in Santo Domingo. During the evacuation, which started on April 27, there was some shooting and rough handling of American civilians by 'Constitutionalists', who suspected that a key anti-Bosch Dominican was being evacuated. This proved false and the 'Constitutionalists' withdrew, but the Americans were left feeling resentful.

Wessin managed to cross the river by a bridge a few miles north of Duarte bridge and was soon driving the rebels south into the old city. The position of the rebels was precarious, and they appealed to the US Ambassador to mediate, but without effect. The 'Constitutionalists' informed the Ambassador that they could no longer guarantee the safety of US citizens and of the diplomatic community. The Wessin group, who had set up a three-man Junta at San Isidro air base headed by Colonel Pedro Bartolomé Benoit, requested the United States to intervene. President Johnson immediately ordered 1,500 marines from USS *Boxer* ashore on April 28, and they rapidly gained control of the diplomatic residential area.

The United States informed the Council of the OAS and the UN Security Council of the action taken. As a fellow-member of the same regional organization as the Dominican Republic, the United States had by its unilateral action violated the organization's principle of non-intervention by one member-state in the domestic affairs of another, but this did not evoke any apparent reaction by the OAS, which simply called for an immediate ceasefire and the establishment of an international security zone for the protection of foreign embassies. This decision was reached by a majority of one vote, i.e. by the Wessin group nominee from the Dominican Republic. Clearly there was little consensus in support of the US intervention.

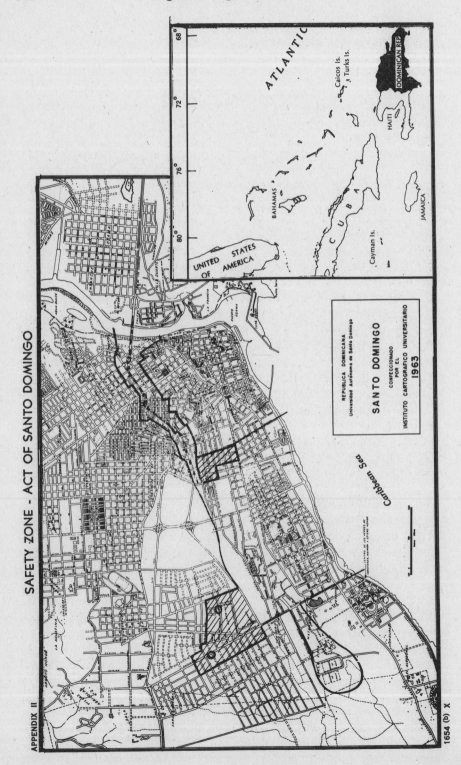

APPENDIX II

SAFETY ZONE - ACT OF SANTO DOMINGO

1654 (b) X

Despite these moves, fighting continued, and the United States reinforced its troops by bringing the 82nd Airborne Division by air transport to San Isidro. These troops immediately seized the Duarte bridge to link with the Marines guarding the International Security Zone, thereby trapping the 'Constitutionalists' in the old city. Taking advantage of this situation, the Wessin forces increased their pressure on the northern part of the city which had been cut off from the main rebel forces.

Fighting continued despite a diplomatic approach by the Papal Nuncio Mgr Clerizio for a ceasefire. The Wessin group now became the 'Government of National Reconstruction' headed by General Antonio Imbert Barrara. It was persuaded to sign the ceasefire agreement, but the 'Constitutionalists' refused to sign on the grounds that the United States and the OAS had intervened on the Wessin group's side and were now supportive of the government headed by Imbert.

On April 28, 1965, the United States reported these developments to the UN Security Council, justifying the intervention on the grounds that it had been in the interest of law and order, a protective measure for its own and foreign nationals and at the request of at least one party to the conflict. During the Security Council debate that started on May 3, the Soviet Union hotly contested the United States interference while other Council members felt that the OAS should have dealt with the situation and that a UN involvement was undesirable.

Following the OAS appeal to halt fighting, the organization's Secretary-General José A. Mora arrived in Santo Domingo. On May 1, a meeting of the OAS Council of Foreign Ministers established a Special Committee comprising the representatives of five states — Argentina, Brazil, Colombia, Guatemala and Panama. It immediately proceeded to Santo Domingo and offered its good offices to the rival factions to achieve a ceasefire and an orderly evacuation of foreign nationals and Dominicans granted asylum in foreign embassies from the fighting zone. The OAS also requested its members to make available land, air, naval and police forces for the formation of an Inter-American Peace Force (IAPF) which would operate under the authority of the OAS. On May 5 the OAS Special Committee succeeded in obtaining the signatures of the rival factions to the Act of Santo Domingo formalizing the ceasefire arrangements initiated by the Papal Nuncio. The agreement, besides providing a ceasefire, delineated an international security zone with a corridor connecting San Isidro with the International Zone in the capital. This formalized separation of the opposing forces proved an aggravation rather than a palliative and was the cause of further fighting.

The United States was aware of the international opposition and domestic criticism of its intervention in the Dominican Republic and started vigorous efforts to resolve the crisis. Its former Ambassador to the Dominican Republic during the Bosch Presidency, John Bartlow Martin, was despatched by President Johnson as his special envoy to negotiate a ceasefire and bring the opposing factions together. When Martin's mission failed, McGeorge Bundy, the President's Special Assistant for National Security Affairs, was sent in his place. Bundy put forward Antonio Guzmán, who was to be President many years later, as a compromise candidate for the Dominican Presidency. Guzmán, a wealthy farmer, was a respected PRD leader, but he was rejected by the Junta, who thought he would be weak in dealing with the 'Communists'. It was now clearly for the OAS to resolve the stalemate.

The United States soon had about 15,000 troops in and around Santo Domingo. In explaining to the OAS the initial United States unilateral intervention, Ambassador Ellsworth Bunker explained that in the absence of a readily available Inter-American force, his country had had to act alone. It was therefore essential, he added, that an Inter-American force be established under the OAS; the United States troops in the Dominican Republic would be placed at the disposal of this combined force.

After a protracted debate and by a bare two-thirds majority vote (the Dominican Republic representative taking orders from the anti-'Constitutionalists'), a request was made to 'member-states that are willing and capable of doing so to make contingents of their land, naval, air and police forces available to the Organization of American States, within their capabilities and to the extent they can do so, to form an inter-American force that will operate under the authority of the Tenth Meeting of Consultation'.[11] The purpose of the force would be, 'in a spirit of democratic impartiality, that of co-operating in the restoration of normal conditions in the Dominican Republic, in maintaining the security of its inhabitants and the inviolability of human rights, and in the establishment of an atmosphere of peace and conciliation that will permit the functioning of democratic institutions'. As to the decision to withdraw the force, the resolution left it to be determined by the Tenth Meeting of Consultation of the Foreign Ministers, but later amended to include a co-ordinated role for the government of the Dominican Republic.

The Inter-American Peace Force (IAPF) was the first peacekeeping force in the experience of the OAS. Brazil, Costa Rica, Honduras, Nicaragua and Paraguay agreed to contribute contingents, and of these only Brazil had previous peacekeeping experience with the UN. However, the Commander, General Hugo Panasco Alvim of Brazil, who had never served with the UN, proved inflexible and was openly hostile to the 'Constitutionalists' from the start. The Commander of the United States forces, Lt.-Gen. Bruce Palmer, Jr., was appointed Deputy Commander. Palmer, an experienced paratrooper, had already proved sensitive to the politics of the crisis and played a dominant role in the management of the IAPF, whose mandate, as in the UN type of peacekeeping operations, was vague and rhetorical. Notwithstanding appeals by the OAS and the Nuncio, shooting incidents of varying degrees of seriousness occurred in the coming months. However, due to the presence of the IAPF, the efforts of the OAS *Ad Hoc* Committee and especially Ambassador Bunker, the guidance of General Palmer and the responsive leadership of General Meira Mattos, who had served with UNEF in Gaza and was now in command of the Brazilians who formed the majority of Latin American troops, the conflict was finally resolved.

Meanwhile, as the IAPF was being assembled and deployed in the International Security Zone, fighting continued unabated. On May 13 General Imbert, in violation of the truce, launched a successful attack against the positions of the 'Constitutionalists' in the northern part of Santo Domingo. On May 14, the 'Constitutionalists' called for a meeting of the UN Security Council, charging that US forces had moved outside their positions and that radio stations had been bombed by the pro-Wessin air force. The Security Council called for a ceasefire and for the dispatch of a representative to Santo Domingo to report developments. U Thant immediately sent a small advance party under the present author, and a few days later José Antonio Mayobre was appointed his Special Representative.

Soon after his arrival, in accordance with his instructions, Mayobre notified all parties concerned of the Security Council's call for a ceasefire. On May 18 he met both sides but had little luck in persuading them to end the fighting. Colonel Caamaño, the 'Constitutionalist' Commander, had asserted that the United States was giving military assistance to the Imbert force who were attacking the city. Imbert blamed Caamaño for the fighting. That evening heavy fighting broke out, and Mayobre, in conjunction with the Nuncio, pressed hard to negotiate a ceasefire to facilitate the work of the International Red Cross in searching for and evacuating the dead and wounded; on May 21, Mayobre succeeded in introducing a twenty-four hour ceasefire for this purpose, which he proved unable to prolong.

The OAS proposed the holding of elections, a general amnesty for those who had taken part in the fighting, the surrender of unauthorized arms, and the convening of a constitutional assembly within six months of an elected government taking office. Although during 1965 there were repeated violations, the OAS proceeded to implement its proposal. The UN Observer Team concentrated on supporting the Latin American UN Human Rights Commission. The OAS mediation effort also persuaded rival Dominican groups to agree on Garcia Godoy, a non-controversial, respected senior diplomat, becoming the interim President, which did much to heal wounds. On June 1, 1966, Joaquin Balaguer was elected President and the IAPF started its withdrawal. On October 22, 1966, the UN Mission was withdrawn.

The appointment of a representative of the Secretary-General at the Security Council's request to observe and report on a situation which was already being dealt with by the OAS was unprecedented. The crisis in the Dominican Republic presented an unusually complex situation that had considerable international repercussions, particularly with regard to the unilateral military involvement of the United States in the initial stage and the later role of the IAPF.

While Mayobre had a limited mandate, the effect of his mission was significant. He played a major role in arranging a ceasefire on May 21, 1965, and reported on the situation in Santo Domingo and the interior. The presence of the Secretary-General's representative, however much disliked by the OAS and right-wing leaders in Santo Domingo, did prove to be a moderating factor in a difficult and dangerous situation. Such a UN presence, when a regional organization already had responsibility, created a conflict in spheres of responsibility and prejudiced the ability of the OAS to act.

When the civil war in the Dominican Republic led to unilateral military intervention by the United States on April 29, 1965, the OAS immediately tried to establish a ceasefire through its good offices, and within days, after intense US lobbying, approval was given by the organization for the creation of an Inter-American Peace Force. Controversy between the OAS and the UN started on May 1, 1965, when the Security Council took up the question at the insistence of the Soviet Union, and a debate on jurisdictional matters was started. On May 14, after the OAS had negotiated a ceasefire which quickly collapsed, the Security Council unanimously approved the establishment of a UN presence. The sponsors of the resolution recognized that the OAS had the primary role in dealing with this problem.

The United Nations Charter, Chapter VIII, describing regional arrangements in Article 52 (1), does not preclude the existence of regional organizations for dealing with matters relating to maintenance of international peace and security as long as their actions comply with the Charter. Article 52 (2) states that 'member-states entering into regional arrangements shall make every effort to achieve peaceful settlement of local disputes through such regional arrangements . . . before referring them to the Security Council.' And Article 52 (3) calls on the Council to encourage the regional organizations to solve disputes peacefully, either on their own initiative or when referred to them by the Council. Therefore, it would be legitimate for member-states to give preference to regional systems and this principle has generally prevailed. However, the argument in the Dominican case arose over the jurisdictional question: whether, at the same time or as a priority, the UN could deal with such cases. The Charter does not pre-empt the field in favour of the regional systems.

It is not intended to make a comprehensive examination of related legal and constitutional issues. However, this analysis is intended to highlight the impact of the UN-OAS controversy on peacekeeping operations, so as to enable diplomats and military officers engaged in such operations on behalf of the international organizations to avoid the kind of pitfalls that were encountered in the Dominican situation.

The military intervention of the United States in the Dominican Republic caused serious concern to several members of the Security Council. The initial US support for the military junta was obvious, as was its opposition to the 'Constitutionalists', whom it suspected of having Communist support and inspiration. The UN could not ignore these activities, and what bothered some Security Council members, including Uruguay, was that the OAS, instead of condemning the US action, was about to legitimize it by including the interventionist American forces in the IAPF. Hence the Special Committee appointed by the Meeting of Consultation of Ministers, the OAS Secretary-General and later the IAPF, between whom good relations had been emerging, found itself at odds with the UN Mission in the Dominican Republic. At the UN, the United States, unlike the Soviet Union in situations relating to its direct interests, e.g. Hungary and Czechoslovakia, had accepted a UN Observer Mission. It was a hard pill to swallow for those who were obliged to witness the UN flag flying over Santo Domingo, and UN personnel in the city.

Shortly after the arrival of the UN Mission in Santo Domingo, the OAS Special Committee abruptly left the scene and reported to the Tenth Meeting of Consultation that the UN Mission had 'greatly obstructed' its peacemaking efforts. The OAS Consultation called on the Security Council to suspend its activities and to give the regional organization time to deal with the problem until all efforts were exhausted.

As soon as the UN Mission submitted its first reports to the Security Council, they were at variance with the OAS reports. Mayobre, the UN Secretary-General's representative, reported soon after his arrival that certain actions of the IAPF, including the use of force, could not be considered impartial, whereas the daily reports of the OAS indicated only peacekeeping efforts. Obviously the UN Mission and IAPF had different views on the methodology of peacekeeping and indeed on its very definition. This controversy only further exacerbated relations. On the basis of Mayobre's reports, many members questioned the impartiality of the OAS and at one time seriously considered enlarging the UN Mission and its mandate.

The competence of the UN to deal with issues in which regional organizations have already become involved is clearly stated in the Charter. According to Article 53 (1), no enforcement action shall be taken by a regional system without the authorization of the Security Council. In any event, Article 52 (3) states that it in no way impairs the application of Articles 34 and 35. Article 36 states that the Council 'may investigate any dispute', and Article 35 specifies that 'any member of the United Nations may bring any dispute . . . to the attention of the Security Council or the General Assembly.'

The Guatemalan crisis in 1954 resulted from the policies of Col. Jacobo Arbenz, which included introduction of land reforms. Consequently the US said at the OAS that Guatemala was under growing communist influence. Subsequently, when border incidents developed, Guatemala complained to the Security Council that there was disruption of peace and international security by interference from Honduras and Nicaragua. Several Latin American countries strongly opposed the Security Council's refusal to listen to Guatemala's complaint, by contrast with the actions of the OAS Consultation Meeting. They endorsed the right of UN organizations to hear and act at any time on a complaint involving matters affecting international peace and security: In the introduction to his annual report to the 9th Session of the General Assembly, Dag Hammarskjöld emphasized that the importance of regional arrangements was fully recognized, but that when resort to such arrangements was already chosen, that choice could not be permitted to cast any doubt on the ultimate responsibility of the UN.[12] Once political violence subsided and the Special Committee of five was replaced by a three-man OAS committee which included the able US Ambassador Ellsworth Bunker, relations gradually improved, leading to co-operation.

It would be perfectly in order for the Security Council to continue exercising its right to examine any threat to peace and to insist that any coercive measures receive its approval. However, in the light of its difficulties in resolving peacekeeping issues, the UN should encourage regional peacekeeping provided that the non-use of force principle is complied with. The UN and the OAS have become increasingly aware of the need to co-operate. The changing dynamics of interrelationships between Latin American states and the relationship between the United States and Latin America, are trends leading to co-operation between the international organizations. Efforts to improve this co-operation must not be allowed to lag.

A number of lessons were learned from the IAPF experience. Its Commander was given operational control over all its contingents. Members of the force remained integral to their national contingents in the same way as in the UN peacekeeping operations. A combined headquarters staff was established. Brazil provided an infantry battalion and a marine company; Honduras, Nicaragua and Paraguay each provided a rifle company; and Costa Rica, having no military, sent a platoon of Civil Guards to act as military police. The Latin Americans were placed in a brigade under General Meira Mattos, of which the total strength was about 2,000. The United States had a total of 21,500 in the field on May 22, but their naval forces were excluded from the IAPF and so 11,935 were under the IAPF by June.

Differing from the UN operations, the OAS Foreign Ministers' Consultation Meeting nominated the Commander and entrusted him with complete powers relating to operations and administration and for making financial arrangements for the force. Since neither of the two parties to the conflict was recognized by any government, a status of forces agreement could not be negotiated with them. Such an arrangement was not even made with the provisional government of the Dominican Republic when it came into office on September 3, 1965. The OAS Secretary-General had no authority over the IAPF. His role, unlike that of the UN Secretary-General, was essentially administrative, despite attempts by the United States to strengthen it.

The United States provided the bulk of logistical and financial support for the Dominican operation, but as well as US air transport support, the Brazilian and Honduran air forces also participated. The US Navy carried out all sea lifting, and US forces provided nearly all supplies and services. The cost of this operation to the United States was $38,269,185.

The initial US military intervention was intended, first to evacuate their own and other nationals, and secondly to thwart a possible 'Communist takeover' by the rebels. The first is permissible under international law but the second was in contravention of the OAS Charter. Notwithstanding this violation, the OAS legitimized the US military intervention by establishing an IAPF, to be built around the US forces already in the country. This experience has in fact caused the OAS members to shy away from planning a standby arrangement.

The IAPF had previously been a United States operation, and participation by the Latin American states was essential. It succeeded in preventing a victory by either party, and following agreement on an 'Act of Dominican Reconciliation', it helped disarm the 'Constitutionalists' and controlled movements of arms. It quelled lawlessness, prevented further *coups*, and supported the provisional government.

The OAS members have more recently considered peacekeeping needs in the region. Given the political climate and urgency, an OAS peacekeeping force could play a useful role. It would have to be truly an inter-American affair, i.e. not dominated by the United States or even by one of the larger Latin American states. It could be planned along the lines of the Nordic standby forces,* earmarked but kept under the control of their respective governments until requested by

---

* At the Sixth General Assembly of the UN in 1952, it was proposed that national standby forces should be formed and that their services could be called upon in the event of an international crisis. Subsequent to this proposal, no action was taken until it was referred to Secretary-General Dag Hammerskjöld, in his report to the Thirteenth General Assembly. Later, in a letter dated June 12, 1959, Hammerskjöld approached the nations which were participating or had participated in UNEF I with a petition that these member-states should include in their national military planning considerations for possible future UN requests for peacekeeping forces. Denmark, Finland, Norway and Sweden agreed in 1964 to establish a Nordic Standby Force for the United Nations, to be made available when requested and if accepted by the contributing countries.

the OAS. The ready availability of such a force would inhibit unilateral intervention and act as a deterrent to armed conflicts. Thus its
establishment would be of significant interest to the inter-American
community.

The UN Charter does not provide clear answers to the question of
the concurrent, overlapping and somewhat confusing responsibilities
of the UN and the regional organizations, which the Dominican crisis
forcefully highlighted. The United States was the great power in the
region with its own security concerns, and regional interests of a political ideological nature (in common with Cuba and to some degree
Nicaragua since the overthrow of the Somoza regime). OAS members
prefer dealing with their own disputes. The exact moment when
member-states, obliged to submit local conflicts to regional organizations, can feel free to appeal to the UN, and the extent to which the UN
should defer to the regional organizations as a first resort, are
questions to which clear answers have yet to be given. The problem
therefore deserves international attention.

The Organization of African Unity

General. The Organization of African Unity (OAU) was established
in May 1963 with headquarters at Addis Ababa. It is unique in its
inclination to combine Pan-Africanism with nationalism, a quest for
autonomy in solving African problems, and a drive to free the entire
continent from all traces of colonialism and racial discrimination.[13]
The basic principles of the OAU are equality among its member-
states, non-interference in fellow-members' internal affairs, respect
for the sovereignty and territorial integrity of each state, peaceful
settlement of disputes, unreserved condemnation of subversive activities, dedication to the total emancipation of dependent African territories, and non-alignment with regard to major power blocs.

Soon after becoming independent, the African states formed into
two groups. One was the Casablanca group, consisting of five West
and North African states and the 'Algerian Provisional Government'
before its independence from France; the other was the Monrovia
group consisting of twenty regional members, including twelve
francophone states which were members of the *Union Africaine et
Malagache* (UAM), known as the Brazzaville group. The first
(1960–4) Congo crisis created a sharp division among the groups.
When the OAU was established, the two groups merged, although the
Brazzaville group has retained its distinctiveness in one form or
another. The UAM transformed itself into the *Union Africaine et
Malagache de Coopération Economique* (UAMCE). However, due to
differences among OAU members over interference in states' internal
affairs, specifically in the second Congo crisis in 1965, the UAMCE
changed into a political organization, named *Organisation Commune*

Africaine, Malagache et Mauricienne (OCAM) as a group within the OAU to reinforce co-operation and solidarity among their own members.

The establishment of OCAM created a further cleavage between the OAU members already divided by the Sahara, i.e. the North African and the sub-Saharan groups. From the point of view of the latter, all the francophone states except Guinea, Mali, Burundi, Mauritania, Zaire and Congo (Brazzaville) were members of OCAM, but the others also had some ties with France. The OCAM states and some others were affiliated to the European Economic Community (EEC) under the Yaoundé Convention of Association (1963 and 1969). Not until the enlargement of the EEC to include Britain did the division between the anglophone and francophone states south of the Sahara begin to decline. In addition, the six Arab states of North Africa are members of the League of Arab States, thus exposing Africa to the full fury of the Arab-Israeli conflict. Most francophone states favoured a modest role for the OAU, whereas others have adopted attitudes ranging from modest to strong. As to the North-South division, while the Arab League members would like to see a stronger OAU involvement in the Arab-Israeli conflict, the others have preferred a symbolic support for Egypt's efforts in this conflict, even after the Camp David agreement.

Unlike the OAS, which may take all necessary measures to reestablish or maintain peace and security between two or more members, according to Article 7 of the Inter-American Treaty of Reciprocal Assistance, the OAU may only use the weight of the opinions of its members. It is a co-ordinator of African policies on regional problems but not a defence alliance, and it is an agent for African nonalignment on East-West issues.

The OAU has been involved in three types of peace and security problems: (1) disputes involving only its members; (2) situations involving members with colonial or settler regimes; and (3) situations resulting from relations between its members and states outside Africa.

As to the first type of problem, these are territorial and other disputes between member-states or disputes with ethnic, political or religious causes. Internal disputes, except when they have international overtones, are outside the sphere of the OAU or the UN. In the second category, both the OAU and the UN become involved, as for example in Namibia. On such issues there is in fact a greater reliance on the UN. The third category consists of experiences, as in the Congo in 1960–2 and Nigeria in 1967–70, when there was large-scale outside interference. Here both the OAU and the UN have striven towards excluding such interference. The arms race is another related issue. The demilitarization of Africa has been a goal of both the OAU and the UN.

Boundary disputes. The two main disputes in the 1960s were those between Algeria and Morocco and between Somalia and both Ethiopia and Kenya. The first of these two disputes is described here because peace observation machinery was established and played a significant role in resolving the conflict, which did not happen in the second case.

The French colonial regime in North Africa had only demarcated the northern sector of the boundary between Algeria and Morocco. On gaining its independence in 1956, Morocco claimed part of the Sahara now within Algeria as being part of its own territory in pre-colonial times. In 1961 the Algerian provisional government recognized the border problem and both countries agreed to deal with it after Algeria became independent. However, after independence political differences between the two countries increased, and heightened tensions led to war. Moroccan forces invaded the disputed territory on October 14, 1963. There was an attempt to resolve the problem bilaterally, but it had failed by October 18: Algeria had insisted that Morocco should withdraw its troops and recognize the borders as they had been in colonial times. An initiative by the Arab League also failed, and both parties agreed to call on the OAU to deal with the dispute. Algeria sought consideration by the OAU Council of Ministers, and Morocco informed the provisional Secretary-General of the OAU and the UN Secretary-General.

After consideration of whether the UN Security Council should be involved because of the fact that OAU members favoured the preservation of existing boundaries, and because an attempt by some North African heads of states to deal with the problem had failed, the OAU members remained determined to seek a solution within an African framework. Emperor Haile Selassie of Ethiopia, acting in his own capacity and on behalf of the Provisional Secretariat of the OAU which had been entrusted to his country, and the President of Mali concluded an agreement at Bamako, Mali, on October 29, 1963, between the King of Morocco and the President of Algeria.

The Bamako Agreement included: (1) a ceasefire from November 1, 1963; (2) establishment of a commission of Algerian, Moroccan, Ethiopian and Malian officers (the 'Bamako Commission') to determine a demilitarized zone; (3) observers from Ethiopia and Mali to supervise the ceasefire and watch over the security and the neutrality of the demilitarized zone; (4) the OAU Council of Ministers to appoint a commission to deal with all the frontier issues and make a proposal for a settlement; and (5) the two parties to stop public and press attacks on each other and interference in each other's internal affairs. This agreement was endorsed by a meeting of the OAU Council of Ministers. An *ad hoc* commission of seven states was appointed to seek a solution, and the Bamako Commission was asked to stay in being and to maintain contact with the OAU *ad hoc* commission.

On February 20, 1964, the Bamako Commission obtained an agreement from the two parties to withdraw their troops to the positions they had occupied before the start of fighting and to establish a demilitarized zone. By May 1964 the relations between the two countries had improved sufficiently for their ambassadors to form a joint committee, and it was possible for agreements to be concluded on a number of issues to normalize relations. Although the *ad hoc* commission did not succeed, it was able to help in clarifying issues and reducing differences. This modest contribution helped towards a subsequent general treaty of solidarity and co-operation concluded bilaterally between the two states and a final agreement on the boundary question in May 1970.

The role of the military officers in peace observation played a significant part in creating the conditions for this conflict to be resolved.

Situations involving OAU members with colonial and settler regimes. The differences between the OAU members over the future of non-self-governing territories have been handled more frequently at the level of the UN than by the OAU. Among the two main examples of such conflicts were the French Territory of the Afars and the Issas (which was formerly French Somaliland, now Djibouti) and the Spanish Sahara.

In the former territory, the Afars are linked with the Danakils of Ethiopia and the Issas are ethnically Somali. The two populations are of approximately equal size, and were thus claimed respectively by Ethiopia and Somalia, but Ethiopia further stressed its claim because of the importance to it of Djibouti as a port. The OAU and the UN became involved. The UN General Assembly called for a referendum and a UN presence, which finally led to the Territory's independence.

The dispute over the future of Spanish Sahara originated in 1958 when Morocco claimed the territory. The conflict was further fuelled by counterclaims from Mauritania and by the aspirations of the indigenous Sahrawi people, nomads of Moorish origin, for the territory's independence — in spite of which Spain summarily divided it in 1975, by the Treaty of Madrid, between Morocco and Mauritania. This arid desert land is rich in phosphate deposits, with a major mining facility at Bu Craa. Some 75,000 Sahrawis live in the territory and many thousands more are refugees in Algeria, Mauritania and Morocco.

The *Frente Popular para la Liberación de Saguia el Hamra y Rio de Oro* (Polisario Front) was founded in 1973 and became the military arm of the Saharan Arab Democratic Republic (SADR) after it was proclaimed on February 27, 1976, by virtue of the right to self-determination expressed in the UN and OAU Charters and reaffirmed by the Resolutions of those bodies on Western Sahara. Fighting had broken out in November 1975 after the signing of the Treaty of Madrid. Polisario, based on and supported by Algeria, started guerrilla operations to free the territory from the control of Mauritania and Morocco.

Spain had gained entry to the area after the Berlin Congress in the 1880s, although it did not completely establish its control until the 1950s.[14] When Morocco became independent from France, King Mohammed V called for a 'greater Morocco' to incorporate Spanish Sahara, Mauritania and border regions of Algeria. In 1965 the General Assembly requested Spain to take all necessary measures for the liberation of Ifni and Spanish Sahara,[14] but the conflicting claims of all the parties involved were not conducive to an easy decision on its future. A Resolution at the General Assembly session in 1966 invited 'the administering power [Spain] to determine at the earliest possible date, in conformity with the aspirations of the indigenous people of Spanish Sahara and in consultation with the governments of Mauritania and Morocco and other interested parties, the procedures for holding a referendum under the United Nations auspices with a view to enabling the indigenious population of the territory to exercise freely its right to self-determination.'[15]

In 1974 Spain entered into bilateral negotiations with Morocco and Mauritania over the holding of a referendum in Western Sahara. At the General Assembly session that year, Morocco obtained approval for the postponement of the referendum, the sending of a UN visiting mission and for an advisory opinion to be obtained from the International Court of Justice.[16] The subsequent verdict of the UN mission was that 'there was no overwhelming consensus among the Saharans within the Territory in favour of independence and opposing integration with any neighbouring country'.[17] The ICJ ruled that at the time of the Spanish colonization there were 'legalities of allegiance' between the Sultan of Morocco and some of the tribes living in Western Sahara. There existed some rights which 'constituted legal ties' between the Mauritanian entity and the territory of Western Sahara. However, 'the Court has not found legal ties of such a nature as might effect the application of Resolution 1514(XV) in the decolonization of Western Sahara and in particular of the principle of self-determination through free and genuine expression of the will of the territory.'[18]

On October 17, 1975, the day after the ICJ ruling, the Moroccan government, hailing the Court's recognition of its claims, announced a 'Green March' to show the commitment of the people of Morocco to their right to sovereignty over the territory. With Franco dying and the Spanish government in disarray, the Treaty of Madrid was concluded:

this established an interim administration until February 28, 1976, when Spain would withdraw. In fact, control of the territory passed immediately to Morocco and Mauritania, with Spain retaining 35 per cent of the phosphate and some fishing rights. The Treaty required consultations with the tribally-elected *Yema'a* (the General Assembly of Spanish Sahara), but the members fled the territory to join Polisario.[19] These developments prompted Spain to hurry its withdrawal, and the battle of the Sahara was in full swing.

The Polisario force numbers about 15,000, organized in armoured Jeep columns of 3,000–5,000 men; their Jeeps and trucks are mostly captured from the Moroccans. They also have Soviet armaments provided by Algeria and Libya, including light surface-to-air missiles. Polisario has scored some notable successes. In January 1979 it briefly occupied Tan-Tan, far inside western Morocco, by denying Moroccans control of the Djibal Zini passes. The traffic between Tan-Tan and El Aaiún has been interrupted periodically. In March 1980 Polisario forced the Moroccans to withdraw from Zag, in western Morocco. Within the Western Sahara, the Moroccans, after being forced to evacuate Mahbés at the end of 1979, have not since held any positions east of Semara. Polisario are able to move about over some three-quarters of the Western Sahara, while the Moroccans control the economic and population centres.

Since Morocco completed the building of the *berm*, a defensive wall of sand enclosing the triangle of El Aaiún, Bu Craa, Semara, Ras el Kharifra and Tan-Tan, the conduct of war has changed. The *berm* is reported to be 6–10 feet high and to have strong positions with mines and barbed wire every few miles. It has enabled roads to be reopened between Morocco and the territory. Because of the *berm*, Polisario have had to switch to fighting in the south near Mauritania.

King Hassan of Morocco is deeply involved in the Sahara war; but the terrain, the difficulties of maintaining a large force in the field, and the mobile nature of Polisario operations, make this war a difficult one for the Moroccans to win. Although King Hassan, in a suprise declaration at the OAU summit earlier in 1981, agreed to a referendum in the Sahara, the war reached a dangerous level in October of that year. In a five-day battle at Guelta Zemmour, so the Moroccans alleged, Polisario had advanced from Mauritanian territory and had used Soviet SAMs to shoot down a Moroccan transport plane and a 'Mirage' jet fighter. Morocco also complained that Polisario was using non-African advisers. The King, claiming total freedom of action, strafed Polisario troops in Mauritania.

Since its Council of Ministers meeting at Port Louis in June 1976, the OAU has been saddled with the Western Sahara issue. On that occasion the Co-ordination Committee for the Liberation of Africa affirmed the right of the Sahrawi people to self-determination and called for the withdrawal of all foreign (i.e. Moroccan) troops. Subse-

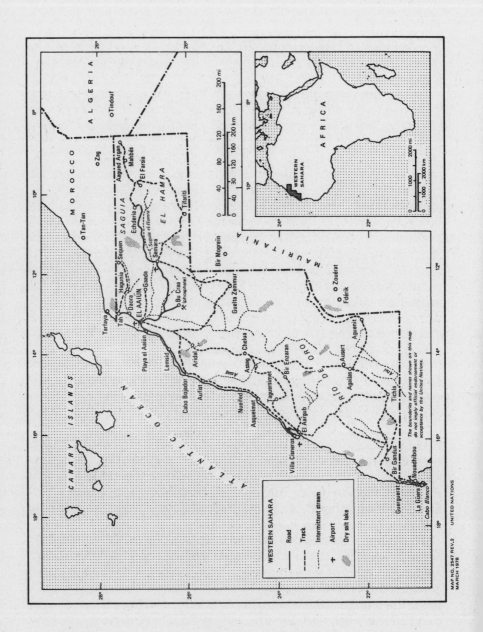

WESTERN SAHARA

	Road
	Track
	Intermittent stream
+	Airport
	Dry salt lake

The boundaries and names shown on this map do not imply official endorsement or acceptance by the United Nations.

MAP NO. 2547 REV.2   UNITED NATIONS
MARCH 1978

quently, the Assembly of Heads of States in Port Louis called for an extraordinary summit on the issue, but although this resolution was reaffirmed at the Khartoum Summit in 1978, no such summit was held. The Monrovia Summit in 1979 resulted in a consensus in support of Polisario. An *ad hoc* committee, formed in December 1979, recommended a ceasefire, the withdrawal of Moroccan administration and troops from Rio de Oro, and establishment of an OAU peacekeeping force.

At the summit meeting at Freetown in 1980, differences remained. Twenty-eight states supported SADR's application for OAU membership. Only when Morocco threatened to walk out and take another five states with it was an *ad hoc* committee set up for further consideration of this question. After a meeting on September 9–12, 1980, under the chairmanship of President Siaka Stevens of Sierra Leone, a six-point plan was adopted calling for a ceasefire by December 1980. It had little effect. Then in a surprise move King Hassan, after a lapse of many years, came to the summit meeting at Nairobi on June 26, 1981, and announced that he had decided on 'a procedure of controlled referendum' which would meet both the OAU's resolutions and Moroccan views. The heads of state, when they approved Hassan's commitment to a referendum in Resolution 103(XVIII), called for an immediate ceasefire, established an Implementation Committee to work out how the referendum was to be conducted and administered, and requested the UN to co-operate with the OAU in setting up a peacekeeping force in Western Sahara.

The SADR rejected the King's proposal, alleging that it was an attempt to legitimize Morocco's military occupation. Rabat, maintaining that a referendum would favour integration with Morocco, countered by declaring that it had no intention of giving up 'one grain of sand'. The SADR, realizing that it had to respond more constructively, now announced conditions for the implementation of the OAU resolution for a referendum. The OAU's Implementation Committee met the two parties — separately, because Morocco refused to meet Polisario face to face. The SADR expected direct negotiations, Moroccan withdrawal, an interim administration and the return of refugees. Morocco saw it differently.

The Committee decided on voter registration based on the 1974 Spanish census, the records of UNHRC and internationally-recognized rates of growth of population. The referendum would be conducted by the Committee in collaboration with the UN, and an impartial administration would be established with civil and security elements, to work with existing administrative structures. An OAU and/or UN peacekeeping force would maintain peace for this period.

At the Nairobi Conference in February 1982, the OAU agreed on a peace plan to end the six-year desert war between Morocco and Polisario. The plan included timing for a ceasefire and administration of a referendum, but the OAU rejected direct negotiations between the warring parties, a condition on which Polisario had insisted. Polisario rejected the OAU plan, which the Moroccan Foreign Minister welcomed, and this rejection without direct negotiations made any possibility of immediate peace in the Western Sahara seem doubtful. The leaders from the seven African nations which were members of a special OAU Committee on Western Sahara had directed the President of Kenya, Daniel arap Moi, to negotiate with all parties to create conditions for a ceasefire and a referendum. Because of the attitude of Polisario, President Moi was expected to consult separately with the parties. Morocco continued to maintain that Algeria was financing Polisario's guerrilla attacks, and that a solution would be to close its borders to Algeria and Mauritania to prevent the infiltration of mercenaries. Mauritania relinquished all claims to the former Spanish Sahara in 1979. The Secretary-General of Polisario, Mohammed Abdulaziz, complained that the work of the seven-nation OAU Implementation Committee had not led, as it should have done, to a peace agreement between the two warring parties — Morocco and Polisario; this was because Morocco had preserved its intransigience, while Polisario was always ready to negotiate to achieve a just and definite solution to the problem.

The Foreign Ministers, meeting in advance of the mini-summit of the OAU, had recommended that Polisario and Morocco be named for the first time as the 'warring parties', which would have constituted a victory for Polisario since it would have given them official OAU recognition, a status it had previously failed to achieve.

On a visit to Morocco in 1982, the US Secretary of State, Alexander Haig, called for a prompt settlement of the Western Sahara war so as to keep Colonel Qaddafi of Libya from meddling directly in the conflict. However, African and Western diplomats have been known to stress that as long as the United States continued to supply arms to Morocco, there would be no pressure on King Hassan to negotiate with Polisario. Morocco continues to insist on negotiating with Algeria, which backs Polisario, rather than with Polisario itself. During a visit to the United States early in 1982, the King said that Morocco would be prepared to mount a referendum giving the inhabitants of the Western Sahara a choice between integration with Morocco and independence, even without Polisario participation — but the Moroccan government maintains that a referendum is impossible unless Polisario agrees to a ceasefire.

At the annual Council of Ministers meeting to discuss the OAU budget, held at Addis Ababa early in 1982, Polisario was seated by the Secretariat, on the ground that a majority of the member-states had recognised the Saharan Arab Democratic Republic. This decision was opposed by a number of member-states and by the Chairman, President arap Moi of Kenya, who held that the decision to seat Polisario undermined efforts to resolve the armed conflict. Morocco and eighteen other member-states walked out of the budget meeting in protest. Since then further efforts have been made to resolve the conflict, but without success so far.

Lt.-Col. Mengistu Haile Mariam, the OAU chairman for 1983, had called a meeting of the summit bureau, the Organization's executive arm in Addis Ababa, on July 15 and 16, 1982. Already King Hassan had declared in a speech marking his birthday that Polisario should understand that, even in the unlikely event of the referendum going in its favour, he did not intend to offer the Western Sahara to it 'on a plate'. An OAU delegation (Chad implementation committee) was in Rabat. This became the occasion for Polisario to launch its first attack in a year by 1,000 guerrillas against Moroccan positions at Maghdar Soltani, M'Sied and other points along King Hassan's defensive line. A Polisario communiqué declared that its action was in self-defence. Polisario also maintained that a meeting of the implementation committee was premature, as direct talks should take place first.

Mohammed Abdulaziz, the head of SADR, told the Pan-African News Agency in Addis Ababa (issue of October 3, 1983) that Morocco had so far refused to implement the Resolution adopted by the OAU 19th Summit that direct negotiations were a pre-condition to the organization of a referendum. He said that there should be a negotiated ceasefire to define the modalities for organizing the referendum and to determine the population of Western Sahara, for which we have our own statistics.

Chad. While a number of serious situations had occurred — e.g. friction between Rwanda and Burundi, the Congo (Zaire) civil war and the attendant mercenary problem (1964–8), and the Nigerian civil war (1967–70) — peace observation or peacekeeping played no role. Only in the Nigerian civil war was there an invitation to the UN, the OAU and the governments of Canada, Poland, Sweden and the United Kingdom from the Federal military government of Nigeria to observe the conduct of its troops' operations against the Biafran rebels. The military observers reported that there was no basis for the Biafran charges of genocide against their people by Federal troops.

In spite of many difficulties, the OAU has maintained the principle of 'try OAU first', in the search for peaceful solutions, which the UN has consistently supported. More recently, the situation in Chad had demanded OAU and UN attention and here too the OAU role has remained pre-eminent.

The first OAU peacekeeping force in Chad was established, following the 'Lagos Accords' of August 1979, and took up its positions in December 1981. Composed of troops from the Congo, Benin and Guinea, it replaced the Libyans, who had previously assisted the government in its efforts to cope with the breakdown of law and order, and whose withdrawal was requested by GUNT (the Traditional Government of National Unity).

Chad became independent from France in 1960, although French military administration of the Borkou-Ennedi-Tibesti (BET) region in the north continued till 1965. Since then, Chadian factions, with foreign assistance, have resorted to fighting, making the functioning of a central government impossible. Within the country are at least twenty different tribes with as many languages. The sub-tropical south is dominated by the sedentary Sara peoples who form the largest single group. These are mostly Christians, and Western in outlook, and they have dominated central government affairs. The central section is populated by the Sahelian people who are nomadic or semi-nomadic and depend on livestock and part-time agriculture; they are Arabized Muslims who maintain links with the neighbouring countries Sudan, Niger and Nigeria. In the BET prefecture, which consists of rocky desert, live the Toubou, some of whose sub-groups, like the Teda in the far north, have little interaction beyond their own groups, while the Daza have established relations with semi-secondary farmers of the Sahel.

Chadian independence was gained under the leadership of François Tombalbaye of the *Parti Progressiste Tchadien* (PPT) in alliance with the *Union pour le Progrès du Tchad* (UPT), a grouping of Muslim parties. But the struggle for power in the new state prevented the establishment of an effective central government; in this the north and central regions suffered especially. The army suffered from administrative inefficiency and corruption. Attempts at national reconciliation and an end to civil rebellion failed; although some guerrilla groups rallied to the government, Frolinat, the most important of these groups, rejected the plea. In 1968 the French military were invited to return to help restore order and attempts were made to improve administration.

The government of General Felix Malloum (President, 1975–9), did not fare any better than that of Tombalbaye, and when the French withdrew their troops in 1975, Chad faced inevitable breakdown. In February 1978, anti-Libyan leaders from the north, together with their guerrilla army, joined the Malloum government. By August that year their leader Hissène Habré had become Prime Minister and in February 1979 he turned against Malloum. Fighting broke out in N'Djamena, the Chadian capital, causing extensive damage and putting an end to central government. Habré followed Malloum to the south, which brought him face to face with Colonel Wadal Kamougué, the commander of the *Forces Armées Tchadiennes* (FAT), a Sara military unit in the south of the country. The Sara fled south, and many Muslims were massacred in the southern towns in the process.

A Nigerian initiative led to two meetings at Kano of a number of

Chadian leaders. Habré and Goukouni Oueddei, leader of the *Forces Armées Populaires* (FAP) of north-west Chad, agreed to a cessation of hostilities and the formation of a new government. Kamougué reluctantly agreed to participate in the new government, and Malloum agreed to relinquish his position and retire. However, the terms of the agreement were not respected and there were infractions of the peace, which led to renewed efforts to deal with unresolved issues. The meeting of OAU heads of state at Monrovia in 1979 assumed that Nigeria had taken upon itself a peacemaking responsibility, and in a conference at Lagos in August that year, all the factions were persuaded to join in a coalition government under Goukouni. However, the OAU had realized that a neutral military force would be needed to separate the warring factions. An earlier attempt by Nigeria to use its troops unilaterally in N'Djamena had been unsuccessful because of Chad's insistence on its sovereignty. Thus any further peacekeeping had to be under the OAU umbrella. However, offers for troops were not matched by offers of funds — and the African insistence on African questions being handled by Africans precluded any outside assistance. Realizing its resource constraints, the OAU sought UN support in providing financing and logistics for the force.

The UN had two major reservations. First, its Congo experience caused considerable hesitation over becoming involved in an internal situation; and secondly, certain procedures would have to be followed if there were to be a UN-supported operation. Meanwhile, France and the United States offered bilateral assistance to the OAU, which the OAU hesitated to accept.

Late in 1979, four pro-Libyan groups joined forces against Habré. Perceiving a threat to his supply lines from Abéché to N'Djamena through the Biltine, Habré on January 12, 1980, attacked the pro-Libyan forces in Ouaddai and captured Am Dam. Soon afterwards, exchanges of gunfire were heard in N'Djamena. By March, the two rival groups were engulfed in bitter fighting, with each struggling for positions in the capital.

Early in 1980, a succession of ceasefires were negotiated by the French Ambassador in N'Djamena and President Eyadema of Togo, the last of which took effect on April 6 but lasted only three days. After this failure, conciliatory efforts were abandoned. Kamougué's forces joined the anti-Habré forces but never got past the outskirts of N'Djamena. On April 25, Goukouni dismissed Habré from the coalition government.

Early in May, Libya sent 2,000 troops of Chadian descent to support Goukouni as fighting spread to other cities in central Chad. On June 15, 1980, the Secretary-General of Frolinat, Ibrahim Youssouf, signed on behalf of the Chadian government a co-operation agreement with Libya which included a defence treaty. Although Youssouf was not a regular member of the government,

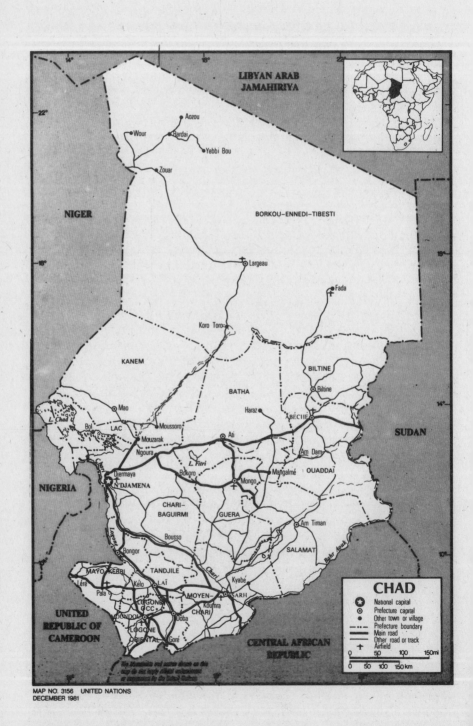

the agreement was ratified by Libya towards the end of 1980 and deposited with the UN. At the beginning of November, the Libyans intervened directly in support of the government forces under cover of the collective defence clause of the treaty. They despatched 3,000 heavily-armed troops, who routed Habré's forces and drove them out of N'Djamena. Habré signed the ceasefire agreement, which he had previously refused to sign, on December 16.

On December 23, 1980, President Shagari of Nigeria called a meeting of the OAU Standing Committee on Chad to discuss recent developments — specifically the extent of Libyan involvement and the failure of the latest ceasefire to take effect. Presidents Stevens of Sierra Leone and Shagari of Nigeria refused to condemn the Libyan role explicitly, as the other members demanded.

Then on January 6, 1981, a press conference was held in Tripoli to announce an agreement on working to achieve the 'full unity' of Chad and Libya. This drew furious condemnation from the international community, although this was something of a misinterpretation: outside observers paid little attention to the first clause of the agreement, which affirmed 'the continuation of [Libyan] support for the fraternal republic of Chad in order to ensure the freedom and independence of its people and to eliminate the remnants of the agents of reaction which co-operated with colonialism inside and outside the country'. More disturbing was the ambivalent reaction of the major power-brokers in the equation, with Qaddafi insinuating that he had a 'gentleman's agreement' with France over his intervention.

At a special OAU meeting on Chad in Lomé on January 14, twelve African states — Togo, Ivory Coast, Benin, Nigeria, Niger, Sierra Leone, Guinea, the Central African Republic, Senegal, Congo, Ghana and Cameroon — condemned the recent Libyan actions and rejected the so-called 'proposed merger'. The Libyan Foreign Minister walked out of the meeting, objecting only to the part of the condemnation requesting the withdrawal of Libyan troops, which he felt should be Goukouni's prerogative. At the end of January 1981, the French strengthened their military presence in Bouar and Bangui in the Central African Republic, stressing at the same time that they had no intention of intervening in Chad.

As the issue of the 'proposed merger' heated up, numerous members of the coalition government expressed reservation. The Vice-President, Kamougué, who preferred to remain outside the capital, was quoted as saying that 'no marriage was possible' and that it would be difficult for 'negro-Africa' to tolerate political rule by 'Arabo-Berbers'. Towards the middle of January, Qaddafi was reported to have said that when he wanted to withdraw his troops at the end of the rebellion, Goukouni prevailed on him to keep them in Chad; he also said of the merger that it was 'neither a political union nor a fusion' but a 'union of the masses' which would only take place if sanctioned through a general referendum. It had become evident by March 1981 that Egypt would support Habré in his efforts to regroup and resume guerrilla attacks on Goukouni's government and against Libyan forces in Chad.

On April 13, 1981, the Presidents of Chad, Nigeria, and Algeria conferred in Lagos after a six-nation summit due to be held there had been cancelled on Qaddafi's refusal to attend because he felt it to have no useful purpose. Late in April, Nigeria was beginning publicly to express its belief that most of the furore aroused by the Libyan role in Chad had been exaggerated and that Libya constituted no real or diplomatic threat in the African continent.

Meanwhile, relations among the pro-Libyan factions were not going smoothly and some clashes were reported; pro-Libyan and pro-French groups too were polarizing and a new struggle was brewing. Fighting broke out too between the pro-Libyan groups CDR and FPL.

In May, President Stevens on a visit to Libya acknowledged that Libya's efforts were 'not contrary to those exerted by the OAU for the establishment of peace in Chad'. On May 22, 1981, a mini-summit was held in N'Djamena attended by Presidents Stevens, Shagari and Goukouni and Colonel Qaddafi. It was reported that the meeting stalled because Nigeria and Sierra Leone could not agree on how a Libyan withdrawal should be arranged. The OAU meeting of heads of state in Nairobi in June considered the Chad question and agreed to accept Chad's choice of troop-contributing countries that would bear most of the costs themselves. UN assistance was also to be sought.

On a visit to the UN in mid-October, Ahmat Acyl, the Chadian Foreign Minister, appealed to the United States not to encourage the exploitation of the Libyan presence in Chad. He stressed that GUNT forces were 'victims of aggression on the part of Sudan when Chadian dissidents supported by regular Sudanese troops infiltrated Chadian territory'. Late in October, at the Cancun conference on world development, the French expressed concern over Libya putting pressure on Goukouni and attempting to consolidate its control over the country's affairs, and offered to help offset the cost of despatching an OAU peacekeeping force. On his return from Cancun, President Shagari of Nigeria indicated that his country was prepared to send troops to Chad if invited by the OAU. The OAU agreed to raise a peacekeeping force of about 5,000 men from Nigeria, Guinea, Benin, Togo, Senegal and Zaire. Goukouni indicated at the outset that he expected the OAU troops to enforce peace, but raised the question of whether the force would fight to establish the central government's control; the OAU answered that its troops were for a peacekeeping role and not to fight.

By December an advance element of 400 Nigerians had joined 600 troops from Senegal and 700 from Zaire, who had arrived in November. Each contingent was to be deployed in a specified area, e.g. the Nigerians in the east, based on Abéché; Zairean troops in the north, based on Largeau; and the Senegalese in the central zone with their base at Mongo. France assisted the Sengalese and Zairean troops, while Britain and the United States assisted the Nigerian contingent. The United States also aided the Zaireans. Each of the troop-contributing countries had accepted responsibility for their own direct costs. Negotiations were begun for UN assistance, and bilateral assistance to troop-contributing countries from friendly Western powers. An administrative committee, headed by the OAU Secretary-General's representative in Chad, Egziabher Dawit (Ethiopia), and including representatives from Benin, Congo, Guinea and Kenya, was made responsible for the operations in Chad. Observer states included Kenya, Gabon, Guinea-Bissau, Zambia and Algeria.

But meanwhile, the delay in the arrival and deployment of the OAU from after the withdrawal of Libyan forces provided the opportunity for Hissène Habré, the former Defence Minister, with some 4,000 armed men, to defeat the disorganized government troops and capture Oum Hadjer and Oum Madjeun, east of Ati. Habré had received military assistance from Egypt and the Sudan as long as the Libyans had been present in Chad, but after the Libyans' withdrawal Goukouni obtained the support of the Sudanese President. However, he had yet to reach agreement with Habré.

The OAU Nigerian forces were deployed at Ati to head off an attempt by Habré to move further south-west from Abéché along the road to N'Djamena. The Zairean contingent, which had been ear-marked for the strategic northern settlement of Largeau, was also sent to Ati, thus leaving Largeau defended by a weak Chadian force. Habré took advantage of the situation and seized Largeau in January 1982, thereby further complicating the task of the OAU force and making an agreement with Goukouni even more difficult.

By the beginning of 1982, the strength of the OAU peacekeeping force under its Nigerian commander, Maj.-Gen. Geoffrey Ejiga, had reached about 3,500. However, some 3,000 more were needed — the promised troops from Benin, Guinea and Togo and more from Nigeria — for the force to reach its minimal required capability. In February 1982 the OAU held a mini-summit at N'Djamena on the future of its peacekeeping operation. The current situation in Chad was that some 4,000 troops under Habré were in control of most of northern and eastern Chad; this had come about in the ten weeks since Libya had withdrawn its troops supporting President Goukouni. The Chadian President resented the non-combative role of the OAU force; he feared that he was losing ground to his rival, and had been pressing the OAU troops to take more determined action to enforce peace, i.e. by dealing with Habré in northern and eastern Chad. This continued to be rejected by the OAU. The mini-summit decided on a five-point plan for implementation of the ceasefire, the holding of a constitutional convention to form a new government, and the holding of free elections.

In order to implement these decisions, the main points were (1) a ceasefire to take place at midnight on February 28; (2) peace talks to be held from March 15 under OAU guidance in a neutral African country between the Chad government and all parties concerned, to achieve national reconciliation; (3) to prepare during April a provisional constitution, to be adopted by all the parties; (4) between March and April 30 to prepare nationwide elections in Chad to be held under OAU supervision; and (5) the OAU peacekeeping force in Chad to be withdrawn by June 30. By setting these dates for the end of hostilities in Chad, the OAU gave itself the chance to be rid of its huge financial burden in maintaining the peace force. The estimated cost of the operation so far exceeded US$162m., whereas nothing at all had been collected from OAU member-states. President arap Moi appealed to the fifty-member OAU to donate to the cause, and appealed to the UN also to help finance the operation.

Goukouni left the mini-conference and flew home to N'Djamena, rejecting the OAU offer. He said: 'We shall find a solution to the Chad problem here among ourselves and with the help of friendly countries and brothers.' He accused a number of African heads of state present in Nairobi of allowing themselves to be 'manipulated by imperialism', adding: 'We are not a protectorate of the OAU.' President Sekou Touré of Guinea said to this that Goukouni could not ignore decisions adopted by the OAU calling for a truce and a peace accord; he recalled that it was under OAU auspices that agreement had been reached, following the 1979 Lagos Accords, to set up the Chad provisional government with Goukouni as President, and this had received the consensus of the country's eleven armed political factions (including Habré's FAN) which made up the government. If Goukouni now chose to ignore the OAU's Committee on Chad, the OAU could not consider Goukouni as anything more than the leader of one of the factions.

The OAU thus faced enormous problems in Chad, and whether or not it was going to see the implementation of its plan depended on what financial assistance would be offered by the international community, and the extent to which it could persuade the various Chadian groups to resolve their acute differences.

Late in April, it became uncertain whether Nigeria, faced with economic cutbacks at home, could afford the financial burden of keeping its troops in Chad any longer. The OAU and President Goukouni then made a formal request for financial assistance to the UN Security Council. After informal consultations, the Security Council met on April 30, and a Resolution (S/RES/504) was passed creating a Voluntary Fund to be put at the disposal of the OAU force under coordinate management between both organizations. This

Resolution improved the chances that the pan-African peacekeeping force in Chad could continue to function. The problem on the ground, however, was that GUNT's unity was cracking at the seams.

In May the troop-contributing countries met in Lagos and set two conditions for their continued presence. First, a ceasefire had to be agreed to by June 10, and secondly reconciliation talks had to begin immediately after that. If these conditions were not met, the OAU force would pull out by June 30. It was also stated that $36,000,000 was needed from the UN to guarantee their stay. However the UN Voluntary Fund had not received the much-needed contributions by the beginning of June. As OAU troops grew weary and frustrated, Nigeria had begun to withdraw her troops, which were now down to two battalions.

Positions on the ground were suddenly altered drastically as Habré's forces (FAN) captured N'Djamena on June 7, 1982. Goukouni was forced to seek political refuge outside the country. The need for a political solution involving all the factions was now still more important; the OAU did not believe that Habré's military victory offered a long-term solution. Meanwhile, the OAU Chairman ordered the organization's peacekeeping force to withdraw from Chad, and Habré requested that its mandate be prolonged. Most observers felt that its presence would make a quick reconciliation easier. However, the OAU reaffirmed its belief that a solution would only be possible if the factions were willing to arrive at one. The OAU force in fact left Chad at the end of June, except for the troops from Zaire, whose basis for remaining was not clear.

Early in 1983 there were reports that forces opposed to Habré had made military gains in the north. The former GUNT leader Goukouni had set up his government in exile in Bardaim, his loyalist Toubou county in the Tibesti mountains, in October 1982. Col. Kamougué, the southern leader who too opposed Habré, had joined Goukouni. Since the abortive OAU summit at Tripoli in November 1982 on the Chad issue, Libya's support for the Goukouni-Kamougué alliance was important.

As the fighting intensified between government troops and rebels, the OAU splintered again, dividing the so-called moderates from the radicals. Habré called for assistance from King Hassan of Morocco, but this appeared unlikely to be forthcoming. Zaire immediately dispatched 250 troops and three fighter aircraft to N'Djamena, an action that was strongly criticised by Lt.-Col. Mengistu. In April Habré complained to the UN Security Council of Libyan illegal occupation of the Azou strip. However, it was generally thought that Habré was looking for a way of obtaining recognition by the international community. The Council instead called on Libya and Chad on April 6 to settle their dispute through the OAU.

By June heavy fighting broken out again in northern Chad, and

Goukouni's ANIL had overrun Largeau and occupied Abéché. Since mid-July, government troops led by Habré recaptured Abéché and had retaken Beltrini, Fada and Oum Chilouba between Abéché and Largeau. This had been made possible by French military assistance, including 1,000 soldiers, twenty Jaguar aircraft, and technical advisers. Zaire had already reinforced their troops in N'Djamena to 700 paratroopers so that Habré could leave his capital safely. By the end of July US military aid, worth a total of $10 million, had also started to arrive. Egypt stepped up its military aid to Chad as well. Egypt and Sudan, bound by close ties to Habré's government, threatened to take what they called appropriate measures if the alleged presence of Libyans continued. Col. Qaddafi is known to desire a pro-Libyan regime in Chad and a formal annexation of the northern border area, which he occupied some time ago.

The politics of Chad present some hard choices for the west and especially the French. In the 1970s Habré led the revolt in the north against a French-backed regime in N'Djamena, kidnapped a French ethnologist and killed a French major sent to negotiate her release. But since he gained control of the capital, the French have backed him. However, he lacks the support of the south. The francophone African leaders had urged France to support Habré as they opposed Qaddafi's expansionist policy. Victory for a pro-Qaddafi leader in Chad would provide Qaddafi with a strategic base to spread ill winds in any direction, and in particular with opportunities to join the rebels in the southern Sudan and then link with Soviet-backed Ethiopia.

The United States view the war from their own global perspective. In August 1983, they sent the aircraft-carrier *Eisenhower* to the Gulf of Sidon, a presence that would place Libya on guard and thereby prevent its air support of Goukouni's forces fighting in northern Chad; also, AWACS were sent to Egypt for exercises with the Egyptian forces. These aircraft could be used to monitor any Libyan air activity over Chad. With military aid and advisers, the United States was committed to support Habré.

On August 12, the Security Council met on Libya's complaint against joint US-Egyptian exercises as well as similar ones in the Sudan, Somalia and Oman. The United States in turn charged that Libya was attempting to cover its aggression against Chad by means of a smokescreen of countercharges.

By the last week of August, the French troops had formed a front-line in the Chadian towns of Salal Arada, Biltine and Abéché, which Libya could only attack at the risk of becoming embroiled in direct combat with France. The French had also placed Jaguar and Mirage F-1 aircraft in the capital, thereby signalling their determination to stop Libya from moving further south.

The control of the north by the Libyan-backed Goukouni and the control of the south by the French-backed Habré indicates a *de facto* division of Chad. This situation is unacceptable to the French and to the West as a whole, as it is to Egypt and Sudan. Efforts are being made to persuade Habré and Goukouni to negotiate with each other, but Goukouni insists that Habré must step down first.

The OAU Chairman for 1983, Lt.-Col. Mengistu Haile Mariam of Ethiopia, was persistent in his efforts to end the war and to seek reconciliation. By the end of November, an OAU delegation had completed meetings with leaders in Paris, N'Djamena and Tripoli in an effort to end the Chadian conflict. Habré's government announced on November 25 that a reconciliation meeting among all factions in the civil war would soon take place in Ethiopia.

Despite setbacks to past attempts to establish a peacekeeping operation in Chad, anoher attempt by the OAU to establish one cannot be ruled out. A French force in N'Djamena and the southern part of Chad will be unacceptable to the so-called radical governments, including Ethiopia — just as Libyan troops will be unacceptable to the West. The OAU flag offers the best hope of maintaining peace after a negotiated settlement in Chad.

On December 10, according to Radio France International (reported by the *New York Times* on December 11), the Foreign Minister of Ethiopia, Goshu Walde, announced that Lt.-Col. Mengistu had postponed the talks between President Habré and former President Goukouni Oueddei originally set for December 21 to January 9, 1984. Much will depend on the outcome of these talks, which may well lead to a new OAU peacekeeping operation in support of a political agreement.

The Commonwealth

General. The Commonwealth was established on December 31, 1931, to give expression to a continuing sense of affinity and to foster cooperation among states then or previously owing allegiance to the British Crown. The original members were the United Kingdom, Australia, New Zealand, Canada, Newfoundland, the Irish Free State and the Union of South Africa. In due course Newfoundland became part of Canada, and Ireland and South Africa became republics outside the Commonwealth. However, the number of member-states expanded greatly as the Indian empire and the Colonies gained their independence. Only South Africa and Pakistan have quit membership; Pakistan now participates in meetings without being a full member.

The Commonwealth is a flexible organization and relies for its decisions on consensus. India set the pace after becoming a republic in 1949, by agreeing to accept the Crown as a symbol of the Commonwealth association and the British sovereign as the Commonwealth's head. Biennial meetings of the heads of state provide opportunities for discussion of important policy issues. Periodic meetings at ministerial level are held to deal with such issues as foreign affairs, defence and finance.

The Nigerian civil war. The civil war in Nigeria which started in 1967 presented the Commonwealth Secretariat with its first major challenge. The UN found it difficult to play an active role in an internal conflict, and furthermore its record in the Congo, where the prime minister of the young nation who had invited international intervention became the first victim, did not inspire confidence among African leaders in the world body's good offices. The OAU set up a consultative committee of six heads of state under the chairmanship of the Emperor of Ethiopia, but this could do little more than provide its good offices to the two opposing leaders.

In contrast, the Commonwealth Secretariat enjoyed considerable flexibility. Arnold Smith, the outstanding Canadian diplomat who was Secretary-General of the Commonwealth, had a simple approach. He brought the Nigerian and the Biafran leaders, or their deputies, together to talk to each other: 'This involved a series of secret meetings in my London office or apartment, scores of telephone calls, visits to Enugu and Lagos by Secretariat staff and talks in other African capitals in the course of other Commonwealth events. It led us on from merely trying to effect meetings between the adversaries to proposing substantial parts of a political settlement and working out plans for a Commonwealth peacekeeping force.'[20]

The Commonwealth Secretary-General worked assiduously in setting up secret meetings with the two sides. At one such meeting, held at London Airport, the plan for a ceasefire and a Commonwealth peacekeeping force was first discussed with the representative of the Biafran leader, Colonel Ojukwu. The idea was that armed Commonwealth troops would move in after agreement on ceasefire conditions and act as military observers in the disputed and occupied areas of the former Eastern Region to ensure both that Ibos were not attacked and that Biafran forces did not use a ceasefire to build up their military strength. But other, often diluted versions were produced later.[21] Smith consulted the Canadian, British, Ghanaian and Indian governments, which expressed their willingness to contribute troops to such a peace force. Biafran representatives indicated their support; however, Lagos questioned the need or the usefulness of a Commonwealth presence. Some senior Nigerian officers simply wished to see the Biafrans disarmed and the Nigerian police made responsible for internal security.

It was during the visit to London of the Biafran Chief Justice, Louis Mbanefo, that Arnold Smith made his opening move to bring the two sides together round a table.[22] His high degree of acceptability and the prestige of his office had provided him with direct channels of communication with the Nigerian and Biafran leaders. There was no clear mandate, and therefore Smith made his own initiatives and acted largely in his own personal capacity.[23] The OAU meeting in Lagos on November 23, 1967, further helped his quiet diplomacy.

General Gowon, the Federal Nigerian leader, had succeeded in halting the Biafrans' military successes of mid-1967 and by the end of the year had turned the tide to the Federal army's advantage. When Ojukwu indicated his willingness to negotiate, Arnold Smith contacted Nigeria to explore the possibility of starting direct negotiations between the two parties. Gowon reiterated his desire for a negotiated settlement, but insisted on the acceptance of a twelve-state structure for the nation. Smith tried to persuade the Nigerians to be flexible on this question, since the Biafrans had not participated in the decision to divide the four regions into twelve states; however, Gowon remained firm. Smith did obtain Nigerian acknowledgement of the need of the Ibos for economic security and for the security of their lives and property in the federated state.

In his attempt to reconcile differences between the two sides, Smith tried to find a face-saving formula which would lead to the Biafrans renouncing secession without having to say so. However, the Federal government did not allow much leeway, except to say that the rebels could call what was to be known as the East Central State within the twelve-state formula by any name of its choosing, provided it was not 'Biafra'. Smith concluded that while the Biafrans showed some flexibility, the Federal side did not.

By April 1968, there were indications that it might be possible to resume serious negotiations. Ojukwu expressed willingness to meet the other side without pre-conditions. But the Nigerians, while expressing their willingness to enter into talks with the rebels, announced their negotiating position, namely that (1) Nigeria should remain one sovereign state with a twelve-state structure; (2) equal opportunity for the Ibos should be guaranteed; (3) there should be acceptable arrangements for internal security within the mainly Ibo state; (4) displaced persons should be rehabilitated, and (5) there should be a constituent assembly to frame a new federal constitution. Ojukwu rejected Nigeria's basic points, but called for immediate talks between the two sides. This led to a meeting at Kampala on May 23–31, 1968.

In spite of flexibility and willingness to reach an agreement, the Kampala talks failed. Arnold Smith played a key role in the talks and attempted to advance negotiations on the basis of a looser federal government for Nigeria. Gowon stood firm on Nigeria's basic points, and Ojukwu made further negotiations impossible by declaring that the Nigerians were negotiating in bad faith and were in fact seeking a military solution.

At the Kampala talks, three different plans were discussed. Biafra suggested an immediate ceasefire and removal of the economic blockade, and removal of troops behind pre-war boundaries. The Lagos representatives suggested a twelve-point plan, which allowed for the orderly withdrawal and disarming of Ibos, while giving them an important role in policing and administering their areas. The third plan, a compromise, was worked out by Smith in meetings with the representatives of the parties: it involved an immediate ceasefire, followed by the establishment of a Commonwealth observer force that could police any no-man's land, relief arrangements including a partial lifting of the blockade, and a constitutional conference.

The failure of the Kampala talks brought the prominent role of the Commonwealth and its Secretary-General to an end. Unexpectedly, within six weeks of the collapse of this effort, the two sides agreed to resume negotiations at the invitation of Emperor Haile Selassie. However, it was not until the final stages of the Rhodesian decolonization process that the Commonwealth had a further opportunity to play an important peacekeeping role, though it was one which was supportive of British diplomacy.

Rhodesia/Zimbabwe. During the colonization of Africa, the British, with the help of Cecil Rhodes, secured large settlement and mining rights on the fertile plateau of the Zambezi river. The immigrants in Southern Rhodesia gained self-government in 1923, although the British government retained some powers including those relating to the rights of the Africans.

The hardships of the Second World War encouraged British and other European immigration, and the white population of Southern Rhodesia grew rapidly. Meanwhile, Africa could not remain aloof from the move towards independence from European rule which had started in Asia. As a preliminary step, Britain in 1953 created the Federation of Northern Rhodesia (Zambia), Southern Rhodesia and Nyasaland (Malawi). By the mid-1960s Zambia and Malawi had both gained their independence, having brought about the break-up of the Federation in 1963. Southern Rhodesia now became known as Rhodesia, and in November 1965 Ian Smith, the Prime Minister elected by the white minority, made a unilateral declaration of independence (UDI) from Britain. However, the British insisted that there could be no legal independence without majority rule and joined a UN-imposed embargo and sanctions against Rhodesia. It was not long before the country's black nationalist leaders resorted to guerrilla warfare with the help of African states from bases in Mozambique and Zambia.

A series of meetings between Harold Wilson, the British Prime Minister at the time of the UDI, and Ian Smith to find a solution proved unsuccessful. Smith made the final break with Britain in 1970 by declaring Rhodesia a republic. However, the liberation war being waged by black guerrilla groups was stepped up, and with the passage of time the issue became of ever more pressing concern to the African states within the OAU and at the UN, and the guerrillas enjoyed increasing support outside Africa, not least in Europe.

A British-sponsored conference in Geneva late in 1976 to discuss Dr Henry Kissinger's proposals for independence in two years failed, as did an attempt to revive this conference. The pace of the guerrilla war intensified, resulting in new efforts to deal with the crisis. In January 1978 the British Foreign Secretary Dr David Owen and the American UN representative Andrew Young met the two Patriotic Front guerrilla leaders, Robert Mugabe of the Zimbabwe African National Union (ZANU) and Joshua Nkomo of the Zimbabwe African People's Union (ZAPU). Fearing an eventual guerrilla victory at the polls, Ian Smith and the three major internal black leaders — Bishop Abel Muzorewa of the United African National Council, Ndabaningi Sithole of ZANU, and Jeremiah Chirau of the Zimbabwe National Front — signed the Salisbury Agreement which promised a new constitution giving major positions to the blacks but with control remaining in white hands. Following a general election, Muzorewa was elected Prime Minister on May 29 with the strings of power retained by Smith. This only escalated the liberation war.

When the Commonwealth heads of government met at Lusaka on August 1–7, 1979, the Rhodesian question was their major concern. They reaffirmed their commitment to majority rule in Rhodesia (Zimbabwe) and therefore rejected the internal solution. They accepted that the British government was constitutionally responsible for the granting of independence and welcomed the British offer to call a constitutional conference to advance independence. This conference would be concerned with the implementation of the Lusaka plan, which included (1) adoption of a democratic constitution with built-in safeguards for the minorities, (2) arrangements for holding a free and fair election under British supervision and Commonwealth observers, and (3) the arrangement of a ceasefire and lifting of sanctions before the elections.

The constitutional conference was held at Lancaster House, London, under the chairmanship of the British Foreign Secretary, Lord Carrington, between September 10 and December 15. The first stage dealt with constitutional issues, the second with the transitional period, and the last with the implementation of the ceasefire. The ceasefire arrangements included (1) quick implementation by providing facilities to both sides to inform their troops; (2) cessation of all military movement, with troops confining their operations to self-defence; (3) no cross-border activity by either side; (4) commanders of both sides to receive their orders from the British Governor Lord Soames and to establish a joint ceasefire commission; and (5) a ceasefire monitoring group to which some Commonwealth countries would contribute.

The ceasefire was signed on December 21, 1979, and provided that at midnight all hostilities would end. The assumption of colonial power by the British sovereign, the ceasefire and the elections were all accomplished with speed. The advance elements of the monitoring force under Maj.-Gen. John Acland had already arrived, and the operation was set in motion within the agreed deadline. The functions of the force were (1) to maintain contact with the command structures of the Rhodesian forces and Patriotic Front forces throughout Zimbabwe, (2) to monitor and observe the maintenance of the cease-fire by the respective forces; and (3) to monitor agreed border-crossing points and the use made of them in accordance with such arrangements as might be agreed in the context of the ceasefire.

The monitoring force had no coercive powers and would not be called upon to enforce the ceasefire. There was a considerable debate over its size. At one time the British had suggested the use of a number of British policemen, while the Patriotic Front had called for a UN force of about 10,000. In the end, the British view prevailed. The Rhodesian police would maintain law and order under Lord Soames, while the monitoring force would keep a watch on the Rhodesian forces on the one side and the liberation armies on the other. It was in fact surprising that the British agreed to the use of the term 'force'; a more accurate term would have been 'observer group'. Initially set at 1,300, the group was increased to 1,548 officers and men. Around a basically British core were 150 Australians, seventy-four New Zealanders, fifty Kenyans and twenty-four Fijians to give it a Commonwealth covering. The command and control lay with the British, who were also responsible for much of the logistics.

The force headquarters was established at Salisbury. The Commander, the Chief of Staff and a small staff were at Government House to be near the Governor and his staff. They were responsible for (1) advising the Governor on military matters, (2) liaison with the Patriotic Front forces, and (3) conduct of the ceasefire commission. The main headquarters, under the Deputy Commander, was just out-side Salisbury for the conduct of all aspects of the force, and the logistics headquarters was at Salisbury airport.

The monitoring force was divided into teams of different sizes according to their tasks. These teams were deployed at the Rhodesian force Commanders' headquarters and at company bases, with the Patriotic Front forces at their assembly points (APs) and during the assembly phase at their rendez-vous (RV) points, with the Rhodesian Air Force at Salisbury and Bulawayo air bases and points on the borders with neighbouring states, and liaison teams in Mozambique and Zambia. Although it was alleged that some 4,000–6,000 guerrillas remained in secure areas outside the camps to maintain political and military control in areas dominated by the Patriotic Front, some 21,000 reported to the APs, many more than had been estimated.

The responsibility for discussing breaches and violations of the ceasefire was vested in the Joint Ceasefire Commission, which was to ensure compliance with the security arrangements, investigate threats to, or breaches of, the ceasefire, and carry out any other tasks related to the maintenance of the ceasefire that the Governor might assign to them. However, the Commission could not give direction to the forces of either side.

Incidents ranged from basic individual disciplinary problems like stealing to death-threats against voters. With such incidents occurring frequently, Lord Soames ordered the Rhodesian Security Forces (RSF) to maintain law and order. The Ceasefire Commission found evidence that most incidents were caused by the Patriotic Front fighters. At one time consideration was given to the use of Rhodesian Auxilliaries to assist the RSF, but the idea was dropped when Kenya threatened to withdraw its contingent.

In order to deal with widespread violence, Joshua Nkomo called for an increase in the Commonwealth monitoring force; this was endorsed by Commonwealth Secretary-General Shridath Ramphal. The British declined because this force was never intended to enforce peace, but Lord Soames did extend the state of emergency which was due to expire on January 19, 1980, for a further period of six months. While the Patriotic Front forces at large caused most of the violations, calm generally prevailed at the APs. And in spite of the various difficulties, the ceasefire held, free and fair elections were held, and the road to majority rule was cleared.

Henry Wiseman and Alastair M. Taylor, in the conclusions to their report *From Rhodesia to Zimbabwe*, pointed to five factors which had contributed to 'the mastery of the situation': (1) although it was called a Commonwealth Monitoring Force, it was inherently British, thereby simplifying organization and command; (2) because Britain was responsible for the negotiations at Lancaster House, it was able to carry out the advance planning for the force; (3) the force had immediate access to Salisbury and London for goods and services and the response was quick and ready, as compared to the UN; (4) close co-ordination between the political and military decisions allowed flexibility; and (5) the neighbouring states fully supported the ceasefire.

It took almost a week to make the ceasefire fully effective. The degree of cooperation of the forces of the two sides had been difficult to anticipate but, as it turned out, General Peter Walls, the RSF Commander, and the leaders of the liberation forces General Rex Nhongo of ZANLA and Commander Lookout Masuku of ZANU (PF) fully cooperated with the British Governor and the Commonwealth monitoring force. Indeed, the very first crisis was averted by the timely intervention of Nhongo when he persuaded 450 guerrillas who were surrounded by the RSF to surrender their arms.

The decision to leave several thousand guerrillas in the bush was surely political and related to the fact that the RSF remained responsible for law and order. While there were reports of intimidation and coercive action by the RSF, it was the guerrillas who were largely responsible for lawlessness and violence. This is what led Soames to call on the RSF to maintain law and order, which under the circumstances could have prejudiced the final outcome. However, Soames had only this one choice and as it turned out that his assumption that ZANU (PF) were guilty of intimidation redounded in their favour.

The responsibility for security during the polling was vested in the RSF under the direct control of Soames. Some 58,000 territorials were mobilized and 8,000 police were augmented by 26,000 auxiliaries. Thus a fully mobilized RSF controlled the nation while the Patriotic Forces (except for their members still on the loose) were confined to APs, causing considerable apprehension. The final results proved such fears to be groundless and indicated the British determination to establish a fair arrangement.

The situation at the APs needed careful handling. The monitoring force teams had to establish their presence, create confidence and, through the Patriotic Force commanders, exercise control. The liberation forces felt exposed, and had therefore established defensive positions. The RSF maintained their own watch by continuous reconnaissance, requiring buffer zones to be established in the APs by the monitoring force.

Towards the end of December, a contentious issue arose. Robert Mugabe claimed that some 1,000 South African troops were present in Zimbabwe, and accused the British of trickery. The African group in the UN called for a Security Council meeting, and Kenya declared that it could not permit its troops to serve alongside South Africans. The British acknowledged that a small group of South African troops was protecting Beit Bridge, a strategically vital railway bridge at the South African border, and announced that it was being withdrawn. This in fact was done. There were a number of South Africans, enjoying dual citizenship, who were serving in the RSF, and they were left alone. However, on February 1, 1980, the Security Council called on the United Kingdom 'to ensure the immediate, complete and unconditional withdrawal of South African troops'.[24]

Despite all apprehensions, the British government managed to achieve the goals of the Lusaka Conference. The government showed great acumen in flexibly accommodating itself to the changing political winds: this won them the complete support of the African groups, in particular the Front Line states. The Commonwealth Secretary-General Shridath Ramphal played an important role during the Lancaster House negotiations by facilitating discussions between the rival groups, and between them and the British government.

The British, having a capability to plan and prepare the Commonwealth monitoring force, were able to do so unhampered, as they were given the responsibility for transferring sovereignty in Zimbabwe. The mandate given to the force was clear and concise, and its interpretation was the responsibility of the Governor and not of a Council. Furthermore, there was a clear chain of command and control.

The Commonwealth monitoring force was not exactly a Commonwealth operation because it was a British responsibility and not under the Commonwealth organization. Yet it indicated a capability which the Commonwealth could easily develop. The Commonwealth has a common language and there is a commonalty of military organizations, procedures and training. Several Commonwealth countries have UN peace observation experience, and Australia, India, Nigeria, Ghana, Canada and Britain have had experience in peacekeeping forces. Thus there is knowledge and a capability to have contingents on a standby arrangement. In the absence of an agreement on the implementation of Article 43 of the UN Charter, such an arrangement could prove useful in creating a Commonwealth component just as one had been set up during the Korean war. A Commonwealth peacekeeping force is also a practical possibility if it is politically desirable. The Commonwealth Secretariat would have the ready availability of the Commonwealth's military attachés in London and could call for support from Commonwealth nations for logistics and administration.

The Commonwealth organization has proved its usefulness as a political organ and an institution to harmonize different views to resolve conflicts. Such an organization, which is international in scope, could be relied on to play a useful role in dealing with conflicts in which its members are, or may become, involved.

NOTES

1. UN S/5007, Nov. 30, 1961.
2. UN Charter, Article 24 (1).
3. UN Charter, Article 24 (2).
4. UN Charter, Article 52 (1).
5. UN Charter, Article 53.
6. UN Charter, Article 54.
7. *Ibid*.
8. OAS Charter, Articles 3.1, 7 and 8, and 6, respectively.
9. UN Security Council Official Records, 9th Year, Supplement for April, May and June 1954. S/3232.
10. Robert F. Kennedy, *Thirteen Days: a Memoir of the Cuban Crisis* (New York: W.W. Norton, 1969).
11. OAS, 10th Meeting of Consultation of Ministers of Foreign Affairs, Resolution adopted in the 3rd Plenary Session, held May 6, 1965.
12. Introduction to Annual Report of the Secretary-General on the Work of the Orga-

nization, July 1, 1953, to June 3, 1954; Official Records of the General Assembly, 9th Session, Supplement 1(A/2663).

13. B. Andemicael, *The OAU and the UN* (New York and London: Africana Publishing Co., 1976).
14. UN General Assembly Resolution 2072 (XX), Dec. 16, 1965.
15. UN General Assembly Resolution 2229 (XXI), Dec. 20, 1966.
16. UN General Assembly Resolution 3292 (XXIX), Dec. 13, 1974.
17. UN 'Report of the Visiting Mission to the Spanish Sahara', Report of the Special Committee on the Situation with Regard to the Implementation of the Declaration on the Granting of Independence to Colonial Countries and Peoples'. (A) 10023/Add. 5, Annex, 1975, p. 48.
18. The Moroccan version of this event was that the Yema'a had gone to Tindouf to explain to Polisario their decision for their approval of the treaty, but were seized by Polisario and taken to Algeria.
19. UN, Advisory Opinion on Western Sahara (1975), International Court of Justice, Report 12, pp. 13–14.
20. Arnold C. Smith (with Clyde Sanger), *Stitches in Time: the Commonwealth in World Politics* (Don Mills, Ontario: General Publishing Co., 1981), p. 78.
21. *Ibid.*, p. 90.
22. John J. Stremlau, *The International Politics of the Nigerian Civil War 1967–1970* (Princeton University Press, 1977), p. 145.
23. Conversation with Ambassador Arnold C. Smith.
24. UN Document S/4166, Feb. 2, 1980.

6

THEORY AND PRACTICE JUXTAPOSED

Charter provision

The Congo peacekeeping operation caused a major financial crisis in the UN. The Soviets and their East European Socialist allies, having been ousted from Leopoldville (Kinsasha) by Colonel Joseph Mobutu after his military takeover from Prime Minister Patrice Lumumba, became strong opponents of the operation, and stopped paying for it. They also protested vigorously at Dag Hammarskjöld's handling of ONUC and called for the post of UN Secretary-General to be replaced by a troika.

The French had refused to pay for UNEF I and now refused to pay for ONUC as well. Their refusal was based principally on their objection to the nature of these operations. During French decolonization in Africa, the French government had excluded the UN, and so in the case of the Congo, while they did not veto the Resolution, they expressed strong reservations. Besides, like the Soviets, the French did not support the idea that the UN Secretary-General's office be given responsibility for the conduct of peacekeeping operations because they preferred direct Security Council control, permitting them to exercise their veto authority.

Faced with a serious shortage of funds, the United States encouraged floating a UN bond, which met with limited success. As U Thant often said, the financial crisis was in fact a political crisis. So it was not surprising that the United States, after its successful predominance in the Congo operation over the Eastern bloc, should have carried the East-West confrontation to the General Assembly. It called for the application of Article 19 of the Charter, viz.

A Member of the United Nations which is in arrears in the payment of its financial contributions to the Organization shall have no vote in the General Assembly if the amount of its arrears equals or exceeds the amount of the contributions due from it for the preceding two full years. The General Assembly may, nevertheless, permit such a Member to vote if it is satisfied that the failure to pay is due to conditions beyond the control of the Member.

While the American confrontation was really with the Soviets, the French could not have escaped the same fate. This was the worst crisis in the UN's history, for if the United States had pressed for a vote, the Soviets and their East European allies, as well as some other states, would have withdrawn from the UN, thus wrecking the world body. Wiser counsels prevailed, and the United States finally did not press for the vote. Instead, the Assembly decided in 1965 to establish a Special Committee on Peacekeeping, commonly known as the

Committee of 33. While differences remain over some key issues, a basis of agreement has emerged on most questions.[1]

Deliberations of the Committee of 33. The members of the Committee have tried to define peacekeeping and place it within the framework of the Charter. It has not been easy because, as Brazil pointed out, no specific provisions exist in the Charter to govern peacekeeping operations; so no agreement in principle has been possible on a definition of the political and juridical scope of a peacekeeping operation. These operations have been quite unlike either the peaceful techniques contemplated in Chapter VI of the Charter or the enforcement measures embodied in Chapter VII. For this reason some countries argue that a new Chapter, incorporating the main conceptual and operational provisions relating to peacekeeping operations, should now be included between Chapters VI and VII of the Charter. It is important to review these discussions in detail, because they describe different points of view of the nations or blocs of nations. These differences still prevail and, given the geopolitical situation, are likely to do so in the foreseeable future. Thus conflict management has to be within the permissible parameters of these views.

The Security Council. Several points of view have been taken by the Committee of 33 concerning the role and responsibility of the Security Council. Most members agree that the Council should exercise general control and overall direction of peacekeeping operations, and the Soviet Union in particular insisted that the Council must determine from the very outset the main issues relating to a particular operation.

Both superpowers, and their allies, agreed that the Security Council should specify the aim of an operation, determine its duration, and lay down the mandate, including the manner of termination. Czechoslovakia, conveying the views of the Soviet bloc, said that the Council should control all aspects of an operation, including decisions on the strength and specification of contingents, the appointment of the Commander and his Deputies, the general direction of the operation, and consideration of reports relating to personnel. Japan (apparently in response to the sudden withdrawal of UNEF I from Sinai and the subsequent June 1967 war) suggested that in terminating an operation the utmost caution should be taken to avoid a large-scale military clash resulting from unilateral notice to quit by one of the parties concerned. Termination should take place only when the organ which had initiated the operation agreed to end it. During discussions as to how decisions should be taken in the Council, the Soviet Union wanted all decisions to be adopted in accordance with Article 27(3) of the Charter.[2]

The United States said that the best interests of the UN and the efficiency of peacekeeping would be served by procedures to ensure that the Security Council is consulted through a committee established under Article 29 of the Charter[3] on key operation decisions, without extending the rule of unanimity to such decisions. In this context the East Europeans said that the Security Council should establish, in accordance with Article 29 of the Charter, a subsidiary organ, namely a 'Committee on Direction of the Operation', responsible for giving the Council advice and assistance. While agreeing that such an organ be established, the Netherlands suggested that it should consist of members of the Council contributing personnel, contingents, facilities, and/or services to the operation, and those member-states on whose territory the peacekeeping operation is to be carried out. The United States preferred that the Committee should hold a 'watching brief' over the conduct of the operation, advise the Secretary-General, and receive reports on the progress of the operations between Council meetings.

The Military Staff Committee. The Committee of 33 devoted considerable time to the question of the role of military experts and their participation in the deliberations of the 'subsidiary organ', or Advisory Committee, of the Security Council. The United States held the view that military experts of permanent members of the Security Council could be included on the Advisory Committee. These experts could be their Military Staff Committee representatives. The United States also expressed the view that the permanent members should be given appropriate weight in the consultations on peacekeeping operations until the full Committee was established in each case: they would serve as a nucleus available for consultation on the initial force composition, selection of a Force Commander, and interpretation of the mandate.

The Soviet Union, on the other hand, said that the Advisory Committee should incorporate a nucleus formed by a sub-committee of permanent members of the Security Council; this sub-committee would work on the basis of agreed decisions of all its members, so that there would be no voting. The decisions of the Advisory Committee would be considered to have been adopted if a majority of the Committee, including all members of the sub-committee (i.e. all permanent members of the Security Council), agreed with them. The Soviet Union said that the Committee should be organized so as to be able to function continuously. It could also be convened at any time at the request of one of its members, or in the light of developments in the region of the operation.

In a lengthy discussion on the role of the Military Staff Committee, Canada recalled that because it was established under Chapter VII of the Charter, covering enforcement actions, its use in peacekeeping operations had long been in dispute. Nothing in the Charter, however, precluded such use; nor need it follow that the use of the Military Staff Committee would impose the character of enforcement on a peacekeeping operation. In Canada's view the Security Council could carry out its functions more effectively if it were to delegate responsibilities for operational direction and control to the Military Staff Committee. This would be supported by an International Headquarters Staff, including a suitable number of military experts, to be established by the Secretary-General as a continuously functioning body, which would assume responsibility for detailed planning and for the day-to-day conduct of the operation.

The Military Staff Committee, the Canadians felt, should make use of proposals developed by the Headquarters Staff. It might, for example, advise the Security Council on the terms of the mandate, the selection of contributing countries, and so on, and the Security Council, if it approved, could then authorize the Secretary-General to conclude such agreements with the respective governments. In addition, the Military Staff Committee could maintain a periodic review of any operation, so as to ensure that it conformed with the mandate authorized by the Security Council. In the light of such reviews the Military Staff Committee might revise the force's instructions according to recommendations made by the Headquarters Staff and issued by the Secretary-General. The Committee, through its Chairman, would report to the Security Council on a regular basis, or at any time considered necessary either by the Committee or by the Secretary-General. If the mandate was proving inadequate, the Committee could refer the matter to the Security Council.

Canada further suggested that, as laid down in Article 47 of the Charter, the Military Staff Committee should be composed of representatives of the permanent members of the Security Council. In addition, and consistent with Article 47 (2),[4] those states contributing to the peacekeeping force would be invited to participate in meetings of the Committee. The Secretary-General or his representative would participate in all such meetings. The Military Staff Committee, thus augmented, would proceed by a majority vote which must include the concurring vote of all its permanent members.

The Soviet Union, commenting on the Canadian suggestions, pointed out that in accordance with the provisions of Article 47 of the Charter, the Military Staff Committee was established to 'advise and assist the Security Council on all questions relating to the Security Council's military requirements for the maintenance of international peace and security'. Such assistance to the Council was related, among other things, to the employment of military personnel or contingents and the command over them. The Military Staff Committee could, in connection with peacekeeping operations, invite any member-state, and in particular any non-permanent member-state, of the Security Council and any state furnishing military personnel or contingents, facilities or services, to be associated with it 'when the efficient discharge of the committee's responsibilities requires the participation of that member in its work'.

As a Third World country, Upper Volta, while agreeing that the Military Staff Committee should be responsible for assisting the Security Council in military aspects of peacekeeping, and consist exclusively of representatives of the permanent members of the Security Council, felt it should be expanded to include three additional members chosen on the basis of equitable geographical distribution. Thus three new seats on the Committee should be assigned respectively to Asia, Africa and Latin America. However, the United States doubted the utility, in consent-type peacekeeping as distinct from enforcement action, of a separate role for the Military Staff Committee.

The Secretary-General. Our description of some of the UN peacekeeping operations has sufficiently indicated that the role of the Secretary-General has been a source of conflict between the Socialist and Western countries. The East Europeans have taken the view that the Secretary-General, as laid down in Article 97 and 98 of the Charter,[5] is very much the servant of the Council: he must assist by all means at his disposal in the implementation of the Resolutions or other forms of authorization by the Council with regard to an operation and he must perform those functions that are entrusted to him by the Council. He must report to the Council as appropriate, or upon its request, on the performance of those functions. Expanding on this, Czechoslovakia said that the Secretary-General's role as Chief Administrative Officer in the conduct of peacekeeping operations is also outlined in the Charter: Article 98 specifies that the Security Council, in directing peacekeeping operations, can entrust to the Secretary-General some particular functions.

The United States view remains that an acceptable balance of responsibility must be maintained among the UN's principal organs for direction and operational control; in particular, rapid and flexible decisions by the Secretary-General would appear to be of the utmost importance for the effectiveness of peacekeeping missions. Canada has said that in the formative stages of an operation, the Secretary-General would naturally be in close consultation with members of the Security Council, and would also bring to bear all means available to him for the implementation of the Security Council's mandate and an eventual peaceful settlement. The Secretary-General would be responsible for all communications between the UN and the host-countries, and between the UN and the troop-countries.

International headquarters. Canada has stressed that the Secretary-General, being responsible for International Headquarters Staff, or his authorized representative, the Chief of International Headquarters Staff, should participate in meetings of the Military Staff

Committee. He should be consulted on all matters relating to the establishment and conduct of a peacekeeping mission, and should implement decisions of the Military Staff Committee concerning the conduct of the mission or force. The Secretary-General would tell the Military Staff Committee which member-states had volunteered Commanders, contingents or services, and keep them informed of the current views of the host-country. He would report to the Security Council as necessary. Furthermore, the Canadians said that, in consultation with the Military Staff Committee, the Secretary-General should establish an International Headquarters Staff consisting of both military and civilian components. When a mission was authorized, he should provide extra civilian officials and clerical personnel for mission headquarters to support the military staff.

The structure, size and composition of the International Headquarters Staff was a matter requiring further study; however, it seemed important that a substantial element of professional military expertise be included in this body. The requirements and qualifications for military personnel would be specified by the Military Staff Committee to the Secretary-General, who would recruit them.

The International Headquarters Staff would have the continuing task of supplying expert advice and information to the Military Staff Committee on all matters affecting peacekeeping missions, in implementation of a mandate from the Security Council. For example, the Headquarters Staff could be asked to prepare Standing Operating Procedures for peacekeeping forces to be submitted to the Military Staff Committee for review. They could carry out whatever advance planning the Committee deemed feasible and necessary. They would be responsible to the Military Staff Committee for its actions in the implementation of the Security Council mandate, and would report to the Committee through the Secretary-General or his authorized representative, the Chief of the Headquarters Staff.

The Force Commander. In describing the requirements for the appointment of a Force Commander, Canada in its proposals recalled that the Secretary-General is requested by the Security Council to compile a list of potential Commanders. Under the Canadian proposal, the Military Staff would receive information from the Secretary-General on potential Force Commanders, as well as personnel, equipment and services which member-states might be prepared to provide if they were acceptable to the host-nation, and would then, together with the Secretary-General, prepare recommendations to the Security Council on the composition of the observer mission or force and its Commander. Canada also emphasized that the Commander should be provided by the Secretary-General with political and other advisers as required.

The United States view was that the Secretary-General should designate the Force Commander after consultation with the host-countries, the parties directly concerned, and the Council's Committee; the Council could always reject the Secretary-General's choice through a procedural vote. In this regard, the United States suggested that the Secretary-General should compile and keep up to date a roster of potential Force Commanders from which, after consultation with the host-government and the Committee, he should select a Force Commander. Given the emergency nature of most peacekeeping operations, the choice normally has to be made quickly, which would help to ensure that it is a good choice.

Czechoslovakia took a similar view on behalf of the East European nations: the Commander should be selected after consultations by the Secretary-General with the host-countries, based on a list of potential Commanders compiled with the Secretary-General's help by the Committee on Direction of the Operation (hereafter 'subsidiary organ') of the Security Council on the basis of information submitted by member-states. The Soviet Union further explained that the Security Council should request the subsidiary organ, with the Secretary-General's assistance, to compile a list of potential Commanders. The Secretary-General, on behalf of the Security Council, would request governments of member-states to suggest the names of potential Commanders from among their own military personnel; this list would be kept up to date to provide a reserve of Commanders available when needed.

Similarly, in appointing the Deputy Commander, the Commander of an operation should submit candidates to the Security Council for approval. In designating the Deputies and in distributing posts of senior officials, the principle of equitable balance among the countries participating in the operation has to be borne in mind.

Troops and Matériel. The Committee of 33 discussed what steps could be taken to improve peacekeeping, irrespective of specific operations. It agreed that with the Security Council's approval, or on a request from it, member-states should inform the Military Staff Committee of the types of personnel and technical services which they might be able to provide for future observer missions and peacekeeping forces authorized by the Security Council.

There was general agreement that the Secretary-General should compile an open roster of information on offers of military manpower, equipment and facilities, on the basis of which the Security Council could respond by telling member-states which of their offers might be most acceptable in future. The Soviet Union supported the notion of such an open roster; however, each state should retain the right to include in, or exclude from, the roster at any time information it had previously furnished in order to maintain the principle of voluntary participation. As soon as possible, agreements should be negotiated in accordance with Article 43 of the Charter between the Security Council and those member-states to be included in the roster.

The United States, although agreeing that it was a good time for member-states to discuss the future possibility of binding agreements with the Security Council within the framework of Article 43, remained sceptical for the time being about the advantage of arrangements on this matter. They felt that potential contributors were much more likely to co-operate with a system of earmarking troops voluntarily rather than binding arrangements under Article 43. But they said they would be willing to examine the feasibility of such arrangements if the Special Committee believed this course to be more practical and acceptable to member-states.

Steps following authorization. The United States said that after the Security Council had authorized an operation, the Secretary-General should simply undertake preliminary contact with the host-government and other governments concerned to ascertain what national contingents would be available and politically acceptable. Soundings should then be made with potential contributing countries to work out an acceptable force agreement.

The Soviet Union had a slightly different emphasis. It said that following Security Council authorization, the Secretary-General on behalf of the Council, acting in contact with the subsidiary organ, should seek contingents by entering consultations with the host-country and those states which had concluded agreements with the Council under Article 43, also with other states included in the roster and with other member-states that showed interest in the operation. The result of these consultations should be submitted to the subsidiary organ.

Composition. The Soviet Union stated that during the consultation following authorization, every effort should be made to reach an equitable balance in the composition of the participants, so that no member-state was excluded because of its political, social or economic system, or because of its geographical location. In response, the United States commented that East Europeans could participate on the same basis as the other participants and did not need any prescribed 'political balance' — whether in the form of a troika or a fixed requirement — to ensure that Socialist countries could always participate. All members should be considered as potential participants on an equal basis. While no member-state should be excluded *a priori*, equally no country or group should have a prescriptive right to participate in a particular operation. The paramount consideration, apart from professional qualifications, appeared to be the acceptability of the contingents or personnel to the host-country and to other parties concerned.

In deciding the strength, structure and composition of a force, the United States said the force composition should be determined by the Secretary-General; and that the Security Council vote on the Secretary-General's recommendation should be a procedural one, and not subject to a veto. It would be the responsibility of the Secretary-General in consultation with the Force Commander, the Council members and the parties to determine the types of forces required, and to make arrangements with nations willing to contribute them. The Canadians have held that the Military Staff Committee, together with the Secretary-General, should prepare recommendations to the Security Council on the composition of the observer mission or force and who should be its Commander. These recommendations would encompass the civilian as well as the military element of the force.

The Soviet view was that it was essential for the subsidiary organ of the Security Council to complete its assessment of what the proper composition of the force should be as early as possible. After selecting the Commander and units, the subsidiary organ, with the assistance of the Secretary-General, would forward a report to the members of the Security Council. The Council would not be obliged to consider this report, and if within forty-eight hours no Council member had requested a meeting to take a decision on it, the report would be considered adopted, and the requests to furnish contingents, personnel and facilities would be sent to the governments concerned. The Socialist countries added that the decision on the use of those contingents, personnel and facilities should be taken by the Security Council with the participation and consent of the member-states providing them, after preliminary consultation with the host-country. Decisions concerning the employment of military personnel or facilities as determined by the agreements concluded under Article 43 of the Charter would be taken with the participation and consent of the member-state providing them.

The United States has suggested that in authorizing an operation the Security Council, on the advice of the Secretary-General, could indicate the approximate size of the force by setting an upper limit to the numbers required. He should be allowed some latitude in this task, for which he should consult the Advisory Committee created under Article 29 of the Charter. In addition he, as executor of the Security Council's mandate, would be responsible for seeking additional contingents, personnel or facilities when needed, as consistent with the Council's mandate. On questions of major importance, such as a substantial increase or cut in the size of the force, the Secretary-General would consult the subsidiary organ of the Security Council and, if necessary, the Security Council itself. The Soviet Union said that if additional contingents, military personnel or facilities were required, only the Committee established by the Council should consider the matter.

Directives. In discussing the direction and control of operations, the United States gave the opinion that the subsidiary organ of the Security Council should provide guidance to the Secretary-General when questions arose over the interpretation of the Council's mandate. The Soviet Union disagreed, arguing that the general direction and command of peacekeeping operations were the prerogative of the Security Council, adding that the directives for Commanders should only be issued by the subsidiary organ within the mandate laid down by the Security Council. These directives should give the Commander a clear understanding of the nature of his responsibilities, of the relationship between the force and the host-country, and of the relationship between contingents and their countries of origin, as well as the reporting requirements. The United States stated that, within the mandate authorized by the Security Council, specific directives on all these subjects should be elaborated by the Secretary-General in consultation with the subsidiary organ.

As to the Commander's authority, the view of the Socialist states was that he should act within the mandate given him by the Security Council and within the directives elaborated by the subsidiary organ. The United States, on the other hand, felt that when problems arose over implementing a mandate, the Commander could consult the Secretary-General. The Soviet Union recommended that the subsidiary organ should periodically send inspection groups to visit the operation, in particular just before the expiration of the mandate.

Financing. On the question of financing, the United States and the Soviet Union have some important differences. The United States believes the Security Council should normally indicate the means for financing an operation, though without prejudice to the General Assembly's authority to apportion expenses among the members. Until a reliable and equitable system of financing is finally agreed, permanent members of the Security Council should undertake to pay their fair share of operations authorized by the Council. The Soviet view clearly places responsibility for decisions about financing on the Security Council alone.

Canada and Japan put forward slightly different formulae. The Canadians believed that when the Security Council authorized a force, it should as far as possible indicate the matter of financing, subject to the authority of the General Assembly, apportioning costs under Article 17 of the Charter.[6] Japan stated that in financing such operations, a special burden should be borne by the states directly concerned, corresponding to their own share of interest and responsibility. The options were (1) special arrangements among the parties concerned; (2) proportional payment by the entire membership of the organization out of the regular budget; (3) voluntary contributions; and (4) financing from a special fund for peacekeeping operations.

Japan felt that since peacekeeping promotes a fundamental objective of the UN, namely the maintenance of international peace and security, it was desirable that financing should in principle be based on the second method. However, in view of the special responsibility of the parties to a dispute, as well as that of Security Council members, there was a case for arguing that such states should bear a heavier financial burden than others.

Japan further stated that it was also possible to envisage a case for voluntary contributions. It could be advisable to employ method (2) as a matter of principle, while authorizing the organ initiating the particular operation to choose any of the four options, or a combination of them. In any case, in view of the financial state of the UN, it was highly desirable to establish a fund from which the initial expenses of peacekeeping operations could be covered on a stop-gap basis. The idea of setting up a 'United Nations Peacekeeping Fund', on the basis of voluntary contributions, merited serious study.

Progress by committee

In April 1968, in its efforts to make progress, the Special Committee on Peacekeeping set up a Working Group to agree on guidelines for military observers, established or authorized by the Security Council ('Model I'), and for UN peacekeeping operations on a large scale ('Model II'). The Working Group first took Model I. During the summer of 1968, the Special Committee adopted a published report to the General Assembly, stating that the topics to be considered in Model I would include (1) the strength and equipment of the group of observers; their recruitment and organization; facilities and services; and related financial questions; (2) the relationship between observers and the state or states or the territory or territories on which they have to operate; and (3) the status of observers; privileges and immunities; and the duration and termination of the mission of observers. By the following year, the Working Group had completed the text of five out of eight chapters of Model I. The three chapters they were unable to complete were those dealing with the establishment of the mission (formation, strength, composition and command, direction and control), and with legal and financial arrangements. The Working Group has still not been able to complete its work because of the political sensitivity of issues.

As for Model II, dealing with peacekeeping operations, progress was not possible in the absence of agreement on the outstanding chapters of Model I. However, the Arab-Israeli war of October 1973 and the establishment of UNEF II in Sinai compelled members of the UN, and particularly the Security Council, to think again. Dr Waldheim, then Secretary-General, concentrated, in his recommendation to the Security Council on various aspects of UNEF II, on the areas of agreement and avoided the areas of conflict.[7] The Security Council's successful launching of a new peacekeeping operation encouraged the UN community, particularly the Special Committee on Peacekeeping Operations, to carry its deliberations a stage further. Early in April 1974 the Chairman of this Committee, Ambassador Ogbu of Nigeria, presented a working paper indicating the items that had been agreed in principle, and those upon which further discussion was still necessary. There was general consensus on most questions, including authorization; definition of purpose and mandate; the kind of advice and assistance required by the Security Council; duration, and related questions; financial arrangements; size; agreements with contributing countries; agreements with host-countries: approval of a roster of potential Commanders; authorization of the appointment of Deputy Commander; ultimate directions and control during the operation, and subsequent alterations. Items requiring further discussion included the manner of termination; composition of the force support facilities; and the appointment of the Commander.

At the first meeting in 1974 of the Special Committee, Waldheim said: 'I believe that there is now a wide agreement among the membership of the United Nations that a peacekeeping operation should be set up speedily and, once set up, should function effectively. The recent experience in the Middle East shows that it is both essential and possible to achieve those objectives. A set of general guidelines which take the most recent experience into account and which command the broad support and agreement of the membership of the United Nations would certainly be of great assistance in establishing and maintaining such operations in the future.'

Ambassador Ogbu in his comments felt that, despite the political differences that had prevented the Committee from fulfilling its mandate in the past, agreement in regard to the laying down of general principles seemed to be close. Because there was no disagreement over the ultimate authority of the Security Council in these matters, 'It should therefore prove possible for the Committee to lay down the broad, general principles on peacekeeping for which the world community had so long been waiting. He added that there was no dispute over the need for operational efficiency and for rapid, flexible decision-making to be provided by the major agents of the Security Council.

On this basis, the Chairman of the Committee proposed for consideration a 12-point programme of draft articles:

Article 1. United Nations Peacekeeping Operations shall be under the ultimate authority of the Security Council.
Article 2. The Security Council will delegate to its agents authority over certain aspects of peacekeeping operations.
Article 3. The agents of the Security Council in peacekeeping matters shall be the Secretary-General and any committee or body.

Article 4. The Secretary-General shall be a principal agent of the United Nations in matters of peacekeeping operations.

Article 5. The Military Commander of a United Nations Peacekeeping Operation shall report to the Secretary-General.

Article 6. Under the authority of the Security Council the Secretary-General shall be the Commander-in-Chief of United Nations Peacekeeping Operations.

Article 7. In matters of peacekeeping the authority of the Secretary-General shall be exercised in conformity with the provisions of resolutions adopted by the Security Council.

Article 8. The Secretary-General shall keep the Security Council fully informed of developments relating to the functioning of peacekeeping operations. All matters which may affect the nature or the continued effective functioning of a peacekeeping force will be referred to the Council for its decision.

Article 9. The costs of peacekeeping operations authorized by the Security Council shall be considered as expenses of the Organization, to be borne by the Members in accordance with Article 17, paragraph 2, of the Charter.

Article 10. In the composition of a peacekeeping force the Secretary-General shall regularly report to the Security Council on the results of his efforts concerning the balanced geographical distribution of that force.

Article 11. United Nations peacekeeping forces shall meet three essential conditions. First, they shall, at all times, have the full confidence and backing of the Security Council. Second, such forces must operate with the full co-operation of the parties concerned. Third, such forces must function as integrated and efficient military units.

Article 12. The Security Council shall have authority over peacekeeping operations in conformity with agreements reached by the Special Committee on Peacekeeping Operations.[8]

The proposal by the Western powers

The establishment of UNIFIL saw the Netherlands and France taking part in a UN peacekeeping force for the first time. The Norwegians contributed troops after a lapse of eleven years, not having participated since the withdrawal of UNEF I. Together with the Irish and the Canadians, who provided logistic support for the first few weeks, four Western European states became involved in UNIFIL. Military observers from these and other European countries have served and continue to be represented in UNTSO.

It was the UNIFIL experience which convinced the Western European community of the need to improve the UN's peacekeeping capability and to link it to the Special Session of the General Assembly on disarmament in 1978. After this session the Western Nine consulted in New York with many states, including the 'Core Group', i.e. states which frequently contribute troops and money.

While not wishing to infringe on the work of the Committee of 33 or any other body dealing with this question, the Nine decided to submit a resolution to the General Assembly in the fall of 1978 to draw to members' attention the importance of peacekeeping for the avoidance and ending of violence, and called on it to strengthen further the UN's peacekeeping capability. The Resolution included the following suggestions: member-states to share costs; member-states to provide supplementary assistance; member-states to supply the Secretary-General with regular information relating to stand-by capacity; and all concerned to ensure the effective formulating of peacekeeping operations, especially the safety of personnel involved. The United States had emphasized the collective responsibility to share expenses, and the Nine took this under consideration.

However, the Soviet Union indicated that it was opposed to the Resolution, but nonetheless offered to continue discussion of the question in the Committee of 33. The Poles, with current experience in the Middle East and past experience in Indochina, were supportive; but they emphasized the paramount importance of Articles 43 and 45 and insisted that the Secretary-General's role should be confined to Article 97 of the Charter.

The Assembly voting was 106 in favour, 11 abstentions and 19 (including the Socialist bloc) against.[9]

Committee discussions continued

Besides the new operation in southern Lebanon, the UN was also engaged in the establishment of the UN Transition Assistance Group for Namibia (UNTAG). With this new incentive in mind, Leslie O. Harriman, Nigeria's Permanent Representative at the UN and Chairman of the Special Committee, reminded the Committee at its meetings in the early part of 1979 that for the past fifteen years it had failed to reach agreement on the guidelines, but that 'given the degree of détente achieved and the high degree of intelligence, experience and education of the members of the Special Committee, the current situation was propitious.'[10]

The Japanese delegate reminded the Committee that there already seemed to be widespread agreement on some points. The Security Council was the organ with primary competence for undertaking and halting peacekeeping operations. The Secretary-General, under the Security Council's authority, directed peacekeeping operations and, with the approval of the Council, appointed the Force's Commander and decided on its composition. The geographic representation of countries which contributed troops to the peacekeeping force was taken into account. And, finally, the General Assembly was competent under Article 17 of the Charter to decide on the expenses to be undertaken in peacekeeping operations and to apportion them among member-states. He therefore urged the Committee to strive harder to elaborate on the guidelines, and added that in this the permanent members of the Council had a crucial role to play.[11]

The Canadian delegate at this meeting argued that the need to reach early agreement on guidelines was clear from the fact that UNIFIL could have been established more quickly if there had already been agreement on guidelines and methods of operation. He added that his delegation was 'interested in improving practical aspects of peace-keeping operations even more than in the completion of guidelines, which it considered an urgent matter'. He said that the existing system had many inadequacies and, with six operations currently in being and UNTAG likely to be established for Namibia, there was a greater need than ever to improve UN performance in supporting troops in the field. The specific areas relating to the practical implementation of peacekeeping operations in which the Canadians saw a need for improvements included earmarking of troops, equipment and services; expanding the use of the Field Operations Service; examining the practicability of contracting services from member-states or private organizations; and training arrangements, including repro-duction of training manuals and the prior training of Commanders and senior staff officers.[12]

The Soviet Union expressed the view that all questions relating to the practical preparations for peacekeeping operations were within the exclusive competence of the Security Council. Therefore, any increase in the Council's readiness to take rapid and effective action could be achieved by concluding agreements provided for in Article 43 of the Charter.

In May 1979 the United States submitted a working paper to the Working Group of the Special Committee, containing some sugges-tions on strengthening UN peacekeeping capabilities. The main points were:

1. A UN peacekeeping reserve should be established. States should have troops on stand-by, or earmarked for availability at short notice and trained for peacekeeping. Contingents should include logistics. Those unable to earmark troops should consider earmarking faci-lities.

2. Arrangements for training of reserves by the UN should be con-sidered. Adequate training of officers and non-commissioned officers was a key element. Appropriate institutes should be sought to organize seminars and field training. Alternatively, some form of UN staff and training college should be considered. Training of UN military observers might be conducted at UNTSO headquarters.

3. The Secretary-General should prepare a study of administrative and logistic problems.

4. Members should fulfil their Charter obligations to pay their assessed contributions for peacekeeping. The whole question of financing should be considered.

5. The United States offered to assist with airlift and equipment when requested; to consider not asking for payment for airlift on a case-by-case basis; to consider assisting the UN in upgrading technical equipment available and enhancing its observation capability through the use of, or access to, modern technologies available in such fields.

By the end of 1979, consensus had still not been achieved on any specific substantive proposal.

The Working Group of the Committee continued its efforts to agree guidelines for carrying out peacekeeping operations in conformity with the UN Charter, and to this end prepared Working Documents 1 and 2, which are described in their Seventh and Eighth reports. These documents listed the main issues, with alternatives. In subsequent years these papers have been revised. The *Draft Formulae for Articles of Agreed Guidelines for United Nations Operations*[13] are as follows:

Title
Draft articles of guidelines for future United Nations peace-keeping operations under the authority of the Security Council and in accordance with the Charter of the United Nations.

Introduction
The aim of the present draft guidelines is to ensure, by the acceptance of principles and the institution of methods, that peace-keeping operations shall be used in the common interests of the United Nations.

Article 1
[(1) The Security Council has the authority over the establishment, direction and control of peace-keeping operations.]
(2) Responsibilities to be exercised directly by the Council in this respect are as follows:
  1. Authorization;
  2. Definition of purpose and mandate;
  3. Kind of advice and assistance required by the Council;
  4. Duration and related questions;
  5. Financial arrangements;
  6. Size (magnitude);
  7. Authorization for appointment of deputy commanders;
  8. Ultimate direction and control during the operation;
  9. Subsequent alterations;
  10. Agreements with contributing countries (model agreement and changes thereto);
  11. Agreements with host-country (including model status of forces agreement and changes thereto);
  12. Approval of roster of potential commanders.

Article 2
The Security Council may, in accordance with the provisions of the Charter of the United Nations, decide to delegate its authority over aspects of peace-keeping operations.

Article 3
In matters of peace-keeping all authority shall be exercised in conformity with relevant decisions of the Security Council.

Article 4
(1) The Security Council may, at the time of establishment of a peace-keeping operation, decide to establish a committee under Article 29 of the Charter in order to assist the Council in the performance of its functions. The committee shall be directly responsible to the Security Council.
(2) The committee shall consist of the following:
  (*a*) The representatives of the five permanent members of the Security Council.
  (*b*) The representatives of five non-permanent members designated by the Security

Council, following a suitable system of rotation.

(c) The representatives of not more than five States designated by the Security Council from among those providing military contingents or personnel, also following a suitable system of rotation.

In the composition of the committee equitable geographical balance shall be one of the guiding principles.

(3) As a general rule, and unless the committee decides otherwise, the representatives of countries where the peace-keeping operation is being conducted may attend the meetings of the committee and participate in the discussions.

(4) Representatives of countries providing voluntarily on a substantial scale financial and other material contributions such as facilities, services and equipment may be invited to attend the meetings of the committee and participate in the discussions.

(5) The Secretary-General or his representative shall attend the meetings of the committee.

(6) The committee shall meet as frequently as necessary for its work. It may also be convened at any time at the request of any one of its members, the Secretary-General, or the representative of a country where a peace-keeping operation is being conducted.

(7) The committee shall report to the Security Council at its request. In addition, the committee may make special reports, with recommendations, if any, on matters regarding the peace-keeping operation requiring decision or the attention of the Council.

(8) Decisions of the committee on procedural matters shall be made by an affirmative vote of a majority of the members of the committee. There will be no voting on other issues, and, in the absence of unanimity, the views expressed in the committee shall be reflected in the reports to the Security Council.

Article 5

The Security Council may delegate responsibilities to, or seek advice and assistance from, the Military Staff Committee established in accordance with Article 47 of the Charter of the United Nations. The Committee may invite any members of the United Nations, in particular any non-permanent members of the Security Council or any States providing contingents or facilities to associate themselves with it, when the efficient discharge of the Committee's responsibilities requires their participation in its work.

Article 6

The Secretary-General, under the authority of the Security Council, [shall direct the implementation of peace-keeping operations] [shall direct peace-keeping operations] [is in charge of the implementation of peace-keeping operations, receiving guidance from a subsidiary body of the Security Council] within the mandate entrusted to him by the United Nations Charter, contributing with all means at his disposal to giving effect to relevant decisions of the Security Council.

Article 7

The Security Council shall receive reports, and may request special reports from, issue instructions to and receive recommendations from the Secretary-General and any subsidiary body which may be established.

Article 8

The command in the field will be exercised by a force commander appointed [on the proposal of the Secretary-General] [by the Secretary-General] [with the consent of] [by] the Security Council. The Commander will be given necessary authority over all elements of the operation within the terms of the mandate and specific directives. The Commander shall co-operate [through appropriate channels] with the subsidiary body which the Security Council may establish to assist the Council.

Article 9
It is essential that throughout the conduct of a United Nations peace-keeping operation it shall have the full confidence and backing of the Security Council. Such forces must operate with the full co-operation of the parties concerned, particularly of the Government of the host-country, due account being taken of its sovereignty. Such forces must function as integrated and efficient military units and act with complete objectivity. It is also of the utmost importance to secure freedom of movement for each unit irrespective of its nationality.

Article 10
In the composition of a peace-keeping force established under the authority of the Security Council equitable geographical balance shall be one of the guiding principles [along with the necessity of securing the over-all efficiency of the force]. [The selection and replacement of the national contingents shall be [undertaken] by the [Secretary-General with the] agreement of the Security Council and the host country.]

Article 11
The costs of peace-keeping operations authorized by the Security Council shall be considered as expenses of the Organization, to be borne by the members in accordance with Article 17, paragraph 2, of the Charter of the United Nations [or any other methods of financing which the Security Council may decide] [unless decided otherwise].

Article 12
[To ensure the state of readiness of the United Nations for prompt and effective establishment of peace-keeping operations, the Security Council may take steps to facilitate the conclusion of agreements, whether for forces, assistance, or facilities under Article 43 or other preparedness arrangements, in order fully to develop its peace-keeping capacity.] Such [agreements] [arrangements] may provide that specific contingents can be employed by the Council in a particular operation with the consent of the respective Governments.

Article 13
To ensure the effective functioning of the operation, United Nations forces will enjoy privileges and immunities in accordance with legal arrangements on the status of forces to be decided by agreement between the United Nations and the host-country.

The above draft did not receive the support of all the members of the Committee, although it was agreed to add it as an appendix to the Eleventh Report of the Working Group.[14] Austria, Canada, Denmark, Finland and Sweden, later joined by Italy — all of which happened to be countries that had provided personnel to UN peace-keeping operations — submitted a working paper that was also attached to the Eleventh Report. The Working paper recommended that

(*a*) member-states consider establishing stand-by forces for United Nations service;
(*b*) member-states include training for United Nations peace-keeping operations in the programmes of their national forces;
(*c*) a training manual or manuals on peace-keeping operations be prepared to facilitate training and to provide guidance for peace-keeping forces in the actual conduct of operations;
(*d*) prior training, under United Nations auspices and/or co-ordination, be given to those officers designated to senior command or staff positions in United Nations peace-keeping operations;

(*e*) the United Nations provide co-operation and assistance to regional/international seminars; and
(*f*) member-states be prepared to assist, if possible, in the preparation of a manual or manuals and in the provision of instructional staff for training.

On November 18, 1982, the General Assembly again urged the Special Committee on Peacekeeping Operations to renew its efforts to work towards the completion of agreed guidelines which would govern the conduct of UN peacekeeping operations, and to give further attention to specific questions related to their practical implementation. Under Resolution 36/37, [15] recommended by the Assembly's Special Political Committee, the Assembly took note of the report of the Special Committee on Peacekeeping Operations, and requested that Committee to report to the Assembly at its 1983 session. It repeated its invitation to member-states to report and to provide information on the experience gained in peacekeeping operations and requested the Secretary-General to prepare a further compilation of those replies.

During consideration of the question in the Special Political Committee, the views expressed by delegations included the following: the mandate of the Peacekeeping Committee must be renewed; financial obligations towards the UN peacekeeping operations must be honoured; peacekeeping was not an end in itself, but created conditions in which the search for a peaceful settlement could be pursued; such operations must at all times have the full support of the UN, particularly the Security Council; primary responsibility to seek settlement lay with the involved states themselves; attention needed to be paid to questions concerning the safety and security of peacekeeping units; agreed guidelines were needed for the conduct of peacekeeping operations; control of security forces had to remain under the Security Council; and the Council alone could decide on its financial operations. There were also certain other proposals: e.g. that a special session of the Assembly be held to assess the existing international peacekeeping machinery; that a new subsidiary body of the Security Council be created to strengthen that machinery; and that a 'ready force' be set up for use by the UN in urgent situations.

In introducing the report of the Special Committee on Peacekeeping Operations, the rapporteur said that that body had been unable to make progress on the substantial issues before it. There continued to be differences in attitude and approach, thus preventing any tangible result. For some members, prior agreement on the guidelines represented a matter of principle, while for others parallel agreement on issues of principle and practical implementation was of equal value. It was evident that long-standing basic differences remained, and that the task before the Committee would continue to be difficult, owing to the fundamental nature of the issues at stake.

In the deliberations of the Special Committee on Peacekeeping

Operations during the fall of 1983, speaking for Egypt, Mr Reda Shehata made some pertinent points that generally recognised the thinking of the UN membership. Shehata said that peacekeeping was an instrument devised to defuse conflicts; peacekeeping operations were based on the principle of peaceful intervention and never coercion; and their effectiveness was due to the support they received from the Security Council and particularly from the superpowers. Because of the paralysis of the Security Council, the General Assembly had assumed a new role in the concept of collective security. He added that certain basic facts had to be recognised, namely that there was a Special Committee for peacekeeping operations, that the primacy of the Security Council could not be eclipsed, and that powers vested in the Council could not be assumed by the Secretary-General. These issues of course are the key ones dividing the superpowers and creating a gap between East and West.

The Special Committee has requested its officers to serve another year on September 13, 1983 (A/38/381), and the General Assembly is expected to renew the Committee's mandate.

The Special Committee on Peacekeeping thus appears to have advanced as far as it possibly can. It has obtained a consensus sufficient to obtain the approval of the Security Council and to establish acceptable guidelines for these operations. It appears obvious that, as differences between the United States and the Soviet Union have widened in recent years, the political will for these two countries to resolve the outstanding differences is lacking. The Committee has served a useful purpose, and the best it can do for the foreseeable future is to be an occasional reminder of what still remains to be done.

The agreed principles drafted by Ambassador Ogbu of Nigeria and adopted by Dr Waldheim in the case of the two UN peacekeeping operations established after the October 1973 Middle East war, namely UNEF II in Sinai and UNDOF on the Golan Heights, worked satisfactorily until the need arose to develop a suitable peacekeeping force in southern Lebanon and another for the implementation of the Camp David Accord.

The UN operation in Lebanon got off to a bad start. The Israelis had never cleared the Palestinians from the area south of the Litani river and from Tyre, and expected UNIFIL to do it for them. Furthermore, they had left Haddad's Christian forces in charge along the Israeli-Lebanese border. The UN could not remove the Christians any more than they could the Palestinians. The Palestinians, seeming to co-operate with the UN, were able to have unarmed civilians return to southern Lebanon who could easily be rearmed from caches in the area. UNIFIL's presence failed to lead to further negotiations, and a renewal of fighting became inevitable. Those responsible for having first created an impossible situation for UNIFIL unfairly heaped blame on the UN.

UNEF II was an integral part of the Camp David process. The Israeli troops were to be withdrawn as UNEF II was to be finally deployed along the international border between Egypt and Israel. But Camp David had excluded the Soviets from the negotiating process; since 1967 they had broken off diplomatic relations with Israel and had become strong champions of the Arab demand that Israel withdraw from all occupied territories. This confirmed Israel's preference for the Soviets to be excluded from any role in the Middle East settlement. The United States had joined the Soviets in ending the October 1973 war and they had acted as Co-Chairmen at the Geneva peace talks. In spite of Soviet exclusion from the Egyptian-Israeli peace negotiations undertaken by President Carter, the Camp David Accord expected UNEF II to continue to play an important role. This was a lot to expect from the Soviets. Under the apparent threat of a Soviet veto, the Security Council declined to redeploy UNEF II, but surprisingly the signatories to the Camp David Accord showed great disappointment, a consequence which should have been apparent all along when they decided to leave the Soviets out of these arrangements.

Thereafter, the UN could no longer serve the diplomacy of Americans and Israelis and, if it was to be used at all, it would be in a minor and marginal role. The United States persuaded its Western allies and some other friendly countries to participate in a multinational force to assure peacekeeping responsibilities in Sinai, and when the Israelis re-invaded Lebanon and occupied Beirut, the Americans and Israelis did not call on the UN, since this would have involved the Soviet Union with its veto authority in the Council. Instead a multinational force not under UN auspices was established to help in the evacuation of the PLO. After the massacre of Palestinians by pro-Israeli Phalangists in September 1982, the multinational force returned to protect civilian life and property in Beirut.

The UN Security Council had decided on August 1 to send UN military observers to West Beirut, but the Israelis refused to permit them in the area. Early in September the Security Council again ordered UN observers to West Beirut. The Americans finally persuaded the Israelis to allow the UN observers in, while the multinational force was being assembled to return. The impasse in the Security Council was because the Americans and the Israelis had no desire to permit the Soviets any role in the Lebanese situation, and therefore the UN was being bypassed.

The setting up of multinational forces outside the framework of the UN to perform peacekeeping tasks is a disturbing trend which has weakened the international organization and has caused the evolution of an international system of peace and security to suffer a setback. There are sufficient indications that the United States accepted the necessity to keep its Marines in Beirut with reluctance, and the needs of all concerned would be better served if the UN were again to be given a prominent peacekeeping role in Lebanon and elsewhere in the Middle East. A UN peacekeeping force was considered for arrangements related to the withdrawal of Israeli and Syrian forces from Lebanon, but where all such possibilities develop, the Security Council must ensure that the mandate for the force is suitable for implementation, and that the force itself is made up in a way that allows it to perform its tasks effectively.

The guidelines carefully worked out by Dr Waldheim remain the best basis for setting up a peacekeeping operation. For as long as the political climate between the United States and the Soviet Union fails to improve, little progress can be made in resolving differences in the development of international peacekeeping operations. However, there are a number of improvements which can and should be made in existing UN peacekeeping operations and by troop-contributing countries. At the political level, a review of the Charter should be undertaken, not necessarily to change it, but to establish how better compliance by the Security Council in the field of peace and security can be obtained. The power balance that exists today between nations is not reflected in the Security Council. There is a need to examine the respective roles of the General Assembly, the Security Council and the Secretary-General.

As long as it remains impossible to develop peacekeeping arrangements under Article 43 of the Charter, member-states should make available, on a volunteer basis, troops, equipment, transportation and facilities for these operations. The contributing nations should organize stand-by forces and facilities, and efforts should be made to rationalize these arrangements co-operatively. It must be recognized that there is no way to force a sovereign state to pay assessments for peacekeeping operations; the only attempt to apply Article 19 of the Charter — in 1964 — caused the most serious crisis in the whole history of the UN, and nothing of the same kind has ever occurred again. A Charter revision is also very hard to bring about. Yet there are enough nations that believe in the usefulness of the UN and need it for their own purposes. An effort is needed on the part of those nations to strengthen the international system of peace and security, which should include the UN and regional arrangements.

NOTES

1. Special Committee on Peacekeeping Operations: a comprehensive listing under specific headings of concrete proposals received and a description of progress

made to date. UN General Assembly Document A/AC.121/L.18, Jan. 23, 1973.
2. *Article 27 (3)*: Decisions of the Security Council on all other matters shall be made by an affirmative vote of 9 members, including the concurring votes of the permanent members; provided that in the decisions under Chapter VI and under paragraph 3 of Article 52, a party to a dispute shall abstain from voting. [The latter refers to encouraging peaceful settlement of local disputes by regional arrangements.]
3. *Article 29*: The Security Council may establish such subsidiary organs as it deems necessary for the performance of its functions.
4. *Article 47*:
   1. There shall be established a Military Staff Committee to advise and assist the Security Council on all questions relating to the Security Council's military requirements for the maintenance of international peace and security, the employment and command of forces placed at its disposal, the regulation of armaments, and possible disarmament.
   2. The Military Staff Committee shall consist of the Chiefs of Staff of the permanent members of the Security Council or their representatives. Any member of the United Nations not permanently represented on the Committee shall be invited by the Committee to be associated with it when the efficient discharge of the Committee's responsibilities requires the participation of that Member in its work.
   3. The Military Staff Committee shall be responsible under the Security Council for the strategic direction of any armed forces placed at the disposal of the Security Council. Questions relating to the command of such forces shall be worked out subsequently.
   4. The Military Staff Committee, with the authorization of the Security Council and after consultation with appropriate regional agencies, may establish regional sub-committees.
5. *Article 97*: The Secretariat shall comprise a Secretary-General and such staff as the Organization may require. The Secretary-General shall be appointed by the General Assembly upon the recommendation of the Security Council. He shall be the Chief Administrative Officer of the Organization.
   Article 98: The Secretary-General shall act in that capacity in all meetings of the General Assembly, of the Security Council, of the Economic and Social Council, and of the Trusteeship Council, and shall perform such other functions as are entrusted to him by these organs. The Secretary-General shall make an annual report to the General Assembly on the work of the Organization.
6. *Article 17*:
   1. The General Assembly shall consider and approve the budget of the Organization.
   2. The expenses of the Organization shall be borne by the Members as appointed by the General Assembly.
   3. The General Assembly shall consider and approve any financial and budgetary arrangements with specialized agencies referred to in Article 57 and shall examine the administrative budgets of such specialized agencies with a view to making recommendations to the agencies concerned.
7. Special Committee on Peacekeeping Operations: Draft Report Document A/AC.121/L.22, Nov. 16, 1973, para. 10, stated: 'Moreover, the current United Nations peacekeeping operations in the Middle East, on the basis of Security Council Resolution 340 (1973), are providing experience and precedents that may assist the Special Committee and its Working Group in making further progress in certain fields in the future.'
8. See Document A/9326 and p. 1 above.
9. UN General Assembly Resolution 33/114, Dec. 8, 1978.
10. UN General Assembly Document A/AC/121/SR.74, April 4, 1979.

11. UN General Assembly Document A/AC/121/SR.75, April 25, 1979.
12. UN General Assembly Document A/AC.121/L.32, July 27, 1979.
13. UN General Assembly Document A/AC.121/L.30, Nov. 28, 1977, Appendix I.
14. UN General Assembly Document A/AC.121/L.30, Nov. 30, 1977.
15. UN General Assembly Resolution 36/37, Nov. 18, 1981.

7

MANAGEMENT: THE ESSENCE

The conduct of peacekeeping operations by the UN has been on an *ad hoc* basis and will remain so for as long as its members are unable to reach agreement on a more permanent system. Such a basis for any organization might well be considered fragile. It is therefore to the credit of the UN that numerous emergency *ad hoc* operations have been successfully established, and in the main have accomplished their objectives. Some use this general success as an argument for leaving things as they are. That view is not supported, however, by the many member-states and individuals who have borne the brunt of the operations. Most of them argue for the need to improve and strengthen them.

Past experience has set a pattern and provided a framework for the conduct of *ad hoc* peacekeeping operations. This means that they are now *ad hoc* only in the manner in which they are authorized and financed. Also they remain *ad hoc* as regards the political framework and purpose, which are different in every operation. The accumulated fund of knowledge and experience available provides guidelines for conducting these operations; lessons learned over the years have been applied to advantage in succeeding operations. The UN, however, has hesitated to resolve a number of problems of organization and administration because of the delicate political context of which they are a part. In order to avoid pitfalls, and with the best of intentions, individuals at UN headquarters and in the field have sometimes used their initiative and by-passed regular institutional procedures.

Once an operation is authorized by the UN, the language of the Resolution must be interpreted into objectives which are as clear as possible, and which will lead in turn to action to comply with the mandate. However, it has to be recognized that Resolutions have often papered over ambiguities that have to be preserved for political reasons. In the initial stages of the process, political considerations are inevitably dominant, but they can not be allowed to overshadow the military and administrative aspects: it is of crucial importance that from the very outset the political, professional military and administrative factors should be integrated.

While it is true that the political circumstances of every operation may be different, it does not follow that the basic principles applicable to these operations should be ignored. The experience of past and current operations has proved beyond any doubt that the mechanics at all levels of peacekeeping operations, except for combat, are no different from those for conventional military operations. There are, of course, certain differences in detail. For example, the low expenditure of ammunition and the low casualty rate in peacekeeping eliminates the need to establish ordnance re-supply and complex evacuation and replacement arrangements. However, the little time available to establish such operations demands specialized skills to organize the force and set up installations and echelons to induct and support the force in the field. Since the force does not have to fight its way in, its organizational and support systems, in comparison with a war situation, are simplified, and thus speedy action is possible.

While it is true that UN peacekeeping operations 'are only semi-military in their functioning,'[1] they are not basically different in composition and organization from normal military operations. The planning and preparation they require are identical to those of regular national operations. Failure to grasp this essential principle will result in the weaknesses of UN peacekeeping being perpetuated rather than its operations being corrected and strengthened. It is quite wrong to assume that UN peacekeeping operations, because they are 'semi-military in their functioning', may be organised on a non-professional basis. It is equally wrong to excuse the inadequacies and weaknesses in organizational and administrative matters that bedevil these operations by blaming them solely on the restrictions imposed by political considerations. It cannot be over-emphasized that the mechanics required for the induction of a predominantly one-nationality force — by, say, the United States in the Dominican Republic in 1965 or in Lebanon in 1958, or by the United Kingdom in East Africa in 1964 — are no different militarily and administratively from the induction of a force in, say, the Congo in 1960 by the UN. In fact, a one-nation force is simpler to manage, because its commander is not faced with many differences in military skills, equipment, training and so on.

UN peacekeeping operations have often been referred to as 'keeping the peace' or 'policing'. These terms can be misleading, since the operations are predominantly carried out by the military. While civilian police forces have been successfully employed in these operations, they have been so only within the limitations of their characteristics, and within the framework of their employment in their own countries. By virtue of their background and training, military personnel have proved better suited than policemen to meet the conditions likely to arise in the conduct of peacekeeping operations, except where large-scale contact with civilians is needed, as in ONUC and UNFICYP. It is neither possible nor practical to employ police in military situations.

This distinction is somewhat confused because UN peacekeeping forces often have a role in the maintenance of law and order. The confusion arises from a lack of understanding that, while police are primarily responsible for law and order, a stage may arise when they lose control of a situation, and troops are called in to assist the civil administration. Such situations are not peculiar to UN peacekeeping operations; they often occur within member-states when troops are called in to aid the civil power. In some UN operations, e.g. the Congo and Cyprus, the restoration of law and order demands their urgent and sometimes their main attention. Such a situation is more often than not due to a breakdown of the internal security and police forces; in other words, the situation is that of civil war.

UN operations, like those in aid of the civil power on a national level, are dominated by political factors, requiring political guidance at every stage. But the mechanics of these operations must be established along professional military lines, and these should be taken into account at the earliest possible stage. The actual moment when this stage occurs is likely to vary with the personality of the chief executive and his immediate assistants, whose methods of working are bound to dictate exactly when the advice of the military is sought. But it is better to call on military expertise too early rather than too late. At the start, the professional military and administrative experts have to play more a listening role than an advisory one. This will give them a grasp of the factors which might develop as the operation takes shape.

The early phases of ONUC are an example of a complex operation that was established, in the face of a grave emergency, with speed and skill. However, serious weaknesses were evident in the command in the field. Whatever the reasons for this, the fact remains that the early phases of the Congo operation were woefully inadequate in both their professional military and their administrative facets. The early failure to establish a well-knit and integrated operation in the Congo can be attributed more to the lack of professional military and administrative coordination and guidance in the field, right from the outset, than to the often-blamed political complexities involved. Once there had been a change of leadership, particularly on the military side, ONUC, especially the operations in Katanga, was well conducted.

An unfortunate example of poor coordination was operation 'Morthor', undertaken by UN troops in Katanga in September 1961. The first operation of this kind, 'Rumpunch', undertaken a few days earlier with the authorization of the Security Council and with the approval of the Secretary-General, was intended to round up mercenaries in Elisabethville, but was halted when the Katangans agreed to co-operate and the Consuls representing the countries from which they had been recruited, promised to help in persuading the mercenaries to leave. When it became evident that neither the Katangans nor the Consuls really intended to help, ONUC planned 'Morthor'. Although Hammarskjöld had told the ONUC Officer-in-Charge, Sture Linner, that while he approved of the plans, they were not to be implemented without his approval, the operation was launched contrary to instructions, with grave consequences for the UN.

UNEF II got off to a much better start, thanks largely to the planning at UN headquarters and support from UNFICYP head-quarters, which provided the first contingents and logistic support. After UNEF II headquarters was established and the force became the direct responsibility of the UN headquarters, many administrative difficulties were encountered due to delays in obtaining and deploying logistic units. Similarly, during the earlier months, the UN force in Lebanon encountered many organizational difficulties in administra-tion and logistics.

During the life-span of the UN, vast experience in peacekeeping has been accumulated. In some instances there is continuity, resulting in the amassing of knowledge and expertise on the part of those at the helm. At the highest political level, knowledge of the professional military and administrative aspects of peacekeeping has been gained. However, at the middle level of administrators, induction of military logistic expertise is essential. It is true that situations have arisen in which political leaders have been able to reproduce experience gained previously from almost identical situations in the maintenance of law and order and the conduct of military operations. But this experience cannot replace the well-established command and staff echelons of these forces. The experience gained should be put to profit by a greater understanding of the problems facing military staffs.

The inclusion of staff planning at an early stage in the West Irian, Cuba and Cyprus situations proved its usefulness, in marked contrast with the Congo operation. In the Congo, the appointment of the Special Representative of the Secretary-General to command the Force in the absence of a Commander had several in-built disadvan-tages. While this operation, like all the others, was *ad hoc* in nature, the procedural detail should have been conventional.

In setting up UNEF II, the UN headquarters relied on its own enormous experience and on the advice of UNFICYP headquarters and the Chief of Staff of UNTSO, Lt.-Gen. Siilasvuo, who was desig-nated Commander of UNEF II. But initially there were no proper military staff and headquarters to assist in the military management and establishment of suitable logistic support for the force. Shortly after being appointed Commander UNEF II, General Siilasvuo, who had many years of experience as a military observer in the Middle East, was involved in complex negotiations with the host-country and was made Chairman of the ceasefire negotiations. This was done at the suggestion of the parties; however, the presence of a Commander in the early phases of an operation is always critical. Therefore, Siilasvuo should not have been absent from his command until routine had been established. Many of the subsequent weaknesses in command and control of UNEF II are attributable to the dual role which Siilasvuo was called upon to perform. A possible solution could have been to appoint an experienced field commander as his deputy.

Two needs in UN peacekeeping are thus evident: the inclusion of military and administrative advice and expertise, along with political expertise, from the very outset; and the incorporation of specialized military experience as soon as an operation is conceived. To this end there is a need to establish suitable and co-ordinated procedures at the highest level within UN headquarters, as well as at the working level.

It has been argued here that UN peacekeeping operations require conventional lines of military planning and preparation. In view of the inability of the UN to utilize formal channels — as, for example, the Military Staff Committee —, experience so far has established beyond a shadow of doubt the necessity to include other military expertise in the conduct of these operations.

The post of the Military Adviser to the UN Secretary-General was abolished in 1969 and replaced by that of a Military Liaison Officer. This downgrading of the post was further emphasized by the fact that its holder was not always available, as he was often given special assignments away from headquarters. The Military Adviser's post was in fact re-established ten years later, albeit at a lower political level.

Another example of the absence of military expertise at head-quarters was Operation UNIPOM (India-Pakistan Observation Mission). The Commander of UNIPOM, Maj.-Gen. Bruce MacDonald, had been selected on the basis of his experience in UNFICYP and was ordered directly to the area of his new responsibility without being given an opportunity to visit UN headquarters for briefing. General MacDonald, an experienced Canadian officer, fully understood his responsibilities as a sector Commander in UNFICYP, but his appointment to an independent post of responsibility within the UN system was a new departure for him. He had no experience of the workings of the UN in New York. Both he and the UN's cause would have been better served had it been possible for an experienced staff officer to be despatched from UN headquarters to brief him and help him establish operations during the difficult early days. The absence of a suitable military advisory staff within the UN thus denied UNIPOM an opportunity which was available to other operations. For example, the present author was attached to Commander ONUC for long periods, and he was available to Commander UNTEA when the latter arrived in West Irian. A member of the Military Adviser's staff was made available to Commander UNFICYP; and later the author was sent to assist at the change of command — all for the purpose of helping the heads of these peacekeeping operations to understand the functioning of the UN, and to establish their own headquarters and forces on the basis of experience gained in the past. The inability of the UN to provide such assistance to UNIPOM was caused by the prevailing political crisis on peacekeeping over the debate on financing in the General Assembly.

We have said that in the Yemen operation, military advice was brought in at a late stage. The officer nominated to head this operation had recommended an organization almost as big as UNEF I. The soundness of this recommendation was questioned by UN headquarters, which wanted a more modest observer group, but also felt that the force should include the capability of sustained ground patrolling. On the basis of information made available to the Military Adviser at UN headquarters, a compromise between the military appraisal — which was thought to be generally unsound — and the UN headquarters view was arrived at; and a small observer group with light aircraft for aerial reconnaissance and a sub-unit for ground reconnaissance were recommended. It was later proved that the light aircraft provided were barely adequate, and the ground reconnaissance sub-unit was unsuited for the role, and could not be adequately maintained in the field. When the Military Adviser was finally dispatched to the area, it became evident that he had not given correct advice, and for once the 'unsound' General in the field had the better of the Secretariat staff, including military experts. All this could have been avoided by allowing the Military Adviser to examine all the factors involved, and by including him or one of his staff in the preliminary planning stage, of which a field trip should have been an essential part.

The introduction to the 1967 Annual Report of the Secretary-General, already mentioned, states: 'It is often said, . . . that lack of military staff and lack of planning in the Secretariat are an important source of weakness. The proponents of this position, based on a misleading equation of United Nations peacekeeping operations — which are only semi-military in their functioning — with normal national military operations, never make clear what they would expect even a limited military staff at United Nations Headquarters to do.' This statement is an over-simplification of the needs of peacekeeping operational planning.

As described earlier, peacekeeping operations are semi-military in their objectives but by no means semi-military in their composition and functions. The above remarks from the 1967 Report do not answer the proponents of the view — which incidentally includes the majority of the delegations of countries involved in peacekeeping — that there are inadequate military staff and military planning in the Secretariat, constituting an important source of weakness.[2] The statement as it stands appears to indicate that the military advisory and other Secretariat staff are required only to plan specific future operations. This perhaps is based on a misunderstanding of the nature of military forces, whether they be in the service of the UN or otherwise. Only a small proportion of any high-level military establishment concerns itself with contingency planning for specific future operations. The majority of staff and establishments in any armed force concern themselves with the detailed preparation and conduct of operations from the highest government level down to all aspects of the care of the individual soldier. A defence staff, including military and civilians representing a whole gamut of professions and skills, is occupied with recruiting personnel, forming them into a variety of units, planning, preparing, procuring and manufacturing supplies, equipment and ordnance. The UN have barely even begun to establish such functions at headquarters, and perhaps for this reason are unable to understand what it is that they are failing to do. The need to fill this gap, however, is more than evident today, not only because there has been a wide expression of views in its support, but also because there is a realization among all who have participated in these operations that adequate planning and preparation are essential for their success.

The inclusion of a military advisory staff on a permanent basis in New York would be advantageous, whether peacekeeping operations continue to be *ad hoc* or develop along the lines envisaged in the Charter. The expertise of the Military Staff Committee has never been available, because an enforcement action, as envisaged in the Charter, by the big powers is most unlikely. But even if its activities were fully restored, the presence of an international military staff within the Secretariat would continue to be an essential requirement. The Military Staff Committee can only act as an inter-governmental committee; it could not be expected to assume staff functions, which would have to remain a Secretariat responsibility. Military staff, integral to this Secretariat, would thus provide a vital link between the political leadership and the Military Staff Committee. There is therefore an obvious requirement for including independent military expertise within the international Secretariat.

At the end of the 1960s, it was said that a military staff would not be able to plan for any specific operation in the future, and therefore it would have little to do unless the UN became involved in another major undertaking like the Congo. In other words, in the circumstances of that time, when the UN's responsibility was limited to two observer operations (UNMOGIP and UNTSO) and one peacekeeping force (UNFICYP), the presence of a military advisory staff of any considerable level and size was thought to be wasteful and politically impossible. In the Introduction to the Secretary-General's 1967 Annual Report (paragraph 34) it was stated: 'In the political circumstances prevailing at the United Nations, it is hard to see how a United Nations military staff, even if authorized by the competent organs, could justify its existence and actually improve very much the quality either of existing operations or of hypothetical future ones.' This raised two main issues: first, in the political circumstances prevailing, i.e. the reservations about strengthening the Secretary-General's office, was it possible to use a Military Advisory Staff? and secondly, even if such a staff were available, could there be enough work to justify its existence?

The fact that the General Assembly had authorized the Secretary-

General to include military personnel within the Secretariat is sufficient evidence of the membership's realization that, if the responsibility for peacekeeping operations involving military personnel were
entrusted to the Secretary-General, he should be provided with
military experts if he needed them. On the other hand, the peacekeeping crisis in the mid-1960s required delicate handling by the Secretary-
General. The other question is whether a military staff would have
enough to do.

The inclusion of a Military Advisory staff on a permanent basis
would provide essential capability to the Organization to meet the
demands frequently made upon it by the recurrent authorization of
peacekeeping operations. It should be obvious that there is a need for
specialized knowledge both in the functioning of the UN and in the
handling of peacekeeping forces. Experience in the field would not be
complete until accompanied by an intimate knowledge of the functioning of Headquarters. This knowledge can be gained only by
military staff working in the Organization. The argument that this
staff cannot be fully utilized in the absence of large-scale operations is
analogous to the situation at national level, where governments may
lament the need to retain expensive defence establishments in times of
peace, but where in wartime the defence establishment is never sufficient to meet its requirements. A military staff retained by the UN on a
permanent basis would be better qualified when new peacekeeping
operations were authorized, or when faced with an emergency arising
from a current operation.

The gathering of information to permit intelligent consideration of
all the factors involved for contingency planning does not require a
great deal of time. Once an operation has been authorized with the co-
operation of the host-country, it is possible to complete plans for the
speedy establishment of a peacekeeping operation. The organization
of the force — including the selection of personnel, production of
tables of organization and establishment of units — and the preparation of the administrative support likely to be required in a future
operation ideally demand long-term planning, but this is usually not
possible. However, in the case of Namibia considerable advance planning has been done. This proves that whenever reasonable advance
notice is available, the Secretariat has now a capability to plan.

Over the years, the UN Secretariat (particularly the Office of the
Under-Secretary-General for Special Political Affairs and the Field
Operations Service) have acquired considerable experience, and most
of their senior staff combine headquarters and field experience. This
staff fulfils a variety of responsibilities which, in the case of a national
military operation, would involve Defence and Foreign Ministries.
The Under-Secretary-General for Special Political Affairs is responsible to the Secretary-General for the day-to-day management of the
operations, whereas the Field Operations Service's responsibility is

confined to administrative and budgetary matters. These two departments must work in unison to implement the mandate given to the Secretary-General. We have already referred to the need for suitable military logistics experts to be included in the Field Operations Service. However, it is the Under-Secretary-General for Special Political Affairs who is at the hub of these operations at the UN Secretariat.

An effective command and control system is vital to the success of any operation. In national military operations, commanders and staff are appointed in advance and given time to train and work together and develop into a well-knit team. Other key personnel who are available are immediately selected and nominated in advance. If they do not have any past experience in the nature of the operations, they are brought together for short periods or despatched to attend specialized courses of training. On mobilization, the team is completed and dispatched to the area of operations.

In UN operations the process of establishing suitable command and control starts 'from cold' with the authorization of the operation. In some cases it has been possible to transfer key personnel from an existing operation to a new one, usually on a temporary basis, and this arrangement has proved fruitful. But the majority of the staff — and, more often than not, the head of the operation — are hurriedly appointed from an existing UN mission. Experience has proved this to be unsatisfactory.

During the Congo operation, the Military Adviser's staff started with great care to prepare a list of requirements of key personnel in advance; and on the basis of previous peacekeeping experience, they prepared an index of qualified personnel. It thus became possible to fill many posts with trained personnel. A military advisory staff of adequate size, as in the past throughout the 1960s and since the establishment of UNEF II, could assume this responsibility for current and future operations, and has actually done so. Such planning greatly assists many member-states which are anxious to support the UN.

The organization tables and establishments for operational units require special study. In the early 1960s the Military Adviser's staff, on an informal basis, successfully helped the Scandinavian countries to plan their standby forces for service in the UN. It is perfectly feasible for such staff (of reasonable size) to plan for some future contingency. The idea, born within the Military Adviser's staff during the 1960s, of working out a block type of organization table and establishment which could be expanded into an observer operation or a peacekeeping force, as required, was enthusiastically received by several member-states when it was first discussed. This could easily be developed into final form and provide a basis on which interested governments could develop their contributions. In fact, this has become a practice as the UN calls upon likely contributing states (e.g.

the Nordic countries with standby units) to participate in planning. The International Peace Academy has also proved helpful in this regard when the UN is unable to undertake advanced planning.

We have already mentioned the problem of administrative support. In the final analysis, the responsibility for the proper administrative and logistics support of a force should belong to the military logistics and civilian administrative units in the field. But here again, despite the UN's enormous experience in the handling of military forces, adequate machinery for advance planning and preparation does not exist. As with the operational units, it should be quite possible to include the logistic echelons within the block pattern, as is often done by national defence establishments. The availability of such units on a standby or readily available basis would be of enormous help to the UN. It is recognized that not many governments have logistic elements for overseas operations. Therefore, there is a need on their part to organize and include such elements for future operations. Logistic support of peacekeeping operations is particularly complex because political factors affect the system of procurement, the use of ports and other transportation facilities. There is thus an even greater requirement for advance planning and preparation.

Not having any standing forces of its own, the UN has to call on member-states to provide logistic units to extend its Field Service into an area of operations. Experience has shown that while it is comparatively easy to obtain individuals for operational duties, it is almost impossible to obtain well-trained logistic units, whether military or civilian. There is thus an urgent need for advance preparation, selection and earmarking of such personnel and units to improve operations and effect economies. Here again, although the UN Field Service has enormous experience and does its best, it relies heavily on the military technical experience of the force in the field — an element which should also be integral to its own establishment. In the case of advance planning for Namibia, the UN Secretariat has largely relied on the United States military planners. The UN also obtained the temporary services of Canadian logistics experts.

Signal communications provide the vital link for effective command and control of a peacekeeping operation, as well as a steady flow of information between the high command and the units in the field. The UN is fortunate in possessing within the Field Service a highly skilled communications service, which was established in the early days of the Organization. Units of this service have been organic to all peacekeeping operations and must continue to provide the back bone of signal communications in any operation. Difficulties arise, however, in establishing suitable signal communications within units, and from units to force headquarters. An infantry battalion is the recognized self-contained unit in an army, and since it is primarily organized for conventional military operations, its signal communications resources are limited. The UN thus has two courses open to it: either to complete plans for the early introduction of suitable signal communications equipment which the units can operate without much training; or to provide these communications on the basis of a rapid expansion of their own communications service.

An up-to-date reference on situation reports and maps, plans, instructions and Standing Operating Procedures (SOPs) is already being maintained. The upkeep and critical perusal of all such material should constitute an important part of the routine work of the Military Adviser and his staff. These tasks were handled during the Congo operations by the Military Adviser, subsequently by the Military Liaison staff, and after the October 1973 war by the Military Adviser again. There is never any shortage of such work to be done. Future plans, instructions and SOPs should be subject to a close review to ensure that they are consistent with Headquarters policy, and kept up-to-date in the light of changing situations which may require fresh instructions from Headquarters to the field. There are also factors influencing the administrative support from Headquarters on logistics in the field, which should be carefully worked out ahead in order to enable their preparation to be completed in advance of an operation.

Supervision by Headquarters is necessary because a Commander and his staff in the field are too close to the situation to be completely objective about their requirements. Detailed checks from UNHQ are essential to improve operations and to ensure economies. Military personnel are accustomed to these controls, and would fall readily into line *if suitable practices were established within the United Nations along prescribed lines*. The present *ad hoc* method of supervision only confuses the military, who are trained to function along orderly and consistent lines. A careful blend of field analysis with Headquarters supervision is the ideal at which to aim. This may be promoted by visits of individuals or small teams from Headquarters to the field for on-the-spot discussions.

A case in point was the planning of the advance of ONUC troops from Elisabethville to Jadotville. Plans for this had been prepared about a year before the operation was actually carried out. For 'political' reasons secrecy shrouded these preparations, and therefore it was thought unwise for the Military Adviser to check on these plans by a visit to the field to make his personal appraisal. As time went by, the need to revise the original plans became obvious, and finally Headquarters checked the situation in the field, but only at a political level (the military advice was excluded). On the basis of the final plans, which appeared sound from the operational point of view but contained several questionable logistics features, requests were submitted to the United States government for logistic support. While agreeing in principle to provide this assistance, the US government proved reluctant to accept the plan in detail until its own high-level military team had visited the area and confirmed its recommendations. There were clearly certain internal political problems about the despatch of an American three-star General (President Kennedy wished to avoid Congressional objections from a strong Katanga lobby by ensuring that the UN operation would be brief and successful), but the US team's visit was also a reflection on the credibility of UN expertise. The United States Mission in New York was aware that, although military expertise at the UN existed, it had in this instance been kept on the periphery of the operations. Such situations can be avoided in the future by proper use of military staff.

While the main responsibility for providing information to delegations and key Secretariat staff rests with the UN political staff, its military staff are subject to questioning on military information. A routine periodic conference is held to disseminate such information to troop-contributing countries, but it would be equally useful if regular briefings for the Secretariat staff were provided by the military to ensure a fuller understanding of developments; this would lead to better co-ordination. Moreover, information is always a two-way street, and a military advisory staff, co-operative with and helpful to the delegations, would create conditions under which the delegations would be equally responsive to providing information of military value to the Secretariat.

The military staff are the ideal link between the Secretariat and the military staffs of the delegations. Not only do some of the permanent members of the Security Council have a large military staff at the UN (the United States, the Soviet Union and China have Military Staff Committee delegates; the remaining two use the military staff at their embassies in Washington, DC), but a number of other delegations also include such expertise, particularly those which have a special interest in peacekeeping. A suitable two-way traffic of mutual assistance, not only with the new information but over the entire field of these operations, could be developed by expanding the military staff in the Secretariat at appropriate levels and numbers. One has only to talk to any of the delegations who evince interest in peacekeeping operations to confirm such a view. Regular contacts between the Secretariat and the delegations are especially valuable when they provide the only channels of information to a troop-contributing government. Timely, detailed information enables these governments to strengthen their support of the operation and to keep their parliaments and public informed. This is in fact being done.

The remarkable manner in which military personnel, regardless of nationality, develop a spirit of camaraderie provides a practical means of overcoming some of the political obstacles of peacekeeping. It has been the author's experience that the interest aroused in the technical aspects of these operations by military experts who have little access to their inner functioning may well be an untapped channel for the flow of such information to their authorities. This exchange of information could in turn result in a greater understanding of, and confidence in, the UN's ability to conduct peacekeeping operations.

Another field which needs overhauling is that of administrative support. The UN has evolved its own methods for the kind of operations which it is called on to perform, and has gained considerable experience. But there is confusion over the division of responsibilities, and a lack of understanding of the need for specialist military expertise. The *political* staff have maintained that general policy should be formulated by them. On the other hand, the *administrative* staff claim that since they are responsible to the organs of the UN for administration, they must formulate policy and be allowed to implement it. Thus the administrative support of a peacekeeping operation is divided between the political and administrative staff of the Secretariat at the expense of unified support for peacekeeping operations. This division adversely affects the functioning of the Commander of the operation, also of the Chief Administrative Officer, and thus of the entire operation.

In an operation's final form, although the Commander is responsible for the entire operation, which should include its administration, the Chief Administrative Officer has been recognized as the representative of the administrative staff at UN Headquarters, and he has *direct* channels for reporting and seeking instructions, relieving the Commander of administrative and financial chores. Generally the Commander is appointed from outside the UN staff, while the Chief Administrative Officer is always a member of it. Not only has this arrangement resulted in the assumption by the Chief Administrative Officer of authority beyond his own functions, but he is also looked on by many elements of the UN Headquarters staff as *their representative*. Thus an element of duplication has crept into the force, in some cases complicating the relationship of these two UN representatives at the highest level in the field. A good Commander and a good Chief Administrative Officer can perform effectively, and have done so. However, when one of them is less able than the other, then the system is of little help.

It is now common practice to include the logistic staff from the field in administrative and budgetary planning at UN Headquarters. A good Chief Administrative Officer should have no difficulty in organizing co-ordination with the military staff in the field. Just as the success of the overall operation depends on the Commander, so it is the Chief Administrative Officer who is the key to success for efficient administration.

The need to have a joint planning staff to co-ordinate and integrate the totality of factors essential to the success of peacekeeping operations is obvious. The office of the Under-Secretary for Special Political Affairs serves as the special staff responsible to the Secretary-

General for the formulation and eventual implementation of policy. Ideally, such a staff must include representation of the various branches of the Secretariat concerned, each branch being responsible thereafter for the detailed application of the policy decisions. At present, representatives of the branches concerned meet frequently to exchange information, formulate policy jointly and eventually implement it. Only in such ways is it possible to co-ordinate and balance the various aspects of a peacekeeping operation at the highest level in a manner which would inject proper coherence into the operation in the field.

The degree of joint planning and co-ordination at the UN Secretariat has varied with the personalties of the main players. Up to the 1960s the two main Under-Secretaries involved — those responsible for Special Political Affairs and General Services respectively — received their guidance from the Secretary-General, met each other as often as they could, and let their staffs co-operate as required. Later, with the reorganisation of the Secretariat, an Assistant Secretary-General for General Services was established, and after a change in personnel, the Director of the Field Operations Service, George Lansky, worked closely with the Under-Secretary for Special Political Affairs, Brian Urquhart, and his staff. The Director of the Field Operations Service was responsible for all the administration of peacekeeping operations, and he co-ordinated with other Secretariat branches: finance, personnel, the agencies, and so on. However, this arrangement remained dependent on personalities instead of being regularized, and thus subject to change with personnel changes.

The high-level Secretariat staff have determinedly avoided the use of a committee system, linking branches of the Secretariat, for joint planning and co-ordination. The usual argument for avoiding this system is the experience of various committees set up by the UN organs. The present practice of about a dozen people co-ordinating various related Secretariat branches has proved efficient.

The United Nations is not unique in its administrative and budgetary practices. Some governments, in order to exercise budgetary control over their forces, have tried to divorce administration from military command, but this has always been detrimental to operations. A peacekeeping operation, like any other military operation, is carried out by men who have to expose themselves to hazards and sometimes extreme danger. UN Headquarters should therefore give proper recognition to the institution of leadership, because only full regard to the position of the Chief of the Mission will restore the necessary confidence, not only in him, but also in the UN as an organization, among the men likely to serve under its flag.

Many of the existing weaknesses in peacekeeping operations are traceable to inadequacies in administrative support. An impression exists among the administrative staff at UN Headquarters that no special knowledge in the field of military logistics is required on a continuing basis because of the *ad hoc* nature of each operation. They argue that what little knowledge is needed is already available in the form of the military experience of staff individuals. While the professional skill and goodwill of the administrative staff is high, there are aspects of administrative support at Headquarters and military logistics in the field which really do require specialized management. The military specialist gains this knowledge from years of on-the-job training and from periodically 'going to school' to study his profession. There are no short cuts to the acquisition of this knowledge.

With the establishment of new peacekeeping operations in the Middle East in the 1970s, two military logistics officers were added to the Field Service. One of them is responsible for air movement. The other is more or less the military specialist, but in practice this appointment has not improved matters much. There is an urgent need for better military logistics expertise at Headquarters, especially in the area of advance planning, practices, standards and inspection.

In any good armed force, leaders are brought up in the tradition that the safety and wellbeing of the men they are commanding must take precedence over their own — always, every time. The command structure at each level, as well as a system of strict supervision and inspection, prevents delinquency in this respect. In the duality of the UN system of administration there is an absence of the personal touch between Headquarters and the men in the field. This situation does not arise in a national force. If management and the wellbeing of the personnel have not suffered more, it has been due mainly to a feeling of commitment to the ideals of the mission on the part of the individuals involved, the unselfish attitude of the national contingent officers, and the additional assistance by governments to supplement inadequate amenities provided by the UN. While it is understandable that, exposed to the political complexities that confront any UN force, some men may return home somewhat disillusioned and cynical about the capabilities of the UN, it should not follow that they need have so much reason to complain about its management capabilities in the field of military operations — operations which are comparatively simple in their nature. The UN has seldom shown a true understanding of this problem, and it is this writer's considered view that the UN should revert to customary military channels for carrying this grave responsibility. The established military tradition demands that administration be the responsibility of the Commander in the field and, directly above him, of the Secretary-General as the Organization's Chief Executive; and that all intermediate echelons should devote their entire energies to helping these two to achieve this end.

As described earlier, the role of the Secretary-General and thus of the Secretariat has emerged as a key factor in the management of peacekeeping operations. As the indisputable primary organ responsible for the maintenance of international peace and security, the Security Council could be likened to the cabinet ministers in a government or the board of directors of a corporation that authorizes, manages and finances a peacekeeping operation. The Council, in turn, invariably calls on the Secretary-General to be responsible for planning, conducting and administering the operation. The office of the Under-Secretaries-General for Special Political Affairs is charged with day-to-day responsibility for peacekeeping operations. Although the Secretary-General's role has always remained critical, credit for the successful higher management of peacekeeping operations belongs to the Under-Secretary-General who is mainly responsible for peacekeeping operations. The first holder of this appointment was Ralph Bunche, and after his death U Thant appointed Brian Urquhart. As one of the chief architects of UN peacekeeping, Bunche had established procedures and practices, many of which carried his own style of working and his own great human qualities. Urquhart, a Second World War paratrooper, had spent years on Bunche's staff and served in the field, so when he was appointed to succeed Bunche, he was able to bring his enormous experience to his assignment. He was able to strengthen co-ordination at the Secretariat and was responsive to the problems of the field, thus knitting the two major elements into a cohesive team. Although differences remain among the member-states on principles and guidelines, it is agreed by all of them that Urquhart (who joined the world organization in 1946) has made and continues to make a vital contribution to global peace and security and that he deserves their fullest support. Urquhart and his highly capable staff have gained the complete confidence and respect of the diplomatic community, as also of the civilian and military peacekeepers in the field.

The Secretary-General appointed in 1982, Javier Pérez de Cuéllar, also brings practical peacekeeping experience to UN Headquarters. He was serving as Peru's delegate on the Security Council when UNEF II was established to end the October 1973 war between the Egyptians and the Israelis. Later he served as President of the Security Council during the most critical phase of the 1974 events in Cyprus, and as the Secretary-General's Special Representative in Cyprus in 1975–7. There he was responsible for negotiations between the parties and for the overall conduct of peacekeeping operations. He later served as the Under-Secretary-General for Special Political Affairs at the UN (1979–81) and as the Secretary-General's Personal Representative for Afghanistan. On his appointment as Secretary-General, his first major act was to place the Field Operations Service, responsible for administration and logistic support of peacekeeping missions, under his direct personal control with James O.C. Jonah of Sierra Leone, a respected UN staff member with long experience in peacekeeping, as the Assistant Secretary-General in charge. Recently a military logistics expert has been added to his staff, which should meet that need in part. Although the administrative and logistic support of peacekeeping operations is beset with inherent problems, this change should certainly make improvements in the weakest link of peacekeeping operations. It is important that the office of the Under-Secretary-General for Special Political Affairs remains the co-ordinating and directing branch of administrative and budgetary matters, as undoubtedly it continues to be. Knowing the bureaucratic difficulties and conflicting interests, the new Secretary-General indicated at the very outset where his priorities lie, an action that deserves credit and the fullest support of the international community.

It is pleasing to note that the UN Military Liaison Officer's appointment has been changed to that of Military Adviser. Since his first posting to the UN, Brig.-Gen. Timothy K. Dibuama of Ghana has in fact played the role of a Military Adviser in the office of the Under-Secretary-General for Special Political Affairs; thus the change in his appointment fittingly recognizes his valuable contribution. With the establishment of this appointment, every encouragement should be given to the Secretary-General to help his staff to maintain and make effective use of it. A Military Adviser can be fully effective only if adequate staff support is provided.

The number of military assistants should be determined by the number and variety of peacekeeping missions and the size of the workload. This staff should include capability to advise and support the Under-Secretary-General for Special Political Affairs in all military matters relating to his responsibilities. In practice, Brian Urquhart is known to recognize fully the need for adequate military staff support, but he has been careful to avoid any apprehensions on the part of the member-states who have so assiduously maintained the primacy of the Security Council.

To summarize, the ultimate responsibility for the effective management of peacekeeping operations is with the UN Secretariat. It is the Secretary-General who is called upon by the Security Council to recommend the size, organization (including command and control), administrative support and finances of the units for any given operation. It is the Secretary-General who interprets the Council's mandate into operational directives and negotiates with the contributing countries and the host-country or countries. While several departments of the Secretariat become involved, it is the Under-Secretary-General for Special Political Affairs responsible for peacekeeping operations who is entrusted by the Secretary-General with the main staff planning preparations, co-ordination, and day-to-day operational responsibilities. Hence this office has remained the key to the success of peacekeeping operations.

Even the UN's strongest critics admit that the Organization deserves praise for its peacekeeping efforts. Although it still has far to go in developing a capability to deal with its primary responsibility — 'to save succeeding generations from the scourge of war' — peacekeeping has taken it in the right direction. The fifth Secretary-General, Pérez de Cuéllar, has shown his determination to strengthen the UN's peacekeeping operations. Because the role of the Secretary-General is the key to a successful peacekeeping operation, member-states should support his efforts to the maximum limits of the policy and political dimensions of each situation. It is now time for the international community to take new initiatives to narrow their differences and provide the UN with the capability that it should have.

NOTES

1. Introduction to the Annual Report of the Secretary-General on the work of the Organization, June 16, 1966–June 15, 1967. Official Records of the General Assembly, 22nd Session, Supplement 1A (A/6701/Add.1).
2. Military advisory staff in the Office of the UN Secretary-General: Military Adviser and one staff officer for UNEF I, from 1956 for a few years. Military Adviser and 3–8 staff officers for ONUC, 1960–4. The same Military Adviser and one assistant continued until 1969. A Military Liaison Officer, 1969–73. A Military Liaison Officer with one or two assistants from 1973 on. The Military Adviser's post was re-established in 1979–80, with a staff of four.

8

THE OVER-RIDING FACTOR: PEACEKEEPING AND THE SUPERPOWERS

The creation of a multinational force for the Sinai by the United States to replace UNEF II, whose mandate the Soviet Union declined to extend because of its opposition to the Egyptian-Israeli treaty of 1979, was perceived by many delegates and senior officials in the UN as a trend that was likely to affect adversely the future of the world organization. The three signatories to the peace treaty would have preferred it otherwise. They had hoped that the Security Council could have authorized a new mandate for UNEF II. But these hopes were based on a naive belief that since UN peacekeeping had proved its usefulness, the member-states would agree, even though the peace treaty had excluded some major parties, particularly Syria, the PLO and, most of all, the Soviet Union.

There was some satisfaction for Israel in the new arrangement. First, other than for a brief period during the civil war in Lebanon in 1958, every US administration, careful of its relations with the Arabs, had kept clear of direct involvement of its troops in the area. Now the United States was to be the main bulwark of the MFO. Secondly, the Soviets had broken diplomatic relations with Israel after the June 1967 war and were strong supporters of Israel's two major enemies, Syria and the PLO. The Israelis hoped to keep the door open to the Russians to promote immigration of Soviet Jews. Prime Minister Menachem Begin had, in all but law, annexed the West Bank, giving the area its old Biblical name of Judea and Samaria. The Israelis had permitted the creation of scores of settlements on the West Bank and had built large-scale housing around Jerusalem; and both of these projects needed immigrants, who were only available from the Soviet Union. But the Soviets had kept the flow below Israel's expectations, and many immigrants had left Israel for the United States or elsewhere. So the Israelis felt they could afford to be tough on the Soviets.

Egypt, virtually isolated from the other Arab states by signing a separate peace treaty with Israel, had hoped to retain the UN presence — as a thread to the international community. Nor was she keen about admitting an American military presence which could further harm her relations with the Arabs and weaken her status as a leading non-aligned nation.

The United States too would have preferred a UN force, even though a foothold in Sinai offered her many strategic advantages. Certainly the United States was not prepared to undertake this task alone. Fiji was glad to provide its second battalion, thus making the

UN responsible for one and the MFO for the other battalion, earning this small nation most of its defence budget. Except for Uruguay, which is a recipient of US military aid, all other MFO contingents are from countries allied to the United States. The MFO headquarters in Rome was headed by Leamon R. Hunt, an American diplomat who was tragically assassinated in February 1984 after showing the highest ability, tact and skill in giving the force a multinational character. In the field Lt.-Gen. Frederick V. Bull-Hansen of Norway, the Force Commander, with his past UN peacekeeping experience, handled the force with a high degree of sensitivity and efficiency. The fact remains that the MFO is largely an American force, financed and supported by the United States.

The role of the MFO is governed by the trilateral Camp David accord, in which the United States is both a mediator and a party. America's support of Israel and its opposition to the Soviet Union's involvement in the region, coupled with Soviet support for Syria and the PLO and the US refusal to deal with the PLO, clearly make the United States an interested party in the Middle East conflict. The saying that superpowers are never neutral because they always have interests applies to the United States in this situation, just as it applies to the Soviet Union.

The operational task of the MFO is to supervise a treaty that ended a state of war between Egypt and Israel. It was established as a confidence-building measure between two countries which had signed the treaty after being in a state of war since 1948, during which period active fighting had broken out five times. Once there is formal peace, there should be no need for peacekeeping in the strict sense.

The practice of peacekeeping as developed by the UN is to bring about and then to supervise an end to fighting and to create an environment that will facilitate negotiations leading to peace. When there is already peace, sealed by a peace treaty, a presence designed to prevent developments that could adversely affect relations and perhaps lead to war might perhaps be called peacekeeping; but it is stretching the definition of peacekeeping unconvincingly.

Thus the MFO is a new phenomenon. It looks like a peacekeeping force, but its role is to build confidence between Egypt and Israel. The UN could have performed such a task well; but the organization should not despair because it was not called upon to do so while the superpowers were at odds. In any case, the Charter permits such bilateral arrangements and allows for another party, or parties, to be included as long as the states involved in the conflict agree. Both the political circumstances and the high capability of the force performance have led to avoidance of incidents. As long as a third-party role, like that of the MFO, is acceptable and functional, it is undoubtably a useful instrument for diplomacy to promote confidence.

It was the creation of the multinational force (MNF) for Beirut that brought the discussion of peacekeeping to the forefront at the United Nations and elsewhere. The choice of a MNF was based on political grounds. In the case of Lebanon — unlike the situation in the Sinai, where the Camp David accord suggested the continuing presence of UNEF II — the Israelis never wanted any role for the UN in peacekeeping, and the US agreed.

The MNF was called a peacekeeping force; yet its losses in personnel killed exceeded many times over the total of those killed in UN peacekeeping operations in Beirut and South Lebanon. This force was daily involved in fighting. A growing body of opinion in the United States wanted the US Marines to depart, but President Ronald Reagan told the nation that the Marines and other MNF troops were performing an essential role in helping the Lebanese government to maintain law and order while its army was organized and trained to assume gradually larger responsibilities. He eventually gave way early in 1984.

Brian Urquhart wrote in the *New York Times* on December 19, 1983: 'The crisis in Lebanon has raised fundamental questions about the concept of peacekeeping — the use of military personnel for control of international conflicts. The success of peacekeeping depends on a sound political base, a well-defined mandate and objective, the co-operation of the conflicting parties, firm but politically sensitive command, and the attitude and understanding of their task by the peacekeeping soldiers.' The MNF does not meet many of these conditions. Urquhart further said that 'in 1982, the United States' objection to a peacekeeping presence [referring to a UN role] was from one side of the East-West divide [meaning the United States]. This year it is, for the moment, from the other.' Urquhart was referring to the Soviet opposition. He hoped that eventually peacekeeping by the UN might be of value in pacifying this uniquely difficult problem.

At his year-end press conference on December 21, 1983, the UN Secretary-General, Javier Pérez de Cuéllar, supported the views expressed by Urquhart. He said that a UN force would be more effective in preserving order in the Beirut area. The Secretary-General, a veteran diplomat, great negotiator, experienced peacekeeper and long-time international civil servant, would not have expressed his views so bluntly unless he felt the situation had become critical.

Historically it is the US, not the Soviet Union, which has promoted UN peacekeeping and helped to develop this novel instrument of diplomacy. Its evolution has also owed a great deal to individuals — Dag Hammarskjöld, Lester Pearson, Ralph Bunche and, for the last decade, Brian Urquhart — and to individual member-states like Canada, the Nordic countries, Austria, Ireland, India, Nigeria and others. But this was largely made possible by the support of the United States. Chapter 1 discussed the political attitude towards peacekeeping of different member-states. The present critical point in

UN peacekeeping has been reached because of the East-West disagreement, and because the United States has opted for bilateral diplomacy and unilateral intervention rather than relying on the international system.

The Reagan Administration's distrust of the UN was the result not only of its difficulties with the Soviet Union, and of opposition by bloc voting in the Assembly on issues like South Africa and Israel. The Administration is also ideologically committed to bilateralism and the use of its influence with the strength it can muster, especially its military power. That has been the recent story. But a brief survey of US attitudes towards UN peacekeeping shows that individual Presidents have not maintained an even policy in this regard. Peacekeeping has been used when it is perceived to serve the best interests of the United States.

It is generally accepted that peacekeeping is a diplomatic key opening the way to further negotiations for a peaceful resolution of conflicts. It is therefore only a part of a whole system, and often only the beginning of a process to halt a conflict. It interacts on the other parts. A poorly organized and conducted peacekeeping operation could jeopardize negotiations. Equally, unsuccessful diplomatic efforts can harm peacekeeping operations and even reduce their ability to a point where their effectiveness is at least questionable if it has not actually been destroyed. The analysis of peacekeeping in the past chapters shows that while peacekeeping operations can and should be improved, they have in fact done their part. The lack of peaceful resolution of conflicts has more often been due to the failure of diplomacy.

The major cause of this failure has been the increased polarization of the world, which in turn is reflected in the actions of international and regional institutions. The great powers, and the superpowers in particular, place a primary reliance on bilateral diplomacy. This process has been blunted by rising tensions and by the resulting confrontation between the United States and the Soviet Union, which then influences relations between East and West and their respective friends elsewhere in the world. This polarization pervades all activities at the UN and regional systems. The first major casualty of the cold war was the UN Security Council, and since the 1950s, with few exceptions, the ability of the Council to perform or not has reflected the attitude of the superpowers. In the last few years up to the time of writing, the potential of the Council has been so reduced that its resolutions go unheeded. The failure of the Council initially led to more reliance on the General Assembly. When the threat of a veto by the Soviets became obvious during the Korean wars, the United States turned to the Assembly for all action related to this situation. After the Suez conflict in 1956, it was again the Assembly that set up the UN's first peacekeeping force.

This situation prevailed until the emergence of many new African states in the 1960s. These countries have consistently resisted any semblance of colonialism or imperialistic trends. They often opposed the United States when it supported the colonial powers, who were part of the Western alliance, or when it took a stand on ideological grounds. Thus the United States lost its assured majority in the Assembly and, like the Soviets, turned to the Security Council for action.

Except on rare occasions, the two superpowers have relentlessly opposed each other in the Council. However, the United States has gradually learned to live with the new Assembly. Even Mrs Jeane Kirkpatrick, the Reagan Administration's Permanent Representative to the UN and the world body's severest critic, acknowledged for the second year in succession, at a press conference concluding the 1983 session, that the Assembly session had been relatively successful. However, the Assembly President, Jorge Illueca of Panama, noted that the Assembly of 158 nations and its committees adopted 63 resolutions on disarmament, 20 resolutions on the Middle East and 11 resolutions on the problem of South African apartheid, all of which were of little effect because the parties to the conflict enjoyed the support of one superpower or the other, and therefore would not comply.

In closing the thirty-eighth session of the General Assembly Illueca, reflecting the views of the large marjority of its members, said: 'I fear we must conclude that in spite of our best efforts, the state of the world has steadily and sharply deteriorated.' He added: 'International violence has increased. We have seen the application of military power. There has been a sharp increase in violent acts of international terrorism, and the nuclear arms race has escalated to a higher and much more dangerous level.'

The architects of the UN Charter, recognizing the importance of the great powers in the maintenance of international peace and security, gave them a permanent place in the Security Council and the authority of the veto. It was not long after the birth of the UN that the United States and the Soviet Union emerged as superpowers. The United States had already developed and used nuclear weapons before the end of the Second World War and therefore became the dominant military power, a position it was able to maintain with its vast economic resources. But the Soviets exploded their first nuclear device in 1947 and altered the whole strategic balance. Not only had they the nuclear weapon know-how, but they had also kept the largest conventional military force in the world. The United States met this challenge through an alliance in the West and by seeking military collaboration elsewhere. It also met the challenge of the spread of Communism by political, economic and even military means, the latter leading to the wars on the Korean peninsula and in Indo-China. Thus, the era of relentless pursuit by the superpowers for influence, political and strategic, and also for resources, started soon after the end of the Second World War.

Each American administration has dealt somewhat differently with the Soviet Union in pursuit of their national interests. Differences between the Democrats and the Republicans were persistent, and some consideration of this subject is required to understand what may be possible in international peacekeeping for the present, and what may be expected in the future.

It was President Harry Truman who first challenged the Soviets and the spread of Communism. The Berlin blockade in 1948 was lifted through a large-scale American airlift; and North Korea's invasion of South Korea across the 38th parallel was dealt with by General Douglas MacArthur's forces, which contained some allied contingents. This action was authorized by the UN Security Council (because the Russians had walked out of the Council chamber over the question of a procedural vote) and became known as the UN Command in Korea. Except for the initial authorization, all subsequent actions of the force in Korea were dealt with by the General Assembly, so as to avoid a Soviet veto. The UN members, wishing to avoid involvement in US-Soviet controversy, turned over all responsibility for this force to the United States. Thus, from the beginning, it was a US operation, led and supported by that power. The façade that this operation is a UN command has been kept up to the present day; the UN flag flies over all military installations, and all vehicles and troops carry the UN insignia. But the Command reports to the Joint Chiefs of Staff at the Pentagon and not to the UN.

The Truman administration did, however, support the early use of UN observer missions to report on ceasefires and other military disengagement agreements, starting with the first in the Balkans; and then in Kashmir, in Palestine between Arabs and Israelis, and in Indonesia. These conflicts resulting from decolonization, a process fully endorsed by the United States, helped America's Western colonial-power allies to obtain a peaceful transfer without serious damage to their future interests. The Soviets too supported decolonization, because newly-independent countries offered them fresh opportunities in areas previously closed to them.

President Eisenhower, on succeeding Truman, was faced with the crisis in the Middle East which eventually led to the Suez war in 1956. Two allies, Britain and France, joined by America's prime aid recipient Israel, had invaded Egypt. The Soviets, having provided arms to President Nasser of Egypt through Czechoslovakia and promised to help build the Aswan dam, answered a call for assistance from the beleaguered Egyptians by announcing the dispatch of volunteers. Faced with the dilemma of having to block the Soviet volunteers by the US Sixth Fleet in the eastern Mediterranean or to compel its friends to leave Egypt, President Eisenhower endorsed the idea of an international force to replace invading troops in the Suez Canal area and in Sinai. Such an idea had been considered earlier by the British and the French, but rejected in favour of the course they finally chose.

It was Lester Pearson, Canada's Minister of External Affairs, and the UN Secretary-General Dag Hammarskjöld who turned this idea into a new, yet highly acceptable, concept of establishing a UN peace-keeping force — UNEF I. The Soviets were not opposed to it as long as it led to the departure of foreign forces. As it turned out, Nasser gained enormously in political prestige as a result of the Suez fiasco.

The Soviet Union gave its consent for UNEF with reservations, reminding the Assembly of its obligations under Article 43 of the Charter, stressing that such operations were the primary responsibility of the Security Council. It was the vetoes by Britain and France that had led the Council to refer the Suez crisis to the Assembly. What was of even greater importance was that the Soviets set their own guide-lines for financing future operations by refusing to pay their share, and insisted that the 'aggressors' should pay. (It took the UN several years to define the term 'aggressor', and even now it remains far from clear.) The French too refused to pay, but for a different reason: they wanted Egypt to pay. Subsequently the United States, realizing the importance of UNEF I, made up the difference by contributing more than its customary share.

Before the end of Eisenhower's second presidential term the Congo (Zaire), on gaining its independence from Belgium, faced a serious crisis. Its army had mutinied and the mineral-rich province Katanga (Shaba) had seceded from Leopoldville (Kinshasa). Patrice Lumumba, the Prime Minister, first turned to Clare Timberlake, the US ambassador, for military assistance. The Eisenhower Administration was reluctant to involve American troops in Africa, but was also determined to keep the Soviets out of the country. Having found the role of UN peacekeeping useful to its foreign policy, the United States encouraged Lumumba to request UN assistance, which he did. This led to the creation of ONUC, the largest peacekeeping operation in the UN's history.

While there were many influences on the nature of UN operations in the Congo, that of the Americans remained predominant. In fact it was pervasive in every aspect in dealing with the local leaders, the national Congolese leaders, the divided Congolese forces, the country's economic and monetary structure, the troop contributors and other states involved, especially the pro-Western Africans, and the Western nations, notably the Belgians, as well as Rhodesia and South Africa. American policy towards the Congo reflected the opposing currents within the Eisenhower administration, as well as the varying forces within the Republican and later the Democratic parties. Timberlake, representing a conservative government, was not long in opposing the fiercely nationalist Lumumba. Wishing to avoid chaos in Katanga and any harm to the extraction of its mineral resources needed by the West, Timberlake was in no hurry to end the secession there. An impatient and highly volatile Lumumba could not wait for a change in US policy, and launched an invasion of Katanga with Soviet-supplied transport. This being intolerable to the Americans and other Western powers, Col. Joseph D. Mobutu (later President Mobutu Sese Seko) was encouraged to remove Lumumba and assume power. The staffs of the Soviet and other East European embassies and several African diplomats opposed to the Mobutu coup, were ignominiously thrown out of the country. The Russians are not likely to forget this period, or the inability of the UN peace-keeping force to take any action to prevent the downing of a legitimately-elected government by a military coup. Many heads of state and government, including Chairman Khrushchev, attended the UN General Assembly session in 1960. The Soviets, deeply hurt by their Congo experience, called for the resignation of Hammarskjöld and the appointment of three persons (a troika) to replace him. The attempt to remove Hammarskjöld was opposed by other permanent powers, and defeated in the Assembly by the solid support of the Third World countries for the able Secretary-General.

A change in US policy was signalled by President John F. Kennedy's inauguration and his appointment of Edmund Gullion as his ambassador to the Congo. Gullion proved to be an able, tactful yet tough negotiator. Kennedy wanted a return to democracy, a negotiated end to Katanga's secession, and the restoration of law and order and of the economic life of the country. He was keen on isolat-ing the Congo from East-West issues, which meant keeping the Russians out and making the Congo safe for the West. While Kennedy moved with caution, seeking the support of different congressional groups, his ambassador in the Congo acted with equal caution but with determination to achieve his President's goals — which he did. Today President Mobutu continues to rule the Congo, and despite many upheavals he has kept it well entrenched in the Western camp.

The Cuban crisis was primarily dealt with between the superpowers. U Thant played a significant role in providing his good offices, but when it came to verifying the departure of the missiles from Cuba, the United States did not rely on any third party, and performed the job with its own navy. However, it did want the UN to monitor any remaining military equipment, which Cuba refused. As it turned out, there was little left to observe beyond the agreed number of Soviet advisors and equipment.

President Johnson inherited the Kennedy legacy of the use of the international organization when it best suited American national interests. In 1962 war erupted between the Dutch and the Indonesians over the future of West Irian; and later there was a war in Yemen when

Egypt sent an army to support a revolutionary military group which opposed the Saudi-supported Yemen Arab Republic. Both these situations were of direct concern to the US. A mediator specially appointed by the President, Ellsworth Bunker, successfully negotiated settlements to both conflicts, which were ratified by the Security Council to permit the use of UN peacekeeping machinery. An observer group in each case was dispatched to supervise an end to fighting. In West Irian, a UN security force was introduced to support a UN temporary administrative authority for a period of six months after which, in accordance with the agreement, the Indonesians were to assume the administration and organize a referendum later. As to Yemen, Egypt and Saudi Arabia came to an agreement about its future, and the UN Observer Group there was withdrawn. In order to avoid any objections from the Soviets, the parties concerned had requested the UN presence and assumed responsibility for all its costs.

The Johnson administration was to support yet another UN peacekeeping operation. At the end of 1963 fighting broke out in Cyprus between the Greek and Turkish communities soon after the island had gained its independence from Britain. Of the powers guaranteeing the independence of Cyprus, only Britain could play a role, once the Greek and Turkish forces in Nicosia joined their respective communities. All efforts to resolve the conflict by the guarantor powers with the help of the United States (which had close ties with all three), and later within NATO, failed. Only then was the Security Council called to assist. A UN force in Cyprus was established. Though much buffeted, notably by the Turkish invasion in 1974, it remains there to the present day.

It was obvious from the outset that the Soviets would not have given their endorsement for this operation had special arrangements for its financing not been made. In this case they were on a voluntary basis. The Cyprus government and those countries directly involved insisted on troops of European origin; however the first Force Commander and two later ones were from India, due to the good relations India enjoyed with the Cypriots, and the past UN experience and outstanding ability of the three Indian generals: Prem Singh Gyani, formerly Commander UNEF; 'Timmy' Thimayya, formerly chief of repatriation of Korean war prisoners; and Prem Chand, formerly UN Commander in Katanga. Their devotion to the UN was unquestionable.

The financing of UN peacekeeping operations took a dramatic turn when the United States moved in the Assembly that the Soviets, having failed to pay their dues for more than two years, should be denied their vote under Article 19 of the Charter. This would have applied equally to the French, who were delinquent in their peacekeeping payments; but the American diplomatic move was primarily against the Soviet Union. Realising that there was considerable sympathy for the Soviets in the Assembly, and that if they continued to insist on such a vote it would lead to the end of the UN, the Americans withdrew their resolution.

Not long after he had escalated the war in Vietnam President Johnson realized the depth of the American people's opposition to it. He chose not to be a candidate for re-election, and it became evident that the nation would not re-elect another Democratic administration. Several attempts were made by leading world statesmen to find a negotiated solution to the war in Indo-China. U Thant's attempts to offer his good offices and a possible role for the UN were derided. An International Control Commission (Canada, India, Poland) had been established after the French withdrawal from the region, but it could not play any significant role because the United States and the Soviet Union were co-chairmen of the Commission, and the former did not wish to discuss the question with the Soviets.

President Richard Nixon, on being elected, mixed tough talk and peace initiatives in Vietnam, and in his dealings with the Russians. He restored relations with China. But he showed little interest in the problems of the Third World. Only the Middle East concerned his National Security Adviser, Henry Kissinger, as it does all US governments because of Israel, Arab oil and other strategic interests. When the Arab-Israeli war broke out in October 1973, a massive air resupply was organized by the United States to replace Israeli losses inflicted by the Egyptians in their successful crossing of the Suez Canal. This timely US support turned the tide against Egypt, particularly at a time when President Sadat was obliged to continue his attack beyond what initially was planned, in order to lessen Israeli attacks against the Syrians in the north. In a brilliant counter-attack the Israeli forces under General Ariel Sharon crossed the Canal and cut off the lines of supply of the Egyptian Third Army in the southern sector. Only the Soviets could have re-supplied this army by air, but this would have required them to deal with the Israeli air force, and would inevitably have led to a global war. Since neither the Soviets nor the Americans wished to go to war over Sinai, they agreed to call on their respective sides to end fighting and jointly called on the Security Council to order a ceasefire.

The circumstances that led to the establishment of UNEF II in Sinai and later UNDOF in the Golan Heights have been described earlier. It was the non-permanent members who called for a peacekeeping force to separate the combatants and supervise a ceasefire. Kissinger, who had little faith in the UN, and the Soviets, who had serious doubts about the relevance of UN peacekeeping to their national interests, went along with a new force because their earlier call for a ceasefire had gone unheeded. However, Kissinger was not relying on the UN alone in Sinai: picking up a suggestion by Sadat for an American presence, he established an American Sinai Support Mission, with electronic surveillance equipment, and deployed it on the vital passes east of the Suez Canal. UNEF II was made responsible for its safety, for which most of a contingent (from Ghana) was detailed.

Kissinger was quick to learn the use of peacekeeping forces as a diplomatic tool in continuing with his peace process. He negotiated a disengagement between the Israelis and Syrians on the Golan Heights, and his subsequent negotiated withdrawals by the Israelis were accomplished with the assistance of UNEF II. Otherwise unhappy with the working of the world organization, Kissinger picked peacekeeping as its most effective function.

The Soviets had agreed to the Middle East peacekeeping forces because the Arabs wanted them to stop further Israeli military success and to regain as much as possible of the territory lost in the recent war. They agreed on the basis of the Waldheim formula discussed in detail in Chapter 6, whereby the Security Council retained control over the operations and an East European contingent from Poland was included. The Soviets were also co-chairman with the United States for the related negotiations in Geneva. After having obtained these arrangements Kissinger, supported by Israel, gradually isolated the Soviets from the negotiation process. The erosion of co-operation between the superpowers later manifested itself in the Soviet refusal to extend UNEF II to implement the Camp David accord negotiated by President Carter. A typical example of the refusal of the superpowers to act together occurred over the rising conflict between India and Pakistan caused by a revolt against the government in East Pakistan, resulting in 10 million refugees flooding into India. Finding that their respective friends were in opposition to each other, the two superpowers failed to prevent a war which could have been prevented.

There was little change in relations with the Soviet Union after the resignation of President Nixon. President Gerald Ford, who succeeded him, continued with Nixon's policies being handled by Kissinger, who had already been appointed Secretary of State.

President Jimmy Carter's policy was to strengthen the American military with limited additional costs; to negotiate with the Soviets, support human rights, assist Third World countries, and negotiate over the use of US military power. While keeping a dialogue going with the Soviets, he turned to deal with conflicts in the Third World. Inevitably the Middle East came first in his attentions, and he personally took charge of the Camp David negotiations. These depended on the redeployment of UNEF II to assist in the final withdrawal of the Israeli forces from Sinai, and then to act as a buffer between the two parties as a confidence-building measure. Having isolated the Soviets earlier from these negotiations, it was not possible to discuss the future of UNEF II, which would have to be approved by the Security Council. Of course Egypt needed a UN force; and even Israel, which usually had little good to say about UN peacekeeping, hoped for one. However, attempts to obtain Soviet consent through intermediaries aborted. When UNEF II was withdrawn, the Americans put together a multinational and observer force to carry out the task. The establishment of MFO marked a new era in the history of international peacekeeping in the Middle East. In Africa, similar multinational interventions had taken place twice in Shaba, and even earlier at Stanleyville in order to rescue Europeans.

When the Israelis invaded Southern Lebanon in 1978, they first wanted US troops to act as a buffer before they would agree to withdraw. Wishing to avoid involving US troops in this sensitive area, Washington persuaded Israel to agree to a UN force — UNIFIL — to assist in Israeli withdrawal and to keep peace in the area south of the Litani river. The Soviets agreed because they supported the Arabs and all UN member-states in wanting an Israeli withdrawal. Only a UN peacekeeping force could provide the pre-conditions that would make it possible. Like UNEF II, this force is kept under Security Council control.

In his efforts to deal with Third World conflicts, President Carter succeeded in helping to negotiate an arrangement for the independence of Namibia. A UN group — UNTAG — would assume temporary administration of the territory from South Africa, conduct a referendum and then transfer power to an elected government. All this was to be supervised by a peacekeeping force. But of all the issues which engaged President Carter's administration towards the end of his term, none loomed larger than the Iranian hostage question, and in fact it caused his defeat at the polls. However, Carter proved the usefulness of international peacekeeping, and made good use of it for furthering American diplomatic efforts.

Ronald Reagan was elected as President with a commitment to make America great again. He proved it by sending the Marines to Lebanon on what was intended as a peacekeeping mission, but kept them there to support the fragile Lebanese government of President Amin Gemayal. He ordered the invasion of Grenada to remove a leftist military regime, and he ordered large-scale military assistance to conservative governments and right-wing groups in Central America, like the Contras fighting the Sandinista regime in Nicaragua. The Reagan Administration's foreign policy is based on the conviction that Soviet-sponsored radicalism is promoting violence and revolution worldwide, and consequently he gave the role of global policemen to US troops. He ordered a US Navy battleship, missile ships and aircraft to attack those who fired at the Marines in Lebanon, and even to support the Lebanese army. He ordered major naval and troop exercises in Central America on a scale not witnessed before. The intervention in Grenada was enough to send anxiety waves into Central America. Reagan's tough approach all but ended the Intermediate Nuclear Forces (INF) and long-range missiles talks (START) in Geneva without a commitment from the Soviets as to when they would return. The Mutual and Balanced Force Reduction — MBFR — talks in Vienna were also suspended.

This style of relations between the superpowers can only be at the expense of the international institutions which rely on their support for efficient functioning. Because negotiations on issues of major concern have made little progress, it is not possible to open a dialogue on peacekeeping — which, at the minimum level, would require Soviet consent. With the Soviets' refusal to change their policies in Afghanistan and Poland, and their support of proxies in Central America and elsewhere, Reagan is determined to show no weakness in the pursuit of his goals.

This policy of confrontation, and of stopping so-called Soviet expansionism, has made Reagan send US troops into Lebanon and keep powerful warships positioned close to its coast. Therefore, the task of separating the Israelis, Syrians and Lebanese warring parties, or for that matter the removal of PLO fighters from Beirut and later from Tripoli, could not be entrusted to the UN, a body of which the Soviet Union is an equal member like the United States.

Israel demanded that the US troops should play the part of peace-keepers for the withdrawal of the PLO from Beirut. The United States, only too willing to keep Soviet influence out, yet not wanting to be on its own, asked the French to join them. The French willingly agreed, because of their traditional ties to Lebanon. The Italians also agreed because of their interest in the Mediterranean, and because of their relations with the Arabs.

On completing its task, the first MNF withdrew after a stay of thirty days in Beirut. In an attempt to reduce their presence in the city, the Israelis turned over the responsibility for Palestinian refugee camps to the Lebanese Christian forces, whose subsequent massacre of many hundreds of the Palestinians in the Chatila and Sabra camps shook the world. The Lebanese President Bashir Gemayel was assassinated and his brother Amin, on succeeding to the office, called for the return of the MNF. Thus the multinational force returned to Beirut to help maintain peace. This time it was augmented by a British contingent.

Throughout this time some fifty UNMOs remained in Beirut quietly performing their various missions of peacekeeping, just as UNIFIL continued with its delicate and vital role in Southern Lebanon. By now even the Israelis, who had little praise for UNIFIL, did not wish to see it depart. The importance of this force increased with the repeated attacks by Shias on the Israelis in Southern Lebanon, indicating that the Israelis would have to pay a heavy price if they wished to occupy this land.

In May 1983 Gemayel signed a treaty with Israel, whereupon fighting between the main Lebanese groups increased. An attempt to bring the factions together in Geneva in the winter of 1983/84 succeeded, but the opposition parties insisted that the treaty with Israel must be abrogated. The United States had hoped that Israel's withdrawal would persuade President Assad of Syria to agree to a similar withdrawal. This did not happen, however, and the Israelis unilaterally withdrew to a general line along the Awali river to reduce their troop commitment and costs.

Meanwhile, fighting had broken out between rival PLO groups in the Beka'a and in Tripoli. Yasir Arafat returned via Syria to lead his troops. The rebels accused Arafat of going soft on Israel, and with Syria's support all but defeated his forces in Tripoli. A ceasefire was arranged, and Arafat with 4,000 PLO troops quit Lebanon for the second time. The fighting in and around Beirut inevitably involved the troops of MNF. Once the American and French governments decided to help the Lebanese army, built around the Christian Phalangists, they were in fact assisting one group among the many in Lebanon. As the Lebanese army took on more responsibility, it became more and more deeply engaged in fighting the other groups. When the American and French troops and their respective naval ships and aircraft gave direct support to the Christians, their mission was no longer perceived as one of peacekeeping by the Lebanese opposition factions. The US Marines and French troops gave fire support to the Lebanese troops in Beirut. In dealing with fire from opposite factions, primary reliance was not on diplomacy but on retaliation. These troops had thus ceased to be peacekeepers. The tragic losses that followed could have been foreseen and avoided, because peacekeeping on the one hand and military support of a government on the other, however legitimate the latter may be, are two different functions. Peacekeepers can afford to act on the general assumption of public acceptance; but law enforcement troops must protect themselves at all times. They must dig and cover themselves against all likely attack.

In his press conference on December 21, 1983 (*New York Times*), President Reagan clarified his Administration's policy in Lebanon, including the role of the Marines. He reaffirmed his support for the Gemayel government. On the mission of the MNF, he said: 'After the Syrians had been asked to come in and help preserve order, because in Lebanon we had and have groups . . . they're fighting each other and at times fighting against the forces of the Lebanese government. We were then asked to come in with an international force, and we went in when the government had been formed, and once the PLO had been ejected.' He described the negotiations that were to lead to the withdrawal of the two foreign forces, Israel and Syria, once the PLO had left. The Lebanese government needed time to build its strength to deal with the internecine fighting groups. He added: 'Israel . . . has announced its willingness and intention to get out. Syria did too and then for some reason reneged on that promise.'

He further clarified the MNF's mission: 'The mission of the Multinational Force is what it was then. We have helped train the Lebanese army, and it is a capable force. We have armed it, and when the other forces, the foreign forces, get out, and the Lebanese military advance to try to establish order in their land, the Multinational Force is supposed to, behind them, try to achieve some stability and maintain order because Lebanon doesn't have the forces to do it.'

The President thus categorically stated that MNF was helping to train and organize the Lebanese army and was needed to back it in maintaining order because Lebanon lacked the forces to do it. This clearly was not a peacekeeping mission, because the Gemayel government exercised authority only in a part of Beirut and some nearby areas, and his army was the Phalangist force over which even he had but little control. Instead of negotiating with the other factions, the Lebanese army, with the help of MNF — more specifically the Americans and French, was attempting to overpower their rivals. Thus Reagan was supporting Gemayel, a Christian leader, against the Druzes and the Muslims, a mission which by no stretch of the imagination could be called peacekeeping. Inevitably it failed.

The UN in the Congo, caught in somewhat similar circumstances, found itself guarding all the rival national leaders and preventing their factions from fighting with each other. This was a far more complex role which ONUC performed with great *élan* and much to the admiration of the world, including Eisenhower, Kennedy and later Johnson. In Cyprus the UN met a similar challenge to protect the Greek and Turkish Cypriots from each other. Peacekeeping demands a true non-partisan role where all are treated alike. The role of the MNF can best be described as peace enforcement.

A country with good security forces can rely on its own troops for aid to the civil power or law enforcement even when there is civil strife. In the absence of adequate security forces, governments usually seek help from outside. Such a role is not peacekeeping. It has been called policing, law enforcement or peace enforcement. In these situations the troops may use force to restore the situation to normality. On the other hand, peacekeeping permits no more than the use of minimum force, and then only when all other means to stop shooting have failed. Peacekeeping troops are equipped with light weapons. Only in Katanga, when specially authorized to deal with Tshombe's mercenary-led forces, were UN troops provided with anti-aircraft guns and fighter aircraft to defend themselves against air attacks.

In the case of Lebanon, President Reagan declared: 'As far as I am concerned, when an American military man is shot at he can shoot back. . . .' The use of field artillery, naval guns and naval fighter and light bomber aircraft to deal with positions from which the MNF was under fire, and the use of such heavy weapons to support Gemayel's troops, is not peacekeeping but waging war. On December 23, 1983, US Defense Secretary Caspar Weinberger was reported as commenting on a special Pentagon report about the Beirut bombing which caused the deaths of 241 American Marines: 'There isn't any way' to guarantee the safety of soldiers 'in a war, and this is a war.'

In an article entitled 'Assad and the Future of the Middle East,' (Winter 1983/4 issue of *Foreign Affairs*) Robert C. Neumann more aptly described the situation in Lebanon: 'The consequences of Israel's invasion of Lebanon in 1982 have significantly changed the entire range of power relationships in the Middle East. . . . They have brought the Soviet Union back into the Middle East in a position of influence from which it will not easily be dislodged. They have profoundly affected American diplomacy, drawing it away from a broadly based peace initiative and sucking the Marines into a narrow, dangerous position in Lebanon, where US forces have already suffered serious casualties. And they have conjured up again the danger of a superpower confrontation in the area which neither power desires, but which the Soviet Union may be less reluctant to avoid than in the past.'

The presence of the US marines in Lebanon became a political campaign issue in the United States. The deployment of foreign troops in Lebanon was reported at 40,000 Syrians (with 7,000 Soviets in Syria of whom a number were with the Syrians in Lebanon) and some 20,000 Israelis in Southern Lebanon. The MFO consisted of French, Italian and British troops as well as 1,600 US Marines. The British and Italians, unhappy over the failures of the Reagan Administration to consult before expanding the role of MFO and facing increasing criticism at home, were obliged to express their contrary views publicly. The Italians cut their 2,000 contingent by nearly half; the French reduced theirs by 482 but sent these to UNIFIL to maintain their overall numbers in Lebanon at the same level. They hoped that a UN umbrella might lead to a reduction in the antagonism against them among the Lebanese opposition fighters.

The Israelis, facing serious domestic economic problems and tired of war, had no will to fight in Lebanon. They witnessed a failure of Sharon's attempts, which had the approval of Begin, to eliminate the PLO from Lebanon and install a pro-Gemayel government in Beirut. They succeeded in removing the military wing of the PLO, but not the thousands of Palestinians whose hatred for Israel has not diminished. They have also added to their problems the intense hatred of the Shia Muslims. The Israelis were let down by the Christians when they arranged to deal with the Druze on the understanding that the Phalangist militia would be pulled out of the Shouf and be replaced by the Lebanese army. When the Israelis withdrew, the Phalangists refused to comply, and heavy fighting resumed.

The fighting in and around Beirut and in the Shouf mountains became a precursor of events, starting in the beginning of 1984. Taking advantage of United States and French support, Gemayel's largely Phalangist-based Lebanese army resorted to force instead of negotiations to deal with the Druze in the mountains and the Muslims in the city. By early February, the opposition factions had cornered the Lebanese forces in the city, reached the Mediterranean coast, and linked their forces in Central Lebanon to access roads to Beirut. This signalled the withdrawal of the Marines to their ships while the British and the Italians returned home. Only the French remained in Beirut to gain time to persuade the UN Security Council to establish a UN peacekeeping force. The United States accepted the French proposal, albeit grudgingly, but the Soviets did not approve because they were not prepared to bale out the West. Subsequently, the French too gave up and left, ending the life of the MNF.

American goodwill in seeking a peaceful solution to the war and the future of the Palestinians is unquestionable. It has been the policy for dealing with these questions that has heightened East-West tensions and minimized the chance of resolving them at a regional level.

It was always clear that the United States should disengage its troops and seek a UN peacekeeping operation, based on a regional effort with US support and Soviet participation to deal with the main issues.

The record of the Reagan Administration shows little faith in the world organization. As Jeane Kirkpatrick said on Capitol Hill in May 1981, the new administration's policy towards the UN was a combination of 'vigilance, straightforwardness and, if necessary, withholding of support'. In a report published by the Heritage Foundation, a Conservative Washington policy research institution, which views the UN with the same scepticism as many in the Reagan Administration, Roger A. Brooks, a policy analyst, claimed that in all the conflicts since 1945 the UN had 'done little to prevent the fighting or to restore peace', and concluded that the UN 'deserved failing grades for peacekeeping'. Brooks charged the UN peacekeeping operations with fuelling violence, supporting wars of liberation, and failing to control international tension. Even more remarkable was his charge that the UN force in Lebanon helped the PLO 'by close and systematic intelligence cooperation'. The *Wall Street Journal*, in commenting on this study in its editorial of May 3, 1983, not only endorsed it but added that it 'shouldn't come as a surprise to anyone who has bothered to look at the generally ineffectual, and sometimes divisive, activities of the UN'.

This study was so full of inaccuracies and preconceived ideas that it cannot be taken seriously. But a newspaper with the prestige of the *Wall Street Journal* carries much influence. This campaign against UN peacekeeping seeks to damage the world organisation's one really effective activity. The intention behind it is obvious: to persuade the United States to turn its back on UN peacekeeping, and to rely only on its own power and might to cope with conflicts such as that in Lebanon. This suggestion is a sure formula for a global war.

In dealing with the situation in Lebanon, the Administration has relied on its own ability and powers of persuasion to obtain the assistance of the Saudis, whose influence in the Middle East comes down to money. The Administration tolerates the presence of UNIFIL in Southern Lebanon because the Lebanese and the Arabs, like the Saudis, insist on a UN presence. Even the Israelis have recognised the usefulness of UNIFIL after their own experience of occupying the south.

Syria opposed a UN role, either in Beirut or for supervising the withdrawal of foreign forces. This was because Syria would have had to make a serious pledge to withdraw once the UN was involved. Also, they would find it impossible to become party to an agreement if the Soviets were to be excluded in the process.

The Soviets did not support a UN peacekeeping role in Beirut because, as a senior Soviet diplomat said in private conversation with the Author at the UN during the 38th General Assembly Session: 'We are not going to agree to pull the American chestnuts out of the fire.' The UN, he added, could not assume the responsibilities of being policemen of the world. Besides, there were questions as to what government the UN would support and what was the basis for accepting such a government.

The Soviet position appeared to be negotiable, as did that of the Syrians. The UN could play a useful peacekeeping role; indeed it would be the best instrument to deal with this complex question. But this would only be practicable if the normal pre-conditions for organizing such an operation were met. This task would not be impossible provided the US government changed its mind and devoted its efforts to negotiating a broad-based government in Lebanon, involving Syria and the Soviet Union in the process. Any solution without the latter two parties could only be temporary. The Soviet Union's borders are near the Middle East; it has historic and strategic interests and relations in the region; it will not agree to be kept out and cannot be kept out without serious consequences for the peace of the region and of the whole world.

In the circumstances, there were some understandable, though necessarily unworthy, reasons for seeking a peacekeeping arrangement outside the UN. Because of the number of occasions that the UN has found fault with the Israelis, the world organization is perceived by the Jewish state as pro-Arab. United States policy to exclude the Soviets from a third-party role is not entirely caused by the East-West ideological divide, but also because there remain important differences between the two superpowers over the conduct of UN peacekeeping, and because the Soviets are perceived by the United States as playing an interventionist rather than a constructive role in the region. The use of a non-UN system can also be argued on the basis that the UN does not exclude such arrangements and in fact encourages them.

These reasons for turning to a non-UN system when evaluated within the overall political and international framework and its effect indicates weaknesses even greater than the UN system.

No one denies that the UN has worked less than perfectly in the maintenance of international peace and security. But the experience of the MFO and MNF has indicated that an authority like the UN is still needed as the main instrument for the maintenance of international peace. Only the UN offers any prospects of a functional international system of collective security. Despite its political limitations, the UN provides the only objective and politically impartial body to deal with complex peace and security issues. The attempts of the United States and other Western nations to give the multilateral peacekeeping forces an impartial façade remained unconvincing. The actions of the United States and the French forces in Beirut have already been discussed. The MFO in Sinai was organized on the UN pattern. However, the American contingent includes troops from the 82nd Airborne Division, which belonged to the Rapid Deployment Force (now part of Central Command) for the Middle East. This force is intended to combat Soviet expansionism and therefore the troop make-up of the MFO, which is largely of NATO or American military aid recipient-states, can do little to allay radical Arab suspicions.

The non-UN forces have shown several advantages over UN forces. Unlike the UN system, multilateral forces are well equipped, well trained and have no financial problems. They are also able to take more risks, whereas the UN system has evolved in such a way that the interpretation of self-defence has become more restrictive. This fact alone makes the UN role questionable in situations like Lebanon. The interpretation of self-defence evolved in the Congo and later in Cyprus gave some validity to the basic principle of UN peacekeeping in a non-force use, where force could be used for self-defence in the last resort after all other means had failed. This kind of arrangement has become greatly eroded as the result of its use in South Lebanon.

The willingness of the United States and the French to use greater force in Lebanon caused the failure of MNF. Therefore, the use of self-defence needs to be judicious to show the determination of peace-keeping troops to do their job yet avoiding the degree of force used at a level where peacekeeping troops are considered hostile and partial. Furthermore, the UN efforts in the Congo and Cyprus have provided the organization with the experience to define the limits of peace-keeping in a divided country. There are limits to intervention in an internal situation. The UN or regional organizations are better suited for such a role than great powers. Thus the Middle East experience of non-UN peacekeeping efforts has only proved the greater efficacy of the UN system despite its limitations.

The fifty UNMOs in Beirut were the only international third-party peacekeeping presence after the departure of MNF. With the modest public relations apparatus at the disposal of the UNMOs and their parent organization UNTSO, the world has given them little attention. Yet theirs was the only group which dealt with all sides, provided humanitarian assistance, helped in quieting the situation, and reported on developments to the Security Council. These UNMOs remain an essential part of the arrangements recently arrived at by the Lebanese to maintain peace in Beirut, and the group could do a lot more were it to be expanded. In fact, it will be the only reliable group for assisting in the achievement of a durable ceasefire in Beirut and areas outside the city. Similarly, UNMOs could play a vital role in future withdrawal agreements involving the Syrians in the Bekaa and the PLO in North Lebanon.

The life of UNIFIL was again wisely extended by the Security Council in April 1984. The Lebanese wish UNIFIL to remain to avoid South Lebanon being turned over to the authority of the newly-created South Lebanese Army with Israeli assistance to replace Haddad's Christian forces. The Lebanese factions, notably AMAL (the strongest in the area), prefer UN troops to dealing with the new Israeli-created Lebanese force. Such a relationship between these two Lebanese forces can be expected to be nothing less than antagonistic.

In Israel the Labour party has already declared its intention, if elected, to withdraw from South Lebanon. But meanwhile the governing Likud has recognised the usefulness of UNIFIL. Some Israelis would wish to extend UNDOF from the Golan Heights to the Mediterranean coast, but this is too complex to achieve politically. It will be simpler to employ UNIFIL to assist in the withdrawal of the IDF, to prevent incursions into Israel from South Lebanon, and to assist in the restoration of Lebanese authority there. Thus UNIFIL in the south and UNMOs in Beirut, in the Bekaa and in the north could together play a useful and much-needed role to assist in bringing peace in this strife-torn land and reduce the threat to peace and security in the entire region.

There are certain essential ingredients in making a UN peacekeeping role useful in Lebanon. First, the Lebanese government must not only give its consent but provide its strong support (the limitations of the Gemayel government are recognised); secondly, the Syrians and the Israelis must agree; thirdly, the consent of the veto powers is essential; and last but not least, the endorsement of the Soviets and the full support of the United States are required. It is not enough to have only a tacit support of the two superpowers, but the support of the United States is a vital ingredient.

The United States, by promoting a Western MNF, attempting to isolate the Soviets and ignoring Syria, did not succeed in resolving the Lebanese conflict. After the MNF's withdrawal and the abrogation of the American-sponsored Israeli-Lebanese agreement, the United States appeared to have taken little interest in developments in

Lebanon. But it is a power very much to be reckoned with in the area, enjoying tremendous prestige. Therefore, for it to pull out of the Lebanese 'ring' at this crucial stage of development is just as critical as were past attempts to bypass the Soviets and ignore Syria. Of course, the United States has recourse to the UN system; but it has said so much against the UN, encouraging conservative groups in the United States to malign the use of the UN, often falsely, this option is not an attractive one for US policy-makers. However, a surrender of the UN option will seriously reduce US ability to influence affairs in the Middle East — or indeed elsewhere in the world. The record proves that the UN, when used effectively, has proved advantageous among the policy choices of the United States.

The United States played a pivotal role in the creation of the UN, but the current indications are that it may in the end so damage its effectiveness that it will cease to be a useful policy option. Thereafter it will be hard to revive it to meet other situations like Korea in 1950, Suez in 1956, the Congo in 1960, Cuba in 1962, Sinai in October 1973, and so on. In fact, an international organization like the UN is needed no less by the United States than by the Soviet Union and diverse other nations in a world where crises are on the increase and the threat of nuclear war is omnipresent.

It is not only in the Middle East that a superpower has bypassed the UN since the beginning of the 1980s. The invasion of Grenada by the United States was based on a request, and undertaken in collaboration with the eastern Caribbean community. This community arrangement was intended to prevent smuggling in the region; but lately the member-states, particularly Barbados and more recently Jamaica, had become concerned with the disproportionate military strength that Marxist Grenada had acquired with Cuban help. However, no security arrangements had been included in the community's agreement, and no consensus existed among them before the US military was asked to intervene. Just as in the case of Santo Domingo in 1965, the United States sought some legitimate basis for intervention: but in neither instance could it be considered anything but a unilateral intervention. Even if one were to accept that Grenada is in the backyard of the United States, just as Eastern Europe is in the front yard of the Soviet Union, such use of force by a superpower makes it difficult to prevent other states from following its example. It is no wonder that scarce attention is nowadays paid to the UN Charter.

During the Falklands/Malvinas crisis, the UN Secretary-General, Javier Pérez de Cuéllar, was at the point of concluding successful negotiations; but Argentina and the United Kingdom, for differing domestic reasons, chose war. A continuing of negotiations to their end would have obliged the Argentinian Junta to resign, and Margaret Thatcher, the British Prime Minister, to face a revolt by backbenchers in her own Conservative party. When the Argentinians occupied the islands, negotiations to get them out were still possible, but this led the British government to decide to invade, a risky operation but a lesser risk for them than the certain alternative: an internal party revolt at a time of declining popularity due to a failing economy.

Margaret Thatcher and Ronald Reagan, using age-old techniques, healed domestic strife, and injected a sense of pride in their respective nations by giving them a military victory. In the British case the victory was won against great odds, in the American case much less so.

In other conflicts — in Africa, Latin America and South-East Asia — direct intervention and negotiations became the US practice. In Central America the Contadora group (Colombia, Panama, Mexico and Venezuela) had yet to conclude its long process of making peace; and meanwhile the United States had involved itself directly with the crisis. The OAS has had little part to play. The UN, other than providing the good offices of the Secretary-General, has not been involved as a third party except for some useful related resolutions by the Security Council and the General Assembly. If the Contadora group eventually succeeds, it will be due to yet another initiative outside the framework of existing international institutions.

In Africa, the UN was involved in Western Sahara and Namibia. In the former, Morocco has shown little willingness to negotiate under the OAU aegis, so that there is no advance towards a UN-supervised referendum.

In Chad, after the failure of OAU peacekeeping, the Egyptians and Sudanese backed Habré's force in the eastern sector. The French provided direct military assistance with troops, aircraft and military equipment; and the United States provided military assistance. They support Habré, who has fought the OAU's choice, Goukhouni. Habré, like Goukhouni, is a Northern leader; but unlike his opponent he is hated in the larger south, which contains most of the country's population. The OAU has yet to wrestle with the new developments in Chad, and has little chance if the great powers involved decide against using this organization.

The future of Namibia hangs on a number of factors. South Africa has attempted to end the cross-border war between its forces in Namibia and Angola (as also with Mozambique) by taking a series of initiatives that led to the Lusaka agreement in March 1984. This arrangement called for a ceasefire and a monitoring commission consisting of Angolan, South African and some US observers. Both parties have agreed to cease support for subversive movements in their respective territories, implying that SWAPO will not operate in areas vacated by South African troops and UNITA will not operate against Angolan troops. There is an apparent shift in the past position of South Africa and the West, notably in the United States which had previously linked the future of the government in Luanda and settlement of the Namibia question to the withdrawal of Cuban forces. The negotiations on Namibia, a responsibility of the Contact Group of five Western States, rest at present with only one of these — the United States, which in turn has assisted South Africa to take the lead.

The Iraq-Iran war has continued unabated as neither East nor West wants either party to win or be defeated. If Iraq were to win, it would become the dominating Arab military power in the Gulf and thereby a threat to Israel; and if Iran won, it would become a potential threat to the security of the region. Recently Shia-sponsored terrorist acts have caused the West to consider aiding Iraq. Whatever may emerge there as the West's final policy, a significant change cannot be expected.

Afghanistan is stalemated as the Soviets have become involved in a long-term role to provide internal security until a government acceptable to them can be evolved. The rebels are badly divided, and Pakistan can do no more than shut its eyes to the flow of men, arms and supplies across its borders for fear of Soviet retaliation. The UN's good offices are unlikely to produce any fruitful results until the question of Afghanistan is negotiated between the superpowers as part of a global discussion of their respective interests.

In some ways Kampuchea presents a picture similar to Afghanistan. The Soviet-backed Vietnamese occupy most of the country, while the Chinese-backed Pol Pot forces camp along the Thai border. Here again a UN mission has all the ingredients of leading the negotiations towards a successful end — but for the lack of will on the part of the three great powers involved. The Chinese and Soviets have moved towards a negotiated solution, but the process is likely to be slow and to stretch over years if not decades. Only the United States, by lending its weight to the UN's mediation efforts could break the deadlock. This will only be possible in the context of a superpower dialogue.

In situations like Central America, Lebanon, the Western Sahara, Chad, Namibia, Afghanistan and Kampuchea, the primary need is for agreements to end hostilities, to arrange a monitoring or supervisory arrangement for the ceasefire, to bring peace and normality and to provide an opportunity to the people in these places to determine their own future. Thus, peacekeeping, particularly by the UN, is an important part of this process. The experience of regional and multinational peacekeeping, with the exception of the Commonwealth's Rhodesia-Zimbabwe operation and the MFO in Sinai, have proved far less successful than UN peacekeeping operations. The UN operations have proved less costly in terms of money and casualties. The financial cost of UNIFIL is only a fraction of that of the MNF. The cost in American and French lives has been staggering for a peacekeeping operation.

In an earlier chapter the possibilities of strengthening the machinery for peacekeeping operations have been discussed. However, while considering the relative merits of the different systems, the need for an alternative system of security — great power roles or the use of military blocs — for the maintenance of international peace and security clearly emerges.

In the Report of the Independent Commission on Disarmament and Security Issues, the Chairman, Olof Palme of Sweden, stated: 'Since then [i.e. the beginning of the work of the Commission in 1980] the international situation has become both more dangerous and increasingly full of hope. Relations between the United States and the Soviet Union have deteriorated sharply in 1981 and 1982. The arms race is accelerating. The development of new nuclear weapons seems to suggest that the nuclear powers may actually consider fighting a nuclear war. In the Middle East and many other parts of the Third World, war is not a threat but a reality.' These words are ominous but true, and the global situation has in fact worsened. The report agreed that there was no such thing as a nuclear war that could be won. A so-called limited nuclear war would almost inevitably develop into total nuclear conflagration. The doctrine of deterrence offered a very fragile protection against the horrors of nuclear war and should in due course be replaced. The alternative suggested was 'common security'.

In explaining 'common security', the Report stated that since 'we live in an increasingly interdependent world,' security cannot be attained unilaterally. The Report provided these guidelines: (1) all nations have a right to security; (2) military force is not a legitimate instrument for resolving disputes between nations; (3) restraint is necessary in the expression of national policy; (4) security cannot be attained through military superiority; (5) reduction and qualitative limitations of armaments are necessary for common security; and (6) linkages between arms negotiations and political events should be avoided.

In the search for common security, the Palme Commission suggested curbing the nuclear arms race between the United States and the Soviet Union, and promoting security in Europe through a balance of conventional forces, limits on nuclear battlefield weapons, agreements on medium-range nuclear weapons, a ban on chemical weapons, co-operation and confidence-building measures, and dealing with the Third World dimension of conflicts by strengthening the UN and regional systems. These are all laudable and attainable objectives. However, what is needed is the political will of the nations and above all wise leadership that looks beyond the immediate present or the next election.

Javier Pérez de Cuéllar, in his report of the UN Secretary-General on the work of the Organization for 1982, put forward useful suggestions to meet objectives similar to what the Palme Commission recommended. He said that people had strayed away from the UN Charter in that there were governments which believed that they could win an international objective by force. The Security Council had frequently been unable to agree, and when it did, it often failed to implement its resolutions. The UN also hesitated to act in crisis *prevention*. The Secretary-General suggested that the Council should seek ways to strengthen the UN's capability to deal with conflicts, e.g. its peacekeeping role. This had proved its effectiveness, but was now being reduced in importance. The Secretary-General had also suggested the implementation of Article 28(2), which provides for the holding of periodic meetings at which each of its members may, if it so wishes, be represented by a member of government or by some other specially designated representative.

Both the Palme Commission and the UN Secretary-General have raised the question of international security, and put forward recommendations for strengthening the present arrangements for maintaining international peace. Their suggestions are pragmatic in nature and will require the willingness of states to co-operate. The development of common security, as the Palme Commission called it, or international security, as it is more generally known, is an essential and vital step towards disarmament and arms control. Experience has already proved the many uses of an international security system.

The uses of peacekeeping and peace observation are manifold. They separate the combatants; establish zones of peace, with limited weapons or with no weapons; supervise ceasefires, and observe ceasefire lines for violations; they can observe behind the lines if the agreement requires it and can provide early warning; and last, but not least, they mobilize the international community to make peacekeeping commitments.

Peacekeeping has proved useful *after* conflicts; it could be equally useful *before* a conflict erupts. Its presence should provide the confidence to remove the need for war preparations and, in turn, an influx of weapons. It could take many forms. Troops could be deployed, civilian or military observers stationed, and surface or air observation established; electronic surveillance could give early warnings; and its physical presence could assist in restoring calm and normality. All these measures would reduce panic, suspicion and the need to arm.

The difficulties should not be overlooked. Although some guidelines have emerged for peacekeeping, the great powers prefer to have it on an *ad hoc* basis rather than institutionalized. This is despite the fact that differences between them on guidelines have been narrowed down to some four points, which could well be resolved if they so chose. Consequently, any UN peacekeeping operation depends — at least tacitly — on their acceptance. Furthermore, if they do not support peacekeeping, it becomes difficult if not impossible to implement agreements. Plans exist to deploy a UN peacekeeping force in Namibia, but South Africa does not yet want it and hence the United States is not ready for it. The United States, Egypt and Israel wanted a

UN peacekeeping force to implement the Camp David accord, but the Soviets, who were excluded from the negotiations, were not prepared to authorize it. Hence the operation was organized outside the UN.

A UN peacekeeping operation, once launched, requires the support of the parties to the conflict and the great powers. It is the reluctance to support these operations that has become a major cause for their failure. The UN Emergency Force in Gaza was withdrawn in 1967, on the request of Egypt, because U Thant concluded that not only was there little support for its continuation by troop-contributing countries, but also that the Soviets would have vetoed any attempt to keep the force in existence once Egyptian consent was withdrawn.

Sometimes peacekeeping operations are not effective because they receive insufficient support from the parties to the conflict. The combatants have different interpretations, each wanting the UN to do its bidding. UNIFIL met such a fate. The Israelis expected that the UN would keep the PLO out and remove its remaining elements, while the PLO hoped that the UN would neutralize the Israeli-supported Christian forces under Major Haddad. Neither of these functions was part of the UNIFIL mandate, and when the superpowers refused to agree on a common policy, UNIFIL was placed in an impossible position.

Furthermore, there are problems of logistics, administration, and most of all financing. Because of these difficulties peacekeeping is not an ideal tool for diplomacy; but neither is war. When given encouragement and support by the great powers, participation and assistance by member-states and the willing co-operation of parties to the conflict, it has proved a useful instrument to manage conflicts and provide a measure of security. It already offers an alternative to the resort to arms and when developed further can become a great improvement compared with security based on national or regional military power.

Disarmament and arms control will be greatly facilitated by the UN member-states, and by the superpowers in particular, if they strengthen their international and regional systems for security. Peacekeeping already has proved its value in ending wars, maintaining armistices and ceasefires, and restoring mutual confidence and trust. The international community should build on past experience to improve similar arrangements in future.

As the need for the security of smaller powers — including those in the Third World where conflicts seem to occur more and more frequently — is met by an international system, the need felt by these states to possess arms will diminish. There will also be less demand by them for military assistance from one or other superpower, and less inclination to enter into military pacts — both of which perceived needs lead to increased tensions and often to conflict.

Thus an international system of security built on past peacekeeping experience will greatly enhance the possibilities of promoting arms control and of a durable peace emerging. Together with such a system of security, the survival of mankind requires that conflicts be resolved through negotiations. An effective machinery for the peaceful settlement of disputes is a prerequisite for effective arms control. In spite of their limitations, United Nations and regional institutional arrangements offer the best hope for resolving conflicts in a dangerous world.

April 1984

INDEX

Abdulaziz, Mohammed, 158, 159
Abdullah, Sheikh Mohammed, 21, 25, 36
Acland, Maj.-Gen. John, 174
Action Front for the Retention of Turnhalle Principles, 122
Acyl, Ahmat, 164
Adoula, Cyrille, 86, 87
Afghanistan, 243
Ahtisaari, Martti, 128
Airborne Warning and Control System (AWACS), 168
Alexander, Maj.-Gen. Henry, 82
Algeria, 152, 155, 158
Al-Isa, Maj.-Gen. Abdullah, 133
Alvim, Lt.-Gen. Hugo Panasco, 144
Angle, Brig. Henry H., 27
Angola, 116, 118; Cuban troops in, 126, 128; and SWAPO, 127; Unita, 119, 242; United States talks with, 127. *See also* Front-line states, South West African People's Organization.
Arab Deterrent Force, 101, 105, 133, 134–6
Arab-Israeli conflicts, 5, 37, 230, 234, 236. *See also* Multinational Force; Palestine; UNEF; UNEF II; UNIFIL; UNTSO
Arab League, *see* League of Arab States
Arabs: in Palestine conflict, 29; in Gaza strip, 33, 34
Arafat, Yassir, 78, 103, 107, 234
Arbenz Guzmán, Jacobo, 148
Argentina, 241; armistice supervision, 28–41. *See also* EIMAC; ILMAC; UN Mixed Armistice Commission; UNSCOP; UN Truce Commission (Palestine); *and* UNTSO
Assad, Lt.-Gen. Hafez al-, 234
Association of South-East Asian Nations (ASEAN), 132
Aswan dam, 47, 226
Atlantic alliance, 7
Austria: in UNDOF, 58; in UNEF II, 67; in UNFICYP, 93
Awali river, 77, 234

Balaguer, Joaquin, 145
Bamako: Agreement, 152–3; Commission, 153
Begin, Menachem, 221
Beirut, 76, 107, 112, 236–40; massacre in, 75; multinational force in, 74–8
Bekaa Valley, 78, 101, 240
Belgium: in the Congo, 8, 80–3; in UNCIP, 21

Benin, 159, 165
Benoit, Col. Pedro Bartolomé, 141
Berlin blockade, 226
Bernadotte, Count Folke, 29–30
Bhutto, Zulfiqar Ali, 25
Botha, Roelof F., 116, 120; on demilitarized zone, 118–19
Botswana, 118. *See also* front-line states
Brazil, 144, 148, 149, 180
Brezhnev, Leonid, 11
Briceno, Brig.-Gen. Gonzalo Z., 58
Britain: and Argentina, 241; in Balkans, 17; in Cyprus, 91, 93, 97; in Jammu and Kashmir, 19, 21; in Kuwait, 133; and Latin America, 140; in Lebanon, 76, 78, 236; London and Zurich agreements, 90; in MNF, 233; and Palestine, 28; and UN, 28, 227; in Zimbabwe, 176–7
Brooks, Roger A., 237
Buffer zone: in Cyprus, 95, 96; interim, 71; in Santo Domingo, 142 (map), 143; in Nicaragua, 139; of UNEF, 54, 63–5
Bull, Gen. Odd, 39
Bull-Hansen, Lt.-Gen. Fredrik V., 72, 222
Bunche, Ralph, 30–1, 218; in Congo, 82
Bundy, McGeorge, 144
Bunker, Ellsworth, 42, 144, 145, 148, 227
Bunker Plan, 45
Burns, General E.L.M., 35, 37, 38

Caamaño Deno, Col. Francisco, 145
Callaghan. Lt.-Gen. William, 66, 110
Camp David Accord, *see* Egypt-Israeli Peace Treaty, 1979
Canada: in Lebanon, 103, 191; on peacekeeping, 188, 192–3; in UNCIP, 21; in UNDOF, 58; in UNEF II, 52, 53, 56, 67; in UNFICYP, 92, 93; and UN Military Staff Committee, 182, 187; and UN Secretary-General, 183–4
Cancun: conference on world development, 164
Carrington, Lord, 173
Carter, Jimmy, 231, 232; administration of, 9; and Iran, 11
Carver, Maj.-Gen. Michael, 91, 92, 97
ceasefire: in Arab-Israeli conflict, 55, 134, 230, 234; in Chad, 161, 163, 165–6, 167; in Congo, 86; in Cyprus, 94, 95; in Dominican Republic, 141, 143, 145, 146; in Jammu and Kashmir dispute, 21, 23, 25; maintenance of,